The Power of Love with Animals

"a magical life communicating with other species"

Debra A Lansdowne

The Power of Love with Animals
A Magical Life Communicating with Other Species

Debra A. Lansdowne

© 2021 Debra A. Lansdowne. All rights reserved.

Self-Published by Debra A. Lansdowne
Editor: Karen Collyer
Book cover Animal Artist: Terri Graham
Back cover Author's Photographer: Lisa Haymes
Book cover background image: By Beautiful landscape ©

Typesetting and design by Publicious Book Publishing
Published with the assistance of Publicious Book Publishing
www.publicious.com.au

All rights reserved. No part of this document may be reproduced or transmitted in any form or by any means, electronic, mechanical, photocopying, recording or otherwise, or by any information storage and retrieval system, without prior written permission of Debra A. Lansdowne or publisher (except by a reviewer, who may quote brief passages and/or show brief video clips in a review).

For permissions:

Debra A. Lansdowne
Email: Heartjourneys006@gmail.com
FB: Author Debra Lansdowne
www.HeartJourneyswithDebra.com

Cataloguing Purposes:
Interspecies Communication
Telepathy/Psychic Abilities
Human and Animal Relationships
New Age Spirituality
Gaia Earth Wisdom

Distributed in paperback and electronic forms.

ISBN 978-0-6451699-0-4 (paperback)
ISBN 978-0-6451699-1-1 (eBook)

The events and stories in this book are all true as the author remembers them, however the names have been changed to protect the privacy of those involved.

Book Reviews
The Power of Love with Animals

I have known Debra for many years, and it's wonderful to see her sweet spirit shining through in her book. To spread the message of the Universal Language of Silence that all beings speak is important work, especially today with the human disconnection from the natural world at such a peak.

For those of us who speak for the unheard, telling our stories is a beautiful way other people can be gently reminded of the rich world of connection we all really live in—and this is crucial.

Debra's sensitive telling of her encounters with animals and the natural world are a delight to read. Enjoy her stories, and remember that we are all part of Nature.

Billie Dean, Author *Secret Animal Business:*
A Celebration of the Secrets of Animals, Their Forgotten
Language and How They Can Help You and the Planet Heal
Shamanic Interspecies Communicator and Teacher,
Co-founder of A Place of Peace (Farm
Animal and Wild Horse Sanctuary).
www.billiedean.com, www.deeppeacetrust.com

What a delight to read this book! The way Debra opens the reader to remembering spirituality and connection to our non-human animal cousins, the pulsations of our hearts and the love which unites us all is both wonderful and healing.

This is especially important at a time when the world appears shrouded in fear, which gives rise to feeling separate from other species, whilst the knowing and the power to transcend to a higher vibration still sits in our collective consciousness.

Flavia Ursino Coleman, Author *Beyond Speciesism* and
Monkey Business: A Story of Soulmates and Primates.

Contents

Author's Message i
Introduction: Communicating with Other Species vii
    Our Relations vii
    How Can we Commune in Practical Ways? x
    What if You Are Not Able to Connect? xii
Healing and Opening Our Hearts xiii
Energetic Frequencies of Animal Companions xvii

My Animal Soul Companions xix
1   Charles: Wisdom and Guidance 1
2   Kindred Souls 10
3   Loyalty and Devotion 14
4   Harley: Our Kitten 24
5   The Reunion 27
6   Love and Compassion 31
7   Bruno: A Child's Love 36
8   Mandy: Love and Grief 38
9   Releasing Wounds 48
10   Remembering Wisdom 55
11   Divine Union 58
12   Sabastian: Finding Joy 61
13   Recalling Wisdom 64

Living With My Companions 68
14   Unconditional Love 69
15   Sharing Our Wounds 74
16   Travelling and Companions 77
17   Compassion and Ageing 79
18   Companion Behaviours 86

My Family of Light **90**
19   Ancestors, Soul Star Family and Past Lives 91
20   My Support Team 98
21   Healing Across Realms of Existence 104

Sound **113**
22   Magical Sound with Other Species 114
23   Shifting Realities at Power Sites 122
24   Hearing the Call 128
25   Seven Days of Whale Play 133

Crystals and Rocks **140**
26   Hearing Crystals and Rocks 141
27   Meeting Ancestral Land Spirits 153
28   Rock Families 157

Wildlife **166**
29   Wildlife Encounters 167
30   Rescue 176

Trees and Plants **185**
31   Trees Support Me 186
32   A Community and a Forest 189
33   How I Commune With Trees 194
34   Conscious Trees and Plants 202
35   The Power of Trees 211

Respect **215**
36   We Are Not Gods 216
37   Human Interference 225
38   Cows, Calves and Karma 231
39   Killing with Kindness 237
40   Horses and Me 240
41   Value all Life 248

My Australian Bushfire Diary 2019/2020 253
42 Apocalyptic Fires—November 2019 254
43 Loss of Habitat, December 2019 259
44 Disrespect, January 2020 263
45 Climate Change, February 2020 267

Honouring in Life 273
46 Honouring and Ceremony 274
47 Communing with Mother Earth and Other Realms 286
48 Nature Mirrors Our Souls 290
49 A Magnificent Conscious Being 293
50 Mother Earth and The Elemental Forces 297
51 Our Evolving Planet 303
52 Power of Feminine Cycles and Earth Mother 308

With Gratitude 318
53 Souls from the Past 319
54 The Joy of Communing with the Others 325
55 A Blessed Life 330
Acknowledgements 343
About the Author 345

This book is lovingly dedicated to all the voiceless species, who have much wisdom and love to share with humans.

Author's Message

Welcome to my magical life journey communicating with other species.

I write to inspire you to know and feel the joy of communicating with other species and our ancestors, that you may know they walk with us in life and are always waiting for us to communicate with them. They want to support our life journey here on earth, to help us to evolve and never feel alone. We can all have a magical and extraordinary life with our animal companions, ancestors and many other species, which helps us to find deeper relationships with everything here on Mother Earth and to explore other realms of existence awaiting us beyond the physical 3D world.

So many are not aware of other worlds around them as they are living unconsciously, limited to the 3D world, while other species (such as our companion animals) live in many realms of existence simultaneously. They see and are aware of energies, thought forms and emotional wave forms that humans can only experience in dreams.

This is my true story of living and communicating with my companion animals, many other species, and my ancestors. They have taken me on an extraordinary ride through life, shifting into other realms of existence to commune and share unconditional love, guidance and heart healing, supporting my soul's journey, and reminding me of my purpose here on earth. I couldn't have made these stories up, not with all the unexpected twists and turns in my life!

I believe our real stories are far more extraordinary and inspiring than fiction. Magic really does exist on earth. If we can go beyond the logical mind, we will find our life is part of a greater divine and infinite force of love that moves in and around us and everything that

Author's Message

exists within the cosmos. By tapping into this infinite force, we can commune with our animal companions through our heart intelligence, the highest vibration of love. That is the universal language of all species that allows communication. My life changed dramatically when I awakened to consciously tap into this force through my heart—I found new realities awaiting me beyond this 3D earthly realm of existence, and I no longer felt alone or separate.

This book may challenge your thinking. I suggest you hold the stories in your heart and ask *can I open my heart to feel the truth of what is being shared here in this book?* If you cannot, perhaps simply accept it as a fantastical adventure to inspire you on your life's journey.

Could there be more to this earthly life you have not yet experienced, or been sensitive enough in your heart to have found for yourself?

As a child, I had no voice and felt disempowered by my family's behaviours. I so needed to be heard! That is when my animal companions came to me and helped me by listening. I felt so much love from them in my heart! My sensitive heart had started to witness the horrible things done by humans to other species. I did not understand why people did cruel things to other species, while appearing to feel no remorse.

I felt the pain of other species as if it were my own, and I felt they had no voice. I could hear them screaming inside and feeling disempowered, but no one else seemed to hear them. I felt like I was strange, as no one else had the reactions as I did. It was very upsetting to feel so much pain on the earth.

My dysfunctional family shared their pain with me too. I tried to take their pain, absorbing it when I witnessed them upset and suffering, but it felt heavy inside of me. I would then go outside to my animal companions to talk with them and feel their love. With their help, my heart always started to feel love again and my joy and lightness returned. That is how I coped with my family's pain. They shared it every day, and I took it on.

It has taken me many years to realise how much I absorbed from my family and the world around me. I was aware of it with my friends and avoided those who were unhappy. I would want to help them, but being so young it was often frustrating as I didn't have the capacity to help everyone who suffered, so I started to block people from my heart. Survival has been a big journey of finding the balance in my life on what I take as mine to look at, or what I release that doesn't belong to me.

With age and experience, I have evolved and shifted to being more conscious of what I'm feeling from others. Even my companion cat, Harley, shows me I still can take on the pain of other species. When I see him suffer with pain at times in his older age, I feel it powerfully in my heart. It's such a tough call—to be vigilant, or be swallowed up with the negativity around us.

> *I am blessed to have a network of conscious, like-minded friends who are proactive in education and campaigns to respect other species and Mother Earth. Thus, I no longer feel different. This gives me strength, and hope for a positive future for our planet to become a place of joy, and a peaceful race of humans who will have respect for other species and Mother Earth.*

My journey has been a long and joyful ride with many species who do not have a voice. It has been my passion and mission to give them a voice. Our companion animals have much love and wisdom to share with us, and much to teach us. Because they commune across many realms of existence while on earth, we can also be taken with them on joyful journeys to other realms of existence.

I wish for my book to inspire you to experience your relationships with your animal companions in new ways and to be more present with them. They always want to commune with us and need us to connect with them fully with our hearts. There is only one language they know—the language of *love*, which can only be accessed beyond our minds of chatter, where one soul knows another through the gateway of the heart. This is where my story begins for this journey.

Would you like to come on a journey with me to meet other species and find out what wisdom and love they have to share with humans?

Author's Message

This book will take you to places in your heart you may have never thought possible, a guide to find a way to places beyond this physical 3D reality, to other realms of existence with many species. If you can bring your heart with you, it will be a most enjoyable journey to feel love like never before and find new dimensions to explore on this earthly plane of existence.

It gives me great joy to share these life experiences. I feel very blessed to have had so many souls come to visit me on my life journey. They've shared so much joy, wisdom and unconditional love with me, a healing balm for my sensitive heart, supporting me to release the pain I've felt and witnessed on this planet that continues to happen with each generation.

I feel passionate to be part of the solution to support changes needed to respect other species and this beautiful home we call Mother Earth or Gaia, who sits like a jewel out in space.

This is my second book. My first book, *Seeker of Freedom and Joy, Inspiring Life Journeys of an Enlightened Heart,* is a road map with landmarks for the reader to gain insights on the winding road to liberate the self from pain and suffering. There I share transparently how my heart and soul guided me to a life of communing with other species.

Here I share my story and hope it inspires you to begin your own journey with your animal companions and other species from a new perspective with new eyes, and to one day share your own stories with many others. As our new earth is being born here and now, we have a great opportunity to change our relationships to respectful ones with all species and Mother Earth. We can support a new cycle for our children and grandchildren to find joy and peace here on earth.

I should explain some labels you will find as you read. Furry companions, animal companions and soul companions are all equally my animal companion friends who are in non-human bodysuits. I use the following labels interrelatedly for my ancestors, soul star galactic family and spiritual guides throughout this book in different contexts. They are all light beings who have made themselves known to me and I communicate with regularly across realms of existence. They originate from the Andromeda Galaxy, where I originate from and will return. They have all lived many past lives with me and know my soul's purpose here on earth.

The Power of Love with Animals

When I look into my animal companion's eyes,
I see their Soul.
When I hug my animal companion,
I feel our hearts become One.
When I see my animal companion suffer,
I feel their Pain.
When I see my animal companion not respected,
I feel them Disempowered.
We Are All One*.*

Debra A. Lansdowne

Introduction: Communicating with Other Species

Our Relations...

> *Many humans are living unconsciously in the 3D world, unaware of the other worlds around them. Other species, including our soul companions, live in many dimensions. They see and are aware of energies, thought forms and emotional wave forms that humans can only imagine.*

Indigenous cultures believe the physical world we live in is the Dream, while our spirit eyes show us our Real world in other dimensional realms of existence, where all our ancestors are in other forms. We chose to come to earth and manifest our own 3D Dream in human bodysuits to journey on earth.

> *To be empowered is to remember—we all create our own reality here in the physical realm, and we can choose to commune with other species across realms at any time.*

You, me, every human being is a love spark from the same infinite force of love that surrounds us all, and we chose our human bodysuits to carry our spirit here on earth. Only a thin veil separates life on earth and life in other realms of existence. Our souls direct us from across the veil of the 3D world to find our own unique journey and the lessons we agreed to come to earth to learn and experience for our souls to evolve. At our deepest connection we are pure love. We know this when we feel the power of unconditional love from other souls.

Introduction: Communicating with Other Species

*What is love? It is the glue that holds us all together,
an energy of highest frequency that keeps us all connected
with everything in the universe, including humans
and other species.*

We all know love when we feel it, for love is the language of our souls. It feeds us, keeps us safe, supports us, and we can share it with others to give them joy and to help them heal. We can access this higher vibration of love when we heal our hearts of the cloudy, heavy energy of not forgiving others, not loving ourselves, of guilt, shame, grief and childhood wounds we carry deep in our hearts. Begin to release the toxic energies from your heart and you create space for the light of your soul to break through the cracks, and then you can function from a higher vibration of love—beyond this limited 3D realm of existence.

*As we raise our vibration to higher frequencies of love,
we can commune through our higher heart intelligence,
and that's when we can commune with other species,
and they with us.*

I have been communing with other species since I was a young child. As an empath, I have been gifted with magical moments with many species, which I found to be a blessing. However, if I feel into the question of *how do we commune with other species*, what follows is what I found to be helpful. I hope it provides you with a starting point to find your own path to communicate with other species.

My own experience has shown me the most helpful way to communicate with other species is to learn meditation and a deep heart connection within yourself.

*Learn how to connect with your soul through the
portal of the heart. First, know yourself well, then you*

> *can start to connect with the souls of other species through the unified field of source consciousness across other realms of existence.*

We cannot know what others are trying to convey to us if we do not know ourselves, and so can be mindful of our own thoughts interfering when communing with other species. Knowing yourself is essential to know what is *not* yours. It can be challenging to learn about yourself deeply, but it is needed to interact with other species. Our soul-to-soul interactions do not relate to logical thinking, as they are simply energetic transmissions of love, respect and reverence for all species.

Love is the energy that holds everything together and makes it interrelated, but most of us do not remember that much of the time. It is simple—love is all there is—anything else is fear masked by many symptoms. Fear is all that keeps us from being connected, separating us from the web of life that is full of magical and unexpected experiences we can receive when we are truly connected in love.

Why is staying connected in love one of the most challenging things to do? Because we have so many wounds, collected in our present and past lifetimes, that cause us pain in our hearts and need to be healed. We also carry ancestral wounds we have agreed to heal as our service to our ancestral families and humanity.

I found meditation most helpful as a starting point because it teaches us how to be centred, in a clear space with no judgement, and from there we can connect through our higher heart intelligence of our souls. Some basic communing skills can be observing our furry companions use of tones, a bit like talking, to express when hungry, sad, angry, protective, warning us, etc. This can be helpful as a first step to practice feeling comfortable to communicate with them.

A little more challenging is when we connect with the other species, such as trees, water, rocks and crystals, earth and the ancestor spirits. For them we need to be more conscious and aware, using our heart portal and intuitive wisdom to help us determine certain ones which are our relations. First though, you must learn within yourself how your body feels energetically, so you will then intuitively know your own soul relations.

Sometimes, I can be sitting with my soul companion and feel

great respect and love, acknowledging them in my heart, then I feel a spontaneous response from my companion in my heart. I must admit, hugging them is the most wonderful part as it fills my heart with unconditional love.

When I sit on the ground outside, connecting with Mother Earth's body, open-hearted and totally present in the moment, another species will often arrive and make themselves known to me.

"Hello, thank you for visiting. Do you have a message for me today?" I ask them.

Sometimes I feel to use sound out in nature to commune with other species, and they love that frequency. I have learnt from their responses it is an invitation, calling out to them to come to me, if they feel to do so. Often, they watch me with curiosity, and I feel they want me to commune with them. I'll attempt to commune if I intuitively feel to do so through my heart intelligence of the soul, or I may simply sit with them in silence together after my sounding, as it changes the vibrational frequency of this reality to peacefulness. We have so much magic waiting for us to tap into.

There are many ways to commune with other species telepathically and intuitively through our senses. The inner visions, our emotional intelligence by feeling, hearing sounds with clarity, our taste sense can help us, we can smell with high sense distinctly, and finally, intuitively trusting ourselves through the hands by writing automatically without engaging the mind of judgment. I have used these forms of communication, with many of the other senses, to intuitively commune with other species. Most humans have many of these senses available to them, but they are like muscles, we need to practice using them for them to be accessible to us.

Do you know what your strongest intuitive sense is?

How Can we Commune in Practical Ways?

I know I am a spark of the divine force of love that surrounds us all, and we are all connected to everything. When I experience love I know it, because love is what I am. I commune with my heart because that's where love is for me, not my little egoic mind that does not know love, only knows logical thinking, doubts and judgments.

Heart open, I begin by being in a meditative space in my head, where my mind is silently chattering in the background without my attention. I can then go beyond that chatter and feel myself tap into my higher aspect of my mind, beyond the egoic mind of logic. The higher mind is beyond words. It is a state of being in peace and harmony, centred within oneself to feel love for self and everything around us. It is where my soul can commune with me through my heart space. When this state of connection to the self is found, I can then focus on connecting to the soul of the species I am communing with. All this is felt in my heart space. Send out unconditional love from your heart and every cell of your body becomes open to receive, and to acknowledge everything with reverence and respect as your equal.

If I give the chatter attention when my mind interferes it stops the flow and I feel stuck, like nothing is happening, or I'm unable to feel if a connection is being made. And then judgment is heard in my mind. Any distortions of emotions that arise in my heart and need healing will also block my feeling of connecting when I open to commune. We need to know our own body and feelings and be able to open the heart with love unconditionally, without fear.

Here I share my practice with you:

1. I suggest learning and practicing meditation will be of great benefit. Practice regularly to control the mind that wants to interfere with your thoughts and feelings of peacefulness.
2. Allow your whole body to feel into the experience, not just your mind. Feel into the peace and centredness with an open heart. You need to know what being centred feels like in your own body. Use breath awareness.
3. Now open heart-to-heart with the other species.
See with eyes of gratitude for the blessings you receive and the beauty in your life and allow your heart to feel love expanding out, for then you can receive the love around you.
4. Invite the other species to commune with you. Remember we are working with free will and respect here, so it may not be the right time for them to be communing with you. Graciously accept the answer, whatever that is.

5. Be prepared for the unexpected. We are not in control of the universal force. You are in the flow of whatever is meant to be for you in the moment.
6. Remember the timing may not be as you expect it to be, taking longer perhaps than you hoped. Everything is in divine timing with the universal force.
7. When you finish communicating, give thanks and gratitude for what you have experienced and received.

If you have an open heart, intuitively aware of your energetic body and feelings, the most direct way is to go to the heart space, as this takes you to your soul. Allow your heart to expand and feel into your pure higher heart of the soul, without judgements of the mind, and send unconditional love from every cell of your body out. Allow yourself to receive, and be open to what presents in your heart space.

What if You Are Not Able to Connect?

If the mind is in control and engaged, you may feel you have had no communication. You probably did commune, but missed the moment because the mind interfered, taking you into judgment and doubt. The engaged mind will stop the flow of connection. It interferes with the soul's journey and stops us from feeling the great joy of life and feeling connected to other species.

> *Connection is all about learning to control the mind and allow the flow of your soul to enter the body's field to find a way to give you the peace and joy we all look for on earth.*

Most people make it more difficult than it is because the mind causes distractions with chatter. That is why we need to learn to disconnect from the mind with a meditative state of being. When you know yourself at a deeper level beyond the mind, with your open heart, you'll know all your own relations (ancestor souls as other species) when they visit to commune with you, supporting your soul's journey.

When we commune with other species and the earth, our soul

reads and connects with other souls in our connectedness. They are not physically connecting in 3D. We are connecting at a soul level through our heart portal—the frequency of *love*—the language and thread of all species. Love travels across the universes, to far-off places in our galaxy and beyond. It is not what we have been told in the past—some believe when we commune with other species it is the 3D reality of language, such as French, German, Italian, English etc. Wouldn't that be limiting!

Healing and Opening Our Hearts

This universe, and other realms of existence, may appear to be way beyond our understanding when we use the mind as a human being, which is why we need to commune from open hearts. Our hearts can be blocked when we carry emotional pain and suffering from past events. You may not even remember events, as I have experienced, until you consciously start to heal. As you remember them, you can release the shadows held deep in the body.

Our soul tries to heal us by showing us strong emotions in our body, which can be triggered unknowingly by another person or event, an innocent comment or another's actions towards you. We don't always need to know the story to let it go, but we can be aware enough to acknowledge how it feels when we are triggered and choose not to react, then to release it. This will allow more light and love in our hearts, giving us that humming vibration within our energetic field that makes us feel peaceful inside and allows us to connect through the heart with the infinite force that surrounds us all.

When we have unhealed emotions in the heart, we have distorted energy spots in our body energetics, causing physical and emotional pain that unconsciously pushes us to feel triggered, not feeling that humming, peaceful vibration within our body. Finding peace within is to heal the distorted parts of our energy within us.

We are not solid forms. We are vibrating energy fields who come to find a bodysuit to experience limitations and emotional intelligence as a human being.

Introduction: Communicating with Other Species

Consciously working with our emotions is the key to greater health and healing—to expand our hearts to receive more light and heal the distorted energy in our bodies and hearts. That is, if we acknowledge strong emotional responses in our body, we can then let them go so we can find the peace we are all want to feel in our bodies. We then begin to experience the universe and our world with all the senses, in a more evolved state of consciousness. This can open us to find magic awaiting us in life, as we will see with our spirit eyes and feel the mysteries of life beyond the limited 3D world. This is how we commune with other species within our universe and world.

Your heart is a portal—the key to communing with all realms of existence, because it's your soul's gateway to learning and experiencing the 3D world, keeping you connected to the bigger universal energy beyond the mind and the 3D bodysuit as a human being. If we work with our hearts, bypassing the mind and bodysuit, all can be revealed to us. Magic happens around us every day, whether we see it or not. We need to awaken from our deep states of not feeling—the time is now.

It is a journey and does not happen overnight. We simply need to keep healing our hearts and allow forgiveness and compassion in the heart to allow more light as we evolve consciously, opening us to a new understanding where our own wisdom can be heard to guide us, not the egoic mind, which is connected to the human bodysuit and keeps us limited. The mind is merely a computer processor of thoughts that we choose to act on, and it will die with the human bodysuit to be recycled back to earth. I share here based on my own experiences, both in this life and remembered from my wisdom of past lives.

Call on your own compassionate ancestors' soul star galactic family, for they will have your back and be keen to help you. I call on my ancestor spirits frequently. They have supported my book writing journey by supporting me to heal my heart. As a sensitive, I have needed this to access those deeper parts of me that challenge me to write my book. My ancestors make it known they wish to help me heal, as I commune with them when I have come across painful feelings from the past that need to be released.

Writing our own book of life in a sacred space from a higher mind can heal us at incredibly deep levels. Having this support, knowing the ancestors are always available to communicate with me, I feel blessed and empowered. They share many subjects, in particular around my soul's journey here on earth. I find it exciting so many of our ancestors are right beside us, waiting for us to commune. They want us to succeed for the soul family, humanity and Mother Earth. It has been such a blessing to journey with them beside me, as I now live in dual worlds as I communicate with them across the veil of illusion, into other realms of existence.

The communication varies. I never know when or what will present. It is not planned. I get an intuitive feeling to call on them and they respond almost immediately, telling me they are always with me and ready to help. Their support can be around questions to help me remember my past lives, if it is relevant, or gives me wisdom about the unfolding of the planet's evolution with humanity at this time. The ancestors made a contract with me before I came to earth that they would fully support me on my soul's journey, but they will not do any healing unless I ask. As they remind me, we all have free will, and that's spiritual law across all species and all realms of existence and time.

When I first started to acknowledge and commune with the ancestors it was outdoors, on my travels across the landscapes in many countries. They would make themselves known through the elements and other species, such as with a strong wind passing me. I could hear their whispers in the trees, through rocks calling me, or by the winged, the four-legged—so many species!

Then I began to acknowledge and call in our ancestors to join my group workshops. The power of love and joy in my workshops was raised noticeably with participants receiving healing when we invited all compassionate ancestors to join us, respectfully, and only after I first acknowledged the original custodians of the land we were journeying on. It became a very crowded room energetically. I have such gratitude for the support and love they have shared with me in my life.

When I began to formally practice interspecies communication in my early forties, all my soul companions returned to me with messages, more complex and at a deeper level of understanding than previously, to remind me of my soul's journey and keep me on track.

In 1998 I had an extraordinary meeting with my ancestors (soul star family) from the Andromeda Galaxy, on a lightship (spacecraft)

Introduction: Communicating with Other Species

in another realm of existence. My group of spiritual friends all felt a tremendous energy vibrating above our friend's house where we were meeting. Her dog had spent the last few days barking at the roof and behaving in strange ways, and she had experienced strange happenings in her home with doors and cupboards opening and closing.

A channel, my friend had been communicating with light beings in past months. This day we sat down to meditate and were all taken to stairs leading up to the roof of my friend's home, assisted by a loving light force field of energy. We were soon inside a lightship that glowed with blinding light and was crowded with many beings waiting to greet us. They did not speak with words, using only telepathic communication, which I could understand immediately. That surprised me at first.

They emanated intense frequency of unconditional love and brilliant light from their energetic field—on reaching my heart it just about exploded! I become emotional, crying joyfully, for I somehow knew those light beings. I felt them so strongly in my heart it was unmistakable. It was so powerful I could have easily stayed on that light vessel. I realized how I had missed that high frequency of unconditional love here on earth. The experience is etched into my memory.

"We are your soul family of light," they shared, "do you not remember us?"

My soul star family. Wow, it was mind blowing. Had I not been with my group, who also felt the intense love and recognized the beings as their soul family, I might not have believed it possible. Later, I found out they were ancestors of my soul star galactic family, from Andromeda Galaxy. They have been watching over me, and their souls have been visiting me here on earth in many forms and species to support my soul's journey here on earth.

Not too long after this awesome event my life took a big turn—my new partner Nigel (who later became my husband) and I had a strong calling in our hearts to travel across Australia to some of the oldest parts of the earth. In remote areas of Australia, billions of years old, we discovered the rocks and landscape that hold records of the planet's beginnings, physically and energetically. This became apparent as we journeyed, leaving crystals and sounding into the landscapes and song lines, and meeting with the Aborigines on their lands. I also found out later that my leaving of crystals has been helping the lightships of my soul star family to connect and heal Mother Earth.

Some years later, my husband and I were guided by our ancestors to go and live in the centre of Australia, where in 2008 I felt to start writing a book. It took three attempts over several years before I took it seriously in 2017, when another ancestor came while I was having a massage, telling me it was time, I must share my stories and not keep these gifts for myself. I felt the calling and began madly writing, no shortage of words! All my ancestors' soul star family started communicating with me to support my journey as an author, telling me I'm meant to share these stories as my soul's mission is to come to the earth to live the stories, then inspire others to take the path of their hearts.

As I share many parts of my life's puzzle, this point is clear to me—trusting the heart is the only journey we need to go on. I can say this from my own experience, as I have never had a plan for my life. I have always known having a conscious plan would limit me, and life unfolds piece by piece as I now journey as an author. The magic keeps unfolding and I keep learning and remembering my past lives, enriching my life here on earth. I now live in dual realities, walking the earth and beyond the 3D world connecting with other realms.

'The more I learn, the more I realise I do not know, and this excites my soul to explore more,' has become my motto. My ancestors have supported and walked with me in this life. I have so much gratitude for them all.

Energetic Frequencies of Animal Companions

Are all our animal companions of the same energetic frequency?

I believe humans are souls who come to earth to experience life in human bodysuits, to feel emotions, and have lessons to learn for the souls to evolve as unique energetic frequencies. The soul companions who resonate within our hearts also come to evolve as unique energetic frequencies. The only difference is they chose to come in an animal bodysuit to support us on our soul's journey through life. Sharing their

Introduction: Communicating with Other Species

wisdom can help us heal our hearts and remind us of who we really are—bigger than this physical human bodysuit!

I have had many soul companions come to me, however I also noticed I didn't have the same deep, soulful knowing connections with all my animal companions from past lives, not like I have experienced with soul companions Charles, Harley, Mandy, Sabastian and Bruno, who felt like my relations. I believe that while We Are All One and part of the same infinite force of love that surrounds us all in the bigger scheme of the universe and beyond, we're all unique sparks of this infinite force of love, with our own unique frequencies. Our vibration is unique, depending on where we are in our evolutionary path, and this determines us attracting similar vibrating frequencies of other souls from other realms of existence to come to help us remember who we really are and that we are not separate from any other species.

Are all species of the same bodysuit of the same frequency and evolutionary path? From my own life experiences and the path I have walked communicating with other species, I do not think so. Does that mean all species come with a unique purpose and mission when their soul arrives to experience the species' bodysuit they have chosen? When we commune with them, we can ask them.

I first heard it said many years ago that according to Buddhist tradition and Indigenous cultures other species are our relatives, and I have always felt a strong resonance to this statement. Indigenous cultures tell us when we tune in to our bodies and know ourselves, we can all tell which species of tree, animal and so on are our relatives in frequency. I resonate with this wisdom, as I have experienced this and know it as my own truth too.

My Animal Soul Companions

1
Charles: Wisdom and Guidance

What if we could be clear channels to receive telepathic messages from our companions?

In September 2007, I returned to the east coast of Australia after many years of travelling and having extraordinary, magical experiences with other species. I felt a strong calling to learn more about interspecies communication and ancient earth wisdom shamanic practices. I believe when the student is ready the teacher presents, as happened to me.

A friend emailed me about a five-day live-in workshop offered by the Rainbow Fianna: Wisdom School of Earth Keepers at a large animal sanctuary 500klms from my home. The work was based on shamanic teachings and initiations based on the Four Winds Society originating from South America, and this was the only place in Australia offering it. I knew straight away this was for me, even though I did not have the full payment available until the funds materialised one month later when I rocked up, ready and excited to take part. This became one of those life-changing events on my earthly spiritual journey.

Below is what I understood a few days into shamanic teachings. My life was about to change, as we were practicing animal communication with our companion animals who had died. Using their photos, we spent quite some time going on shamanic journeys and learning about the three worlds of the spiritual shamanic ancient earth wisdom.

Charles: Wisdom and Guidance

*The lower inner world is very organic.
Often, we meet archetypal animals or go to other dimensions, realms of existence, or other civilizations not of the physical world. They are other earthly realms which we can enter through holes in the earth, trees or tunnels, as they are gateways to these other worlds. Often a guide will meet us, and we can receive healing in these realms. I think of this when I have meditated with the trees or been on a shamanic healing journey and guides take me to an inner earth world.*

The upper world is etheric, beyond the earthly realm. There we can meet light beings, our spiritual guides, ancestors, star family and angels—helpers with a higher vision. We can receive our own guidance from the bigger picture of our existence—feeling through symbols, hearing messages or seeing visions. I experience this when I communicate with my soul star family of light beings and they share their wisdom, or in my deep meditation practice when I receive higher guidance.

*The middle world comprises the spiritual dimensions and soul aspects beyond the veils of our physical world. There we can travel anywhere at any time—past, present and future all at once.
We can commune with other souls, such as other humans we know in the spiritual world, trees, animals, crystals, ancestors of the land and other species' souls. Inter-dimensional soul travel to other realities helps get work done with other humans on earth as we connect with their souls. This I experience when communicating heart-to-heart with other species or doing earth energy healing with other humans.*

As we sat for dinner after a long day of learning, I started sharing with the group about my animal companion Charlie. My shamanic teacher picked up on Charlie pretty much straight away.

"I have a message from Charlie," she said.

Curious, I asked, "What is he saying?"

"This is a very long message. He asks that you get ready for it."

What on earth was this message? I was so excited to hear from him, even when it was coming through my shamanic teacher.

"He was your spiritual teacher in another life, that's why you had such a strong connection and soul memory of one another. It was in Atlantis. You worked with him and crystals to heal and do earth work. This is what you need to do now. Go to the desert and meet up with the Indigenous people and use double terminator crystals. Place them in locations which will become apparent to you."

The message was quite long, and my teacher was having trouble keeping up.

"You better go and get a writing pad to write this down," she instructed.

I missed writing some of the earlier message, but I was listening, and my heart was strongly feeling Charlie. The message continued for some time before the connection was lost. My teacher was surprised at how deep the connection was with my animal companion friend. I did not know why he spoke through her, but later I realised it was my first week of learning interspecies communication and I may not have been open to believe what I was being given.

My teacher had no doubt. "This was an example of why we need to be learning this tool to communicate with our companions, to find the deeper meaning with them. They have so much wisdom to share with us, if we can open our hearts to listen."

Following is part of the channelled message from Charlie that I was able to write down very quickly.

> Charlie tells me he has a lot to say. The soul of a high priest, he came back to earth to learn humility in a dog's bodysuit and did not like the feeling much. He prefers to be called Charles. He was my spiritual partner and teacher in Atlantis, working in the crystal temples. We did much energy work together.

He came back as my teacher mentor to support me to do what I came back here to do on the planet, that is, healing Mother Earth, working with energies, crystals and sounding. Together, we did lots of work with sounding and crystals in my past life in Atlantis.

He said I needed to get on with my sounding and working with crystals, to walk the song lines healing the earth. I must walk without shoes on the land. Lots of walking needed on the land in the desert, and I need to work with the Aboriginal people.

Charlie predicted I would meet an Aboriginal grandmother to help me with energetic work. He said I need to sound with double terminator crystals and then bury them. He will help me when I arrive there, just ask for help. He also asked me to close the energetic cracks around my home, using crystals and sound.

I asked Charlie, "Will you be coming back to here on earth?"

Charlie said he had not deemed if he would be back on earth, but he is with me spiritually now and looks forward to working with me again.

From this point on, I will call Charlie by his preferred name, Charles, to respect his wishes.

What a pleasant surprise to receive this message! It was only my first week of ancient earth wisdom shamanic training, so I could hardly get my head around it all. I eventually did, and became excited to be having these communications with Charles four years after his soul had left the earth. This explained why he always had a knowing about him when he was my soul companion and lived with me. His companionship helped me heal my heart, and to awaken and become more conscious by remembering my past life gifts in 1992. His love healed and supported me through a very deep healing journey and transformation to find a new life awaiting me after releasing my old life.

What an extraordinary soul Charles is to come and help me in this way, even though it was not comfortable for him to be here on earth in the dog's body. I was fascinated to receive his message, for I had been travelling the country for some years with crystals, leaving them intuitively in different locations and using sound when I felt called in my heart to do so. However, I was not consciously working with them in the way he was reminding me from a past life I needed to do.

The interesting part was that on returning home after five days at the shamanic workshop, I shared Charles' message with my husband, and he also had a story. During the week I was away he had been woken in the night by Aboriginal elders telling him to go to the desert. He was being called. I was surprised to hear that, as we had not talked about going until that point, when I shared my message from Charles. How beautifully life unfolds when we are in synchronicity and flowing with our soul's guidance.

We did not hesitate to go, but both thought *that's all very well, but we will need a 4WD vehicle* because we had sold the one we had been travelling Western Australia in. And we would need jobs and a house to live in. You cannot just turn up in the Aboriginal community and decide to live there. These areas are privately owned lands of the Indigenous people—you need permits. We had travelled through some community lands before and had only stayed for an event. Thus, we knew a little about the protocols, but had never lived in a community.

There were hundreds of small remote communities in central Australia—which one were we going to stay in? Many questions arose from our spontaneous decision to go. My husband applied for a job off the internet, a position he had never done before, and was interviewed. When they asked why he should get the job, he said, "You'll not believe this, but I had Aboriginal elders come to me a few weeks ago calling me to go to the desert to see them." They did not seem surprised and showed no reaction over the phone. He thought *oh well, probably missed that job.*

Four weeks later they rang.

"You have the job in a large central desert community, a new 4WD and a house to live in while you work with the Aboriginal Community Service."

Before we went to the desert, we were called to make an overseas trip (more about that in the Harley chapter). This did not dampen our enthusiasm! My husband's new job meant he would be travelling to many communities to support them with housing and environmental care of their communities. Well, that all worked out! The universe was supporting us to go.

When he arrived, the aboriginal corporation discovered his wife (me) was a registered nurse.

"Do you think your wife would be interested to work in the same community as a Remote Area Nurse?"

"I will give you her phone number to call and ask her," he responded. So, I was given an interview and accepted by the same community corporation, administering over twenty communities. I had only dreamt of being a Remote Area Nurse in my nursing career, because it was only available with extra training and I didn't have that qualification. They waived the training, saying with my vast experience I would be suitable.

Before arriving, I received an information package. Because English was not the communities' first language, I needed to learn the native language and cultural customs of that remote region of Australia—an adventure in itself! I loved to learn about other cultures, and now with the guidance of my soul companion Charles, we had found work and a home in the desert to do my work with crystals and sounding. The blessing was I had always wanted to work in this type of nursing role which had so much autonomy to work independently, and it all fell into place reasonably quickly once the decision was made.

I arrived two months after my husband, leaving our rental property on the east coast to travel to the central desert of Australia and live in an Indigenous community, 500klms southwest of Uluru.

After my shamanic training, I began spiritually communicating with Charles on a regular basis. On the first session I did alone, I called him and intuitively felt his big energy around me straight away. Tears of grief rolled down my face as I felt to ask his forgiveness for my ignorance all those years ago—for not consciously communicating to let him know I was going travelling and would leave him with my ex-partner, Kara, for an unknown time.

"I never forgot you. That's why I returned before passing with a message, to show you that you were in my thoughts," was his response.

At that moment, I could feel him sitting on my lap, something he'd loved to do in the past as my companion. My heart expanded so strongly with unconditional love. He also shared that I needed to talk with more animals to get more practice. And I did. I set up an email site where I offered free communication sessions with other people's animal companions. Many people sent me photos of their furry companions with questions they wanted to know about them. Carers found me by word of mouth from other companion carers within Australia, and some found me from overseas, which did surprise me.

I started to notice a pattern. Many of the companions were taking on dis-eases of their carer. I found that many of the questions from the carers relating to behaviour problems resulted from a carer being unable to confidently commune with their companions. Our companions and other species want to commune with us every day and be heard by humans. It takes practice, but we can all do this through our heart connections, beyond the mind, in a meditative state. And we can always ask for help from our ancestors.

I share here one of my communications with Charles about the souls who come to earth in animal bodysuits. This proved to me our connection to everything. We are one—we are not separate to other species.

Communication with Charles.
Subject: Souls in Animal Bodysuits.

Charles: I am so excited and have waited for this moment since I left the planet and I came to you on my last day to let you know I was going. Now that was quite a long time ago.

Debra: Yes, I remember that day you came to me in 2003. It was such a surprise, but I knew it was you. I just so wish I could have been there when you passed over. I hope it was not so painful.

Charles: Oh, it was painful! Those needles are quite a pain to experience. You tell those vets it is not the gentle comfort they tell the carers it is, quite painful to the body, like acid going through the body, if you have ever had that kind of experience. I suspect you may not have.

My message is that many animals are not ready to go. It's crucial for humans to check in with their animals if, or when, they're ready to leave the planet, as they're like human souls—if they leave unexpectedly, they get stuck on the earthly plane and need help to move on to higher realms, being in shock.

So many of your animals are stuck in the pain of the planet, like the animals you eat, they are killed so inhumanely. It is not necessary to be acting and killing them so coldly. All you humans are doing is producing more pain in the energy field of this planet. It needs to be stopped, this killing in cold blood of the animals in such great numbers. So much suffering is in the energetic field of this planet due to this fact.

If you want to help Mother Earth become a peaceful, joyful planet, as she is planning to do with or without the human race, you need to stop and consider your actions towards animals on this planet. They are not respected. If they are your pets, they are killed if too sick, too old or have no carer. So much suffering is sent around this planet.

These souls are here in animal bodies. Just as you come to earth with a human bodysuit, they choose to come with animal suits to learn and experience their evolution. There is no hierarchy to the system. Many of the animals are far more evolved, with greater wisdom than those carers who look after them. Then there are the animals with carers who treat their animals like ornaments and toys, who think they are being kind, but are killing them with kindness.

Life is so full of surprises. You never know where it will take you when you go with the flow of what your heart is guiding you to do. My partner and I have always lived by our heart guidance, travelling and moving homes, intuitively feeling the call in our hearts without knowing why, adventuring into so many wonderful locations and realms of existence, and it continues to this day. The more I keep healing and expanding my heart, the more magic unfolds for me to experience and explore new terrain in life, giving me more depth to my life journey to experience with other species. I always feel so much gratitude, blessed to receive the gifts that have come to me in so many forms.

2
Charles: Kindred Souls

*Would you intuitively know a kindred soul in the form
of another species through your higher heart intelligence?*

Over many weeks, my heart had been calling me to find a furry companion, but I had been travelling a great deal and had no permanent address. Then that all changed. It was 1990, and I was living in a home with my partner Kara and felt it was time to find that special furry companion to share my heart and our home.

That day, in a cold concrete place filled with rows of locked cages, too many sad eyes pleaded with me. Their little faces looked up at me and they jumped up and down to gain my attention as I passed by. I felt each in my heart.

"Is this the one? Can we be friends?" I asked silently of each dog.

"No! She is not the one," I heard their little voices exclaim.

Confused, I did the circuit a second time.

There he was—the one! The feeling in my heart as I looked at him was powerful. As he came to the front of the cage, he caught my attention with his intelligent and curious expression. His face lit up and his little ears stood upright.

"Do I know you?" he asked.

His question went straight to my heart.

"Yes!" I began talking to him.

I felt something between us, and said to Kara, "This is the one!"

A caretaker let him out of the cage. When I picked him up to carry him, he cuddled me, like, "I know you?"

Our hearts connected. Wow, what a hug he gave me! I will never forget his big warm embrace—with all his legs! He was so full of love my heart exploded. That was it, I had no further questions. I loved him, and my heart told me this was the soul I was looking for. I could not leave him in that dog shelter another day. Kara also felt happy with him and loved all animals as I did, so there was no problem with him joining our family.

On the way home he sat in the back of the car like he had always been there. Only a puppy at four months old, he did not even need restraining. He simply sat up proud and tall, looking at us. He never barked or cried, just watched us with such inquisitive eyes and expression. This lovable soul, a collie-cross-cattle dog, had a tan coat with a white patch on his chest. He had been given the name Charlie by his previous family and appeared to already know his name, so we kept it.

I soon noticed that when we were on walks together, although he was very well behaved, he never wanted to mix with other dogs. He had no interest in them. He only wanted to be with me, playing games or sitting with me at home. He always had this knowing I could not quite get my head around. I did not know what he knew, but it was written on his expression and face—he knew me sometimes more than I knew myself! I found him highly intelligent and he learnt quickly, but if he didn't want to chase the ball, he would just look at me. I would intuitively feel and hear his response when I asked, "You want me to get that ball? No! I don't do that game."

One day, as I busily tidied my living room, I was stopped in my tracks by an almighty screeching noise out the front of my apartment, followed by a thud. I ran outside to see my seven-month-old Charles had been hit by a taxi. The driver had driven away. My neighbours all came out and tried to catch the number plate, but he was too fast. I picked Charles up from where he lay on the road and limped back inside with him.

My dearest Charles! We had connected so strongly, and I loved him so much! The vet said he was lucky to escape serious injury, that he must have been rolled so had not broken bones, but had sustained bruising that would slow him down for a while. The nephew of the tenant upstairs had left the side gate open to the yard, and Charles being an energetic and curious pup went out to explore the front of the street, which he must have crossed and collided with the taxi.

I could not believe the callous taxi driver drove off and left him lying in the gutter. The neighbours also felt very upset by what they had witnessed, but were happy to hear he would survive and had only sustained bruising. I was happiest of all, as I had already lost three of my furry companions in the past to fatal car accidents, and each time I was not with them when they passed over. It was an emotional sore point for me, losing so many of my furry companions within two years of having them, and never when I was with them.

My luck had changed! Charles survived and would be with me for some time yet. My heart was so happy! Charles improved, with no major problems. He slowed down for a week or so, and moved around with what I could see were bruised areas. It was unusual for him to be so sleepy, as his cattle dog crossbreeding meant he was a busy dog, highly intelligent and actively curious. He loved life as I did. During those healing weeks I felt his suffering as he looked at me with those sad eyes, filling my heart with sadness. I would remember how lucky I was that he had survived the car accident, that the world was not quite so cruel on that occasion and didn't take him away from me. After all, we had a whole new life to live together yet.

Life carried on as Charles grew into quite a large companion. He was so clever! I trained him to learn language commands to make sure he was safe with me, so he would know what I needed him to do when we were out near roads, walking to parks and so on. We had great fun in the park, where he would jump a little fence and catch the ball mid-air. He loved that game.

One day I took him along a path being built for a new freeway, down the road from home. Most of our dog-walking neighbours had been visiting this vast area. Previously our park, it was now a construction site for a freeway, almost at completion stage. Charles and I were playing along the cement area, where a ramp went off to the side and up to a bridge. It looked like a side road built off the main freeway to enter our suburb. Still under construction, it had a cement base, and the rails were all in place. The ramp meeting the little bridge was about thirty feet above the road below, with steel reinforcement in place for the following week's cement pour.

As we walked up the ramp, Charles became extremely excited. Running ahead of me, he jumped over the rail. As he dropped thirty feet down, I saw his panicked expression as he tried to wind his legs back up mid-air.

Charles landed on his side on the reinforced steel formwork below. I screamed as I ran to him. Winded at first, he must have got his breath, as he sat up and ran off like a crazy dog, back up through the suburb. He seemed confused, not knowing where he was going, in a state of shock. I chased him for a few streets, until finally he must have come to his senses and realised who I was as I called to him, desperately trying to get him to stop before he was run over again. Finally, I caught him, and he let me carry him home.

The vet said it was lucky he fell on his side as it probably saved his life. Due to his breed, he had a sprung rib cage, which meant it did not get broken. The other factor—not being cemented, the steel probably had a little give in it for a landing, which bounced him. Oh my God! This dog was so adventurous! Would he make it to the next stage of life? He was only ten months old. We took him home and again kept him indoors for two weeks and slowed him down while he rehabilitated.

Again, I could not help feeling his pain as he recovered. He would look at me with those loving eyes as he sat in his basket. So much pain I felt for my dear companion. He was my bestie; we did everything together. I so loved him! I was over the moon he'd survived the second trauma, but I couldn't help thinking he'd not made it to two years old yet, by which time my previous animal companions had been taken from me. Once he recovered, I was vigilant with him.

We ended up back at the park, and he played our ball game again, but we never went back to the building site on the new freeway. I remember how he looked at me that day, so excited and loving me, saying, "Look at me, I'll jump this little wall!" which just happened to be a railing thirty foot high, not the wall he'd thought, and this nearly killed him. My heart is raw with love for my furry companions, and Charles was testing me big time with the emotional pain of watching him go through so much trauma before he even reached maturity. Thankfully, I do not remember him causing more harm to himself after the bridge accident.

3
Charles: Loyalty and Devotion

My life changed unexpectedly in the early 1990s when I became seriously unwell, some months after my father passed away. This impacted on Charles too, who became my loyal and supportive companion when my life took a downward turn. I had started to struggle with chronic fatigue and adrenal stress. I had to leave my job and find healing for myself, as I'd been getting quite depressed and my body started to show signs of ill health with serious kidney problems, high blood pressure and ulcers in my gut. It was a low time in my life and kept me in bed, sleeping most of my days in an effort to raise my energy levels.

I guess I was sleeping twenty hours a day, only waking up when Kara came home to cook dinner. My devoted and loyal companion Charles was not going on any walks at all. The fun between us had stopped. I could not even walk him around the block. My life was falling apart. I loved life and would normally be highly active, but the condition took the very life force from me. Charles stayed by my side every day, just sleeping, and when I got up for the toilet, he walked with me. I always felt he was protecting me and showing me not to give up. When I looked over to him, he would give me those adoring eyes of love and my heart would melt. I felt so guilty I could not take him on walks anymore, but he never complained and went along with what I was capable of doing, which was sleeping, unfortunately.

Charles was normally highly active too, but he never took his attention from me. For a dog who loved life so passionately, I felt that was a big sacrifice for him. I don't think he even cared—he just wanted to be with me no matter what my life was dishing out. He was so loyal, and patiently showed me his unconditional love. I so loved him for all the healing and love I felt coming my way, as emotionally I felt hopeless and had become severely depressed with my limitations. Looking at him and feeling his big heart, I would feel motivated not to give up on life, for I had this beautiful, loyal and devoted friend wanting to be with me. I had to do this for him.

Depression took such a hold I was contemplating suicide most days when Kara went to work. *How would I do this*, I thought? Unable to do anything, I felt I had no life, which made me feel I should not stay here on earth any longer. My life force had been drained from me and the long days of resting did not seem to be making any difference. Was my impatient nature causing me to suffer more? The doctor explained, "You do not have any reserves like healthy people have available. You have drained your adrenal reserves, so it's going to take a long time to find some normality to live with this condition."

Live with this condition? I was not going to live with this condition! I would heal or leave this planet. In those moments I thought it was time to leave my body, when I could not cope in life without freedom, my dear Charles would look at me with a curious expression. He would sit beside me, head on my lap, looking up with those loving eyes, and my heart would expand with love.

Charles kept me grounded and sane on this planet. I felt he could read my mind telepathically, and I would telepathically hear him saying, "I love you, it will all change, keep resting. I am not leaving you." I felt intuitively so much healing from his heart and I would begin to feel much better and fall asleep again.

I learnt meditation and researched my condition. One alternative therapy suggestion was to use a mini trampoline to slowly build my body stamina, starting with a few minutes a day. All I could manage at first was bouncing, then building up to jumping, and when I was ready, walking for a few minutes a day. I followed those instructions to slowly exercise, changed my diet and meditated, all of which helped detox my body and mind, while I continued to rest for many hours every day.

Over several months, I made some progress following this healing path, along with rest periods and a meditation practice. This graduated into a simple exercise regime and detoxing, finding the balance to support my body's healing. Eventually, I was walking around the block for ten-minute increments, slowly building up to half-hour sessions. This was so wonderful, because I was taking Charles with me around the block and not once did he ever try to push me to play ball. He simply walked with me very slowly and purposefully, like he knew exactly what I was dealing with.

How did he know so much about my healing? I believe we were connected at a soul level, and when we communicated through our hearts he knew me as a kindred soul. At the time it was hard to explain, but he seemed to have this *knowing*. For him to be so active, then be silently walking with me at my own pace, never pressuring me to take him walking, was extraordinary. He knew what was needed and was with me every step of the way. It was quite incredible how much support he gave me. I don't think I took it in at the time, as I was so focused on my own illness and he wasn't demanding of me in any way. Such a beautiful, intelligent soul. Why he was so attuned to me became clear some years on, after he had passed away.

Interesting that I had no idea of our connection at that time, but something in my heart told me he was helping in ways I didn't understand then. I felt he knew I was seriously ill, and he was going to be there with me. We have so much to learn from other species. The unconditional love shared by them, and the service they give us, helps us to evolve and live our mission on this planet. My heart always knew I was doing the right thing in finding Charles that day at the shelter. As I look back now, I understand that Charles supported my spiritual awakening and life transformation.

Many years later, in 2003, I was travelling in Northern Australia. My then my ex-partner Kara, who loved Charles as I did, had taken over his care after we split up. Travelling around remote areas of the country, I would often think of Charles and could always feel his energy around me, reminding me how much I missed him when at a park or beach, as they were our happy places, walking and playing together with much laughter and joy.

Charles was thirteen years old then. Kara called to catch up and shared that Charles had started to show signs of ageing in recent months, with a couple of lumps on his head. She assured me he was okay otherwise. The next week I was sitting in my caravan, daydreaming, and Charles popped into my head. Telepathically, I immediately picked up his picture from my dresser and thought, *I must get back to the coast to see him over the Easter break in a few weeks.*

Suddenly a message came to me—as strong and clear as a voice in my head!

"It's time for me to leave now, I'm coming to say goodbye. I have not forgotten you. My time here on earth has come to an end. I love you."

I knew immediately it was Charles. I intuitively felt his energy so strongly, all around me. I was surprised to receive this message, and that I actually heard it so loud and clear without a doubt, as though he whispered in my ear as my heart immediately connected with him. I had not experienced that before. What I heard was undeniable. Our souls knew one another very well from the past. My heart always knew the resonance we shared between our souls, from that first day at the dog shelter when we found one another.

Kara rang me a week later to tell me he had passed away at the veterinary clinic. She had finally found the courage to ring, knowing I would be upset. I responded, "Yes, I know." She was a little taken back by my comment, so I explained that he came to me in spirit to say goodbye when he passed over. I pondered how surprisingly calm I was when I received his message. I had been feeling the sadness, but I felt and knew he was still around me and would always be with me. Kara was so relieved to hear this that she started to cry, "I'm so sorry he didn't make it for you to see him on your return trip, but he had lumps on his head and the vet said he wouldn't make it, best to let him go in peace by euthanasing him with the injection."

That really upset me, as I always wanted to be with my soul companions when they left the earth and I did not get the chance, yet again. The opportunity was not there for me to give all my love, but he came to me instead with a message, and that was a huge gift that gave me great comfort, along with feeling him around me.

If you have a furry companion, do you know why they are with you?

I share here some of my many pages of communications with Charles from 2018/2019, whilst writing my books.

Communication with Charles.
Subject: Our Past Life together.

Debra: Charles, how do our souls know one another?

Charles: Our souls met in a time beyond where you are right now. It was also a time when the planet was going through many changes. We came to work together to help with the evolution of this planet. It was a huge time. We were teachers of many people, showing that unconditional love is all that is needed to ride the waves of destruction, and so the time is here again for this to be shared.

As for the animals on your planet, they have so much to share if many would listen to them. So much wisdom is within those other beings who are seen as lesser by the people of earth who don't understand we're all one and we all have a soul. We come back to earth in many forms to experience and learn so much, and to help the planet with our own gifts. You are one of these who came back to help this planet, and many species, find peace and joy.

So many are harmed—the ones without voices. So much cruelty, pain and suffering abounds on the planet. It is up to you, and many others, to let people know we are all the same. We came back to help our carers like you—Mandy, Harley and me. We had to help you in a different form. You never had any children, so we found a way to meet with you and help guide you on the path of evolution with loyalty, love and companionship.

We do not have judgement, as many do towards your animal species. They cannot see what they are throwing out the door when they do not listen to us.

They need to be fully in their hearts and expanded to feel us, as you are, dear one.

I came to help you find your way back to the light, and you know I stayed with you every moment when you were in a dark place, and never let you out of my sight. I never complained, and I sent you so much healing light so you could see there was hope, even in the darkest hours of your life. And I believe that is what you felt, but you were not aware enough to know where it was coming from. But I do believe you were aware my presence in helping you was part of my journey.

You also noticed I was not like other dogs. I never mixed with other dogs and really did not enjoy the life of a dog, but I did enjoy the fun and love you shared with me. We are so destined to be together again for such a great cause of helping humanity and Mother Earth.

We need to get our message out to the wider community to view their furry friends in new ways, and to listen to their calls, as they have much wisdom to share with humans at this time. They are here to help their carers and to help Mother Earth, that is their mission. As I mentioned, I was not much of a dog personality. As you know, I was more a human type of dog and only responded to human interactions.

Debra: Charles, what is our history together?

Charles: We have travelled many lifetimes together. This one I chose to be your companion animal in a dog's body. It wasn't terribly comfortable and I wouldn't put my hand up to do that contract again, but it was an experience. I so loved to be with you, as I proved to you when I came to tell you of my leaving the planet. You knew it was me because we are always connected at the heart. That is all you can be. The most powerful place to be connected is in the heart. No space can change that feeling across many realms of existence.

I came to you later to remind you what you came to do on the planet. That was to connect and place those crystals around the places you visited so we could connect with our lightships, and you did that.

Debra: What do you mean by your lightships? Spacecraft?

Charles: Yes. We are always doing healing work on the planet from our lightships and smaller spacecraft. Do you not remember that from the first contact you had with us?

Debra: Yes, I do. I feel that pain arising in my heart again as I talk with you.

Charles: Dearest, you are just remembering our time together and the love you shared with me. I so loved you and cherished all the fun we had together. I was so glad you found me at the shelter.

Dearest, keep those crystals energised and connected. You need to connect them all together. Remember the things you did in your past life with the crystals. Please tell the people about the crystals and your experiences with them. Crystals are also a species that is not really understood on your planet. Clearing them on the full moon and in the ocean are good for your crystal friends. Talk with them, see what it is they want. You have done this before, just remember all these things so you can help them.

Debra: What would you like to share on the earth crystals?

Charles: So much needs to be shared by you and many others to show how humans are not respecting Mother Earth, or other species, who are also important to help heal Mother Earth and the people.

Crystals can help heal many if they are treated with respect by asking for their wisdom. Many need to know what you have experienced and already know. This has been your calling to come to earth to do this. All these experiences are here in your heart, dearest, keep healing that heart. You have it all inside of you, a lifetime and many other lifetimes to access.

You live from an unconditional heart, dearest, let it be seen for what it truly is. So many need the love you have to share and your passion for this earth and all beings who inhabit it right now.

So much confusion, anger and pain are around the planet from what humans are unconsciously doing to other species and to themselves. They are creating more karma and pain. You know from your own experience what that feels like.

Communication with Charles.
Subject: Past Life With Crystals.

Debra: Charles, what is our history together with crystals?

Charles: Our past life together was in Atlantis. You were in a spiritual school. I also know you from our soul family, that is probably the most significant. Our soul star family reside in Andromeda. You will return there.

You are highly trained to use crystals and commune with them.

You have had many experiences on the earth planet in this life. You need to now share with many so they understand how the rocks, crystals and other species have an intelligence and wisdom that must be considered, for they keep taking them from locations and using them as toys and decorations. They all have a mission to do certain things on this planet.

Dearest, you must share this information you have inside of you, all the experiences that have come to you as gifts to help you remember your past lives, and your experiences with all the stone and crystal families. This is how you can help the many, who will be surprised with what you tell and share with them. They need to know. Others will have forgotten, but you'll help them remember their past with the crystals and stones.

Keep sharing all the experiences you've had on earth, this is our gift, your communing with other species. Many will be surprised and may never have thought they are exploiting the stones, or that they also come with a mission to help the planet. We need to listen to them. They have their own wisdom and intelligence that needs to be respected by the human race.

They are so disrespected by so many humans and not used with sacredness or honour, being used as decorations and toys to play with or to adorn their houses.

Speak with the crystals, ask them what they would like. Share all those passions and times you have had with them, and the sad times that are remembered in your heart when you have experienced the exploitation of such mammoth proportions on your planet.

So many are taken disrespectfully and used for exchange of gold, and this is not honouring their wisdom. They, as you know, come with a family around them to support them. People need to be aware of what they are doing when they remove them without asking them. These are all the things that point towards a healed heart—to hear the voices of these ones.

You can help shed light on this for the many to know and think about when they are collecting them for less sacred purposes. You, dearest, came to be the voice of the unheard. Here is your opportunity to help with that, getting the message out to the world for all to see. It is very different to what many can see, but it all comes down to the heart being healed for them to hear the whispers that they may pick up from the voiceless.

These communications with Charles highlight that if we can heal our hearts to open up to interspecies communication across other realms of existence, we will start to remember wisdom we have forgotten from our past lives.

I remember hearing from an Indigenous elder in South America that when we come to earth in our human bodysuits most of us only have 3% of our consciousness available to us. Our earthly journey is to unveil the illusion and raise our consciousness to remember who we really are and why we came to earth. In saying this, we are part of a unified field, so we have much help available to us from other species, and from light beings in other realms, waiting to commune with us.

4
Harley: Our Kitten

Some months after Charles' bridge accident, my partner Kara found a mother cat with young kittens in the dumpster at her workplace industrial site. She felt compelled in her heart to bring them home, and decided to keep the mother cat, who we named Megsy. She had beautiful ginger markings on her coat and proved to be an incredibly good mum to her kittens. I fell in love with a little beige-coloured kitten from the litter. I felt his cheeky free spirit and our hearts lovingly connected. At the time, Kara had a Harley motorbike and my free spirit enjoyed riding pillion. I thought *yes, this kitten is a free spirit with a big personality, I will call him Harley.* The other kittens all found forever homes with friends.

Charles, then twelve months old, had shown no interest in other animals, but he met and connected with Harley straight away. Inseparable, they slept together every night in Charles' dog basket, played together, and were always around me. Charles protected Harley with his gentle paw motions, never hurting him when they played together.

For a small kitten, Harley had a big personality. He always got everyone's attention and won their hearts with his antics, like meowing with me when I played my music, and finding a way to sit on my shoulder when I played guitar or harmonica. Such a beautiful boy, he also had a cheeky, mischievous streak, which got him into loads of trouble after moving things from one place to another around the home. Harley followed me everywhere like a puppy dog and would play ball games with me. We all loved him and his mother Megsy, who was a passive and gentle wise soul.

We also had another adult cat called Karma, named by Kara's ex who left her with us. Pedigree Persian, Karma was very pretty shades of grey, but she was wild as hell, so we could not pat her or get near her. She would suddenly climb the walls or curtains for no reason we could fathom, then come down, eat her food and disappear outside for the day. None of our other furry companions were interested in or able to get near Karma, as she greeted everyone with much hissing. Apparently, Karma had had that temperament since she was picked up as a kitten, purchased from the breeder. I always felt maybe her name was causing a problem! Karma? She chose to be an outsider in our family of humans and furry companions, but we all accepted her craziness and she seemed happy to keep returning for food and her bed at night.

Our household was full with a large dog, two adult cats and kittens—all in a small 1920's two-bedroom apartment townhouse with a shared backyard. Our home was happy with laughter as we attempted to make some of our own music.

One afternoon in 1993, we had just waved my mother off at the front door. Five minutes later she returned, holding a lifeless bundle of fur in her arms, saying, "Sorry."

"Oh no! Is this my little Harley?" I sadly asked my mother.

"Yes," she responded, "he was in the gutter on the opposite side of the street to your house, near where I was parked."

Harley had only been in the house a couple of hours prior. I knew he liked to go outside exploring, but he usually returned within a short time. That day we had not noticed him missing as my mother visited us and we were deep in conversation for the afternoon. Strange we did not hear any noise of screeching brakes or cat crying sounds. Harley had no injury marks on his body. We could only presume he was hit by a car. I felt he must have been rolled, then gone into shock.

A young cat, his soul likely left his body quickly. His little body was limp, devoid of life. We were devastated. He so entertained us all and we loved him for his affectionate nature and cheekiness. Having been with us since he was a couple of weeks old, at twelve months old he left us. Heartbroken, we felt the loss deeply, as did our other furry companions.

Charles was unusually quiet, and Megsy mother cat was somber for several days after this event. With a little ceremony, we buried Harley in the backyard under the tree he loved to climb and remembered him as our playful little friend who loved music. The loss of the little soul with the big personality and his cheeky, affectionate nature left a hole in all our hearts. And yet, this was just the beginning of Harley's extraordinary life with me.

5
Harley: The Reunion

Could there be realms of existence we can access to give us a deeper meaning to understand why our companions come to us as souls we may already know?

Whilst volunteering in 2007 for a wildlife group, ARC animal rescue care group, where I supported injured animals to rehabilitate in my home and fed rescued fruit bats at a refuge centre, I had a calling. Another volunteer, a veterinary nurse, sent an email to members advising she had just been given a four-year-old male Burmese cat who needed to be homed. He had been living in a shipping container in a shopping centre car park for twelve months. A neighbour loved him and had been feeding him for a few months, but he was antisocial with other cats and she already had many cats in her home. Unable to offer the cat a home, she handed him over to the vet nurse to find a loving home.

I was not looking for a cat, but something about this email got my attention. I felt into my heart, *yes*, something called me to meet this cat and see what he was like, even if it was only out of curiosity. When I met the cat, he was living in the bathroom of the vet nurse's home as he would not tolerate her cats or dogs. He was quite antisocial with other animals, but highly intelligent, very affectionate towards humans and domesticated.

Entering the bathroom, I saw a beautiful beige cat sitting high up on the windowsill. We looked at one another and I felt his big energy straight away in my heart. He was a physically big, proud cat and demanded respect immediately.

"Do you want to come with me?" I put my arms out and up to him.

He jumped straight into my arms and hugged me. My heart expanded, I felt his love so strongly. He was such an affectionate and loving cat—I had to say yes. He sat in the cat cage so proudly during the ride home in the car. He didn't make a sound, and looked like he knew exactly where he was going. *Strange,* I thought, *Charles did exactly the same on his way home with me.*

Once home, he immediately demanded control of the house, walking around like he was the boss and looking at me affectionately. I sat on the lounge and watched him in the dining room, pondering on his name. Harley, an interesting name given to him by a previous carer. Apparently, his ear chip had many details: His name, the Burmese breeder's name, birth date, and the family he was sold to, who gave him to another family because they moved interstate. We had no details on the last family, so never found out how he ended up in the carpark. Was he lost or did he run away?

As he walked and explored the house, I kept thinking of my little kitten Harley who had died many years earlier. His fur coat was remarkably similar, a cream beige colour. Was that just an interesting coincidence? Feeling into his name and the many familiar feelings I felt in my heart with him, I tuned into him while sitting in a meditative state on the couch.

"Harley, are you the same Harley who was my kitten many years ago?"

Wham! Bam! Thud!

Harley had bounded across the room and landed on my lap, cuddled up to me and purred, pushing his head under my hand. He was all over me with affection like he had known me forever. Oh my! I cried as energy created vibrations throughout my body on the recognition of this same soul, Harley, coming home to me. Well, that was 'yes' from me, no doubt in my mind or heart that he was the one and had returned to be with me in this life again.

After about twenty minutes he wandered off around the house to continue his exploration, looking up at me with occasional glances of approval that he was happy to be home. I checked his date of birth on the papers and discovered he was born in 2003. His soul had returned to earth four years earlier, and he found me again in 2007 after living with three previous families. I wondered, was it synchronicity that this soul had found me at the time I was opening to animal communication practices?

After he settled in, I was keen to find out more on my relationship with this furry companion. I tried to make contact at a soul level, but it was very disjointed. I did not feel so confident with my own companion as I was so emotionally charged and connected to him. I had been reading messages for other friend's animals easily, but when I tried with Harley's soul, and being relatively early into my animal communication practices, he challenged me. Curiosity was too much for me, so I asked my shamanic teacher to do a soul reading with him. Two pages later, she had many details on our connection in our past life. And here he was again—after passing over so many years ago, his soul returned to be with me again. (At the time of writing, Harley has been on the earth for eighteen years, thirteen of them with me. This is the longest time I have ever had a soul companion with me.)

What follows is a shortened version of my teacher's message received from Harley. When I first read it, tears welled up in my eyes and my heart melted.

2007: Communication from Harley.

We are old souls and had a past life in Egypt together. I came here to help you move forward on your soul's journey. You need to travel to Egypt to connect with the energies. I suggest you need to return to yoga practices and use art sketching to help find healing. You need to drink more water and to open your third eye more to see me properly.

I am a very superior cat with high intelligence. I would like to be recognised for this, as I will be the chief 'holder of the energy' in the home. I have much to teach you about communication skills with me and energy by observing me and my behaviour.

You need to research the Egyptian cats of Egypt when they were revered. We were on a spiritual path together in Egypt, and I want to be treated as an equal. For my diet, I do not like dried food and want only fresh foods. This diet will keep me healthy for many years to be with you.

And I am really, really, happy and delighted to be back with you again.

Return to yoga and art to help me heal myself? Yes, I would benefit from yoga, my practice had lapsed over the years with all my travels and no routines. As for the art, I started art therapy and that took me on a healing journey I could not have imagined!

I was surprised to read all this, as was my shamanic teacher when I told her I had booked my Egyptian holiday in the past week while waiting for Harley's soul message. This was something I had felt called in my heart to do since childhood and had not pursued. At that time, I had already felt a strong calling to go with a spiritual group I had travelled with in previous years to Mayan temples in Central America. Who would believe it—they were going to Egypt to experience the pyramids and a cruise on the River Nile on a spiritual pilgrimage to access the old master energies of Egypt! It was a strong group energetically, as we had all remembered our past lives in Egypt and felt the calling. Without a doubt, I knew I had to go to Egypt, it was time, I was getting signs from everywhere telling me to do it.

Problem was I needed to place Harley somewhere, and did not want to put him in a cattery after having him for only ten months. I had a few months to organise a place, then without me even discussing it with her, my sister Kim came over and said, "I think I'd like a cat." She agreed straight away to look after Harley for a year while I went to Egypt and the desert. That was a surprise, as my sister was not normally interested in animals, not in the same way I have been all my life. Her husband did not feel much interest in cats, he was wanting a dog, but he came around and did agree to have Harley for the year. After a short time, Harley had him on side, affectionately snuggling up on my brother-in-law's chest every night to sleep on the sofa. Content, Harley happily stayed with my sister and brother-in-law until he returned to us one year later after our Central Australia journey. He has been with me ever since, moving homes happily and adapting to life in our Ford transit van, camping and travelling around this vast country.

6

Harley: Love and Compassion

What if we could communicate with our companions through our highest heart intelligence of unconditional love?

When I commune with other species and feel them respond to me with love, they appear to melt when I shower them with unconditional love from my heart. The response I receive in return is, "Wow, I can take this all day, give me more," and they show such gratitude on their little faces, like Harley when I give him full-hearted acknowledgement in hugs. I feel him melting into my arms and I could do anything to him as he relaxes and goes all limp. It is so beautiful to know he trusts me when I give him whole-hearted affection and compassion from my open heart. If I notice he is unwell I will do this hug and he perks up and appears to be healed. At the moment he has an eye injury causing him discomfort and sleeps a great deal, but when he wakes, he looks for me. I try to stop and share my expanded heart space, and he melts in my arms. As he looks up at me, eye-to-eye, I feel him thanking me.

Even though we do not speak the same 3D language, we do speak the same universal language of love and compassion. When Harley is well, he also gives me all his unconditional love, and I feel healed from his affection and love. Harley has been an extraordinary soul companion friend. He read my energy to tell me what I needed to do through an animal communicator when I first found him, and explained why he came to me. He also shared that his soul has known me through many past lives, in particular from Egypt, when we studied at ancient mystery school together (I was a male in that life). Now he has returned to be with me and help me on my journey to evolve.

As you know, when Harley came into my life I had the urge and opportunity to go and visit Egypt on a spiritual pilgrimage. I did, and it was life changing. I had so many experiences in the temples we travelled to. One was a sounding place, where the group and I connected with a deity in spirit called Isis and we sang in her dedicated temple. We all felt a big shift of conscious energy as we moved into another time and space as we sang. I had never sung in this lifetime, but I appeared to remember the songs as we connected, as did my friends who travelled with me on that trip. It was an extraordinary journey into Egypt that I will not forget in this life.

There is so much to share about Harley, such an awesome soul with so much wisdom to share with me, like teaching me to find new ways to communicate with him to do things. He taught me to check the energy and be sensitive to where I tread, to feel the way with grace—he is a master of that! I must not forget the most obvious, that we have had the honour of his skills in keeping us protected. Harley has been our protector of the energies entering our home at every property we have lived in, and the guardian of the energies. I love the way he turns up out of nowhere when we have a new visitor to check them out with his very 'easy does it' approach.

I know he is checking our visitors' energy frequency when he appears. I can intuitively sense his movements around the person, who thinks he is being a friendly cat, while he is actually checking them energetically. If they do not like cats he always wants to sit on their laps, never interested in the visitors who want to pat and stroke him, only the visitors who do not. He has this wisdom of going straight to the fearful visitors, or anyone who tries to hide their distaste for cats. I laugh, he is certainly too smart for that game! Within minutes of his attention the visitor comes around to liking him and he receives their affection. Harley sure is a master when it comes to knowing how to master energy frequencies. When I asked him once what he felt around my mother, his response was that she was very nervous and fearful, and he did not like that feeling around him too much. So, I could never ask Mum to care for him.

I believe our past life together in Egypt is why he came to me, to remind me of my own wisdom, intuitively working with energy frequencies. This is one of the past life gifts Harley has been helping me to remember. Watching him, I find myself tapping into my old memories. I try to remember what he has taught me, to practice patience reading and sensing subtle energies around me, instead of reacting to what I am feeling. As an empath and sensitive to what is in the field, in childhood I reacted to these experiences, causing me so much harm and pain, and allowing others to drain my energy, leaving me feeling drained of my joy.

To clear my energy field and protect myself at every event is essential, crucial now, as so many are lost and unhappy at this time and looking for someone to latch onto. They drain energy from more joyful and light humans, for they are not strong enough or willing to find their own path to joy. Sometimes referred to as energy vampires, you know them because they can drain your energy, leaving you feeling tired and not uplifted when you spend too long with them. If you are vigilant of your energy exchange and conscious you can avoid the symptoms of being drained.

> *My insight is that you have to find your own freedom, then you will find the joy that follows. I do not rely on anything or anyone outside of me to gain that freedom— that has been my learning experience and message for my life. Make it all happen from within, for it will not come from outside of you. You are the master of your own freedom and joy on this earth, and the life you wish for comes from your own manifesting. Healing the heart and forgiving those who may have given you uncomfortable experiences is the first step, for then you can let love in, and love can then be shared with others, including your furry companions.*

Mother Earth, and many other species' wise ones, have supported me to heal and open my heart. They have supported me all my life in so many ways and continue to. Their hearts are so pure, if you let them in, they can open yours further to let in love and share love. Sitting here now, I feel much discomfort in my heart. I feel there is more healing rising, so I'll keep writing to release it.

**Communication with Harley.
Subject: Our Past Life.**

Debra: Harley, how do our souls know one another?

Harley: We trained together in many lifetimes and you already know me. We are old souls at this time. I am here to help you move on in your soul's journey, and it is working, I noticed you have taken my suggestions from when we first communicated. It took a while, but you have taken them on and now we are at the point you needed to be, writing all about us who do not have a voice.

Work on you, remember all the times we have had together and how that's felt for you to be with me, how it feels in your heart when we are cuddled up, and how I communicate with you every day. Not always do you listen, but I do believe you know what I am saying in a strange way, without words. You can read me, dearest, that is our past together, our hearts are connected. I was so happy when I found you again.

Debra: I was so sorry to lose you all those years ago. When my mother brought you to me that was so devastating, you were such a special little friend to me. Loving my music is what I remember most, and how you played with Charles. Yes, yes! You knew one another—is that right?

Harley: Yes dearest, we all know one another very well, as you will find out soon. We are all so connected in our hearts and come to help you remember. You have many deep wounds that need to be healed. That's why you have trouble remembering so much, dearest one, but the day will come soon where all that will be released and you'll be recognised for your wonderful, compassionate heart. You just need to remember this— keep healing those wounds. We, your soul family, are all here helping you.

7

Bruno: A Child's Love

My first animal love and companion friend as a young child was our family dog. Bruno, chosen and named by my father, was a pedigree dachshund with a shiny black and brown coat. Bruno would come to me when I felt alone, as I often felt disempowered and not heard by my family. I experienced abusive behaviours from my parents and my empathic heart felt the pain emotionally and physically.

My sensitive heart could also feel the pain of other species if I witnessed them suffering or injured for any reason. This became clear to me during a horrific experience at around twelve years of age. I was taking Bruno for his daily walk when a very aggressive dog attacked him. He sustained serious injuries to his body, in particular his neck, where a large bleeding wound gaped open. I could not find any adults to help, so had to carry him home alone, running as fast as I could through the suburban streets with Bruno bleeding and whimpering. My heart was breaking and weeping with him.

I finally arrived home and my parents took him to the vet for treatment. He survived the ordeal, but unfortunately was given the death needle later due to an incurable back injury he sustained. I was extremely sad, as I felt the pain of my best friend and confidante.

I remember looking for love outside of my home by going to the backyard to talk with Bruno. He would always listen to me, showing his love by placing his paw on my lap or leaning up against my body when I cried. He showed me so much love and I felt it so strongly! When I sat with him, I felt like my heart was receiving a healing balm, shifting from a heavy heart to light and open as my joy returned. I so loved him, and spent many hours talking and playing with him. Many times, I packed my bag to run away from home, and always took Bruno with me.

The healing I received from Bruno when I was upset was a healing for my broken heart to feel love and joy return, and it gave me hope to get through another day. After he died, I continued to go outside most days. Missing him, I explored nature and communed with Mother Earth. This kept me feeling inspired with hope for better times ahead, when I would eventually grow old enough to leave home.

My relationship with Bruno showed me how sensitive my heart is, and that I can go to other species to be heard without judgment. Their love reminded me of what unconditional love felt like so I could remember my joy again.

As I grew older, my heart began to shut down love—I could not take any more. Over the years, I had observed great disrespect and mistreatment towards animals by humans, and I felt heartache from my own dysfunctional family with their own unhealed wounds and pain.

I had been intuitively communing with animals at a young age quite naturally, not really aware of this being a gift with the animals, thinking, *why does no one else in my own family, or my relatives, feel the animals' pain, love and joy with strong emotions as I had felt them?*

Do you have memories of how you experienced animals in your childhood?

8
Mandy: Love and Grief

How blessed I felt at sixteen years of age when a beautiful soul unexpectedly found me. On my way home from a day at high school, waiting on a busy main road for a bus ride home, a tiny puppy appeared, wandering around on a high-traffic road. She spotted me and came over to make friends with me. *How adorable*, I thought, and picked her up. Immediately, I felt her little heart and knew she was meant to be with me.

"What are you doing on this busy street with no collar, and so young, with no road sense? You'll be killed here."

I held her in the palm of my hand and fell in love as my heart began to open to her love. I knew I was going to take her home. I asked around the street if anyone knew who her family might be, but no one could help me. I could not, in my heart, leave her lost and running around the main road, it was too dangerous, so I bundled her into my school bag.

My parents didn't agree she was for me and made me take her to a pet shop. They did eventually agree for me to keep her, after repeated pleading by me, "No one wants her, she's still for sale, she has no family." This little soul, who I named Mandy, arrived as a pedigree miniature Fox Terrier, with a white coat and a tan and black patch over each eye. The vet guessed she was eight or nine weeks old and a small breed. I felt I had found my new best friend and cherished our companionship after having a traumatic time with my family.

Mandy gave me unconditional love and loyalty. She made my heart sing, expanding my heart to feel so much more love than I thought could be possible from one furry companion. When I passed my driver's licence exam we travelled together in my car and were inseparable. It was heaven to have such a loyal and loving companion to talk with again and take with me for fun times at the beach, parks or friends' places, as she was very well behaved.

I tried to teach her language skills with some trial-and-error approaches, which I believe did not start in a positive way. Everything changed when I realized that if I showed her lovingly, she would know what I needed her to do. I had been shown discipline through hitting from my parents, so that is what I did to my little soul companion, until one day I woke up to how it felt for me as I received a hitting. It confused me when I was hit, and I knew hitting another being was not a way of showing love. That was not love. How could I do that to her?

I stopped and switched to giving lots of praise with love instead. Mandy knew exactly what I asked, was less confused, and wanted to please me by responding to my requests. I taught her to make sure she knew what my requests meant so I could keep her safe when she was out with me around the roads, as I didn't want her to get run over by a car.

Two years later, I was camping with my boyfriend, Jason, and Mandy. He had taken Mandy to the shops, but when he returned, I couldn't see her with him.

"Where's Mandy?" I panicked.

"I'm so, so, sorry. She was run over at the shops and died instantly."

"What? She is dead! How could that happen? She was very good crossing the road. I never had her run out on the road with me."

"She's in a box in the car," he said.

Oh no! My heart was heavy, then broken. I could not believe she was dead. In fact, over the weeks that followed I had nightmares, believing I had buried her alive. I kept feeling her around me, in my heart, like she was still alive. That was too much pain for my young heart. Empty for her love, I became depressed, would not eat, and could not socialise with anyone. I did not blame my boyfriend, as I knew it was an accident. He loved her too and was also incredibly sad and felt guilty.

I struggled for months to get through the grief. I eventually did, but could never understand why I felt she was still alive. When I shared this with my family, they told me I was being silly, she had gone, which really upset me. They did not understand, but I knew I could feel her around me.

My learning from Mandy was how much love was still in my heart to feel another soul after feeling shutdown. To know the feeling of loss and grief showed me my gift of sensitivity to feel into other realms of existence around me. That is why I could still feel her around me after death. I was upset because I had forgotten in this life that death is just a transformation into another form to exist in another reality, thus Mandy *was* still with me, she had not gone. My heart knew her soul, and that is why I could feel her heart around me.

Many years after Mandy died, she made herself known to me spiritually. What follows is what she initially shared with me.

First communication with Mandy.
Subject: Love at First Sight.

Mandy: We had such a great friendship. We loved one another and knew it was to be at first sight.

I came to you, dearest, to help you feel into your relationship with animals, and to see what happens when they are removed from the earth. The grief you felt was because I was still with you. On a physical level you may not have been able to see me, but I was energetically still around you.

That is what you picked up that many others did not understand, that is what you kept feeling was me still with you. Because we are not gone; we are just in another realm of existence.

Share this with the many, that when their dearest companions leave they are not gone, they are always with them, just in another realm of existence, like a different radio station is needed to connect with them.

You, dearest one, have always been connected to this other realm. That is why you have had so many interactions with so many species, and why you know your companions so well when their souls incarnate with you. It is your gift to see and feel this. So many do not have this gift. It is all about an open heart, dearest one. Please tell your people this. They can access their loved companions at any time, they are always with them.

Debra: Did you choose to reincarnate as a dog in this life with me?

Mandy: Yes dearest, we choose what our contract will be for us and this was my choosing. I am just sorry it wasn't to be for very long as we only had a short time together, but that was my contract—to help you see your gift of feeling and being aware of other realms, especially with the not heard or seen, the voiceless.

We had many past lives together. Do you remember being in Atlantis? I chose to come to you in a dog's body to help you heal your sensitive heart from the trauma of your childhood, as that beautiful heart was beginning to shut down.

Debra: Mandy, are you from my soul family?

Mandy: Yes, I am one of your soul family, and you will know me again soon when you return. We will be face-to-face, so to speak, with our lives in another realm of existence.

Dearest, you are so loved, that is why you have had so many companions come to you. It is your gift. You have communed with other species over many millennia, you just forgot when you came to earth. I was there to remind you of your gift and help you remember what it feels like when another soul family member incarnates with us.

You have always had the knowing, even though you were confused as to what you were feeling—such as the nightmares you had regarding the death of my earthly body. I was not really dead—I just changed form, and have always been with you, dearest. I want you to know I am still here with and for you, until you return in the near future, so we can be together again.

Dearest, it was a big time for you as a teenager. After feeling so much pain in your childhood, I hoped I bought some love and kindness into your heart to let it heal a little more. You were beginning to shut your heart down from all your pain that was experienced as a sensitive heart.

What you saw on the planet, and how you observed others treating their animals, was very painful for you. You were closing your heart down to all the beautiful love that you had inside to make a difference on the planet, to help others see what they need to see through your beautiful eyes as the sensitive soul you are.

Please just share how you saw the beauty and the love from me, and all the other companions who have come to help you open your heart to remember your great love for all beings and species on this planet. Be the way, speak for the species not heard, let people see what they're not sensitive to and why their hearts are needing to be healed, just as yours does, from all you've experienced.

Such a heart-opening message to receive from Mandy! A teenager when she died, I knew I was not going crazy, even though my family thought I was being oversensitive. They did not understand I could feel her soul, that my heart knew the resonance of a kindred soul. That was my first lesson with a soul companion, learning how they are souls who know us well and choose to come to help us heal, as teachers through other species' bodies.

My first experience of deep grief with Mandy taught me that our soul companions do not leave us when they die, they are always around us and we can reach out to them spiritually to help us. Her lesson for me was to remember my past life wisdom, that death does not mean permanently gone, rather it is a transformation into another form of being.

Mandy shared that I could feel her because she was, and has always been, around me. She had changed form but did not really go anywhere, that's why I could feel her energy after her death and felt she was still alive, to the point of worrying I'd buried her alive. Mandy continues to be with me every day, and at this point I know she is around me giving me guidance and healing. My soul feels this connection strongly. Such a heart-opening message to receive from her, to know I was not going crazy as her soul was still around me.

Interesting how our furry companions can open our hearts to great love and compassion, then when they leave us the feeling of emptiness is so painful we lock it deep down, not wanting to go there again. These old wounds we hold in our hearts need to be released.

Death is just a doorway to another way of being, in another realm.

Communication with Mandy.
Subject: Our Past Life.

Debra: What is it you would like to share with me today?

Mandy: Oh yes, we had so much fun together travelling in your car and you took me to so many places to see the world around us. And the way we found one another, it was quite a journey to be with you, and how you kept me in your school bag.

How your heart knew you needed to be with me, you were so tuned to your heart and soul guidance to know this. And you were so persistent to keep this happening until your family came around to let me in to your family. You are to be commended on your determination when you knew in your heart I was meant to be with you. I suspect I would have been run over if you had not found me.

My heart was gentle, and I felt your heart to be also, but you had so much pain from your family life. I could feel it, and I so wanted to help you feel the love around you again. So, I spent much time sending you love and always being available to you, as there was a lot of pain in your home life and you absorbed a lot of it, dearest one. You so deserved to feel the love that was coming your way from us all, and that's why we came down to be with you, so you would remember us all supporting you on your life journey, not to give up and be distracted, to remember your past lives with all species.

Quite a life you have had with the voiceless over many lifetimes. This is just another, but you must share your feeling on the voiceless with the many. It's time to share how you live with them and share your life with them, how you respect them and give them affection and attention, and how you have done that in the past.

Many need to also know this, dearest one. So many do not know what you know with all your experiences. They need to be guided gently from the heart by healing and feeling their hearts. They need to know that our souls are all the same, we just come in different bodysuits.

We often come in many body forms, because we can't access the ones we want to help in any other way except in an animal suit, as you have found by not having any children in your life. You already knew this dearest anyway, so that is how we came to be with you. We could have come in the form of a child, but you weren't going to have children, and you needed to know you were loved very early on as your heart was becoming very wounded from the past. You chose to have these experiences with us and we agreed to come to help you and support you in any way we could. If that meant coming as another species we did that, such as a dog species.

Dearest, keep remembering your time with us so we can come and help you with this important book for the many to learn so much that you already know. Keep remembering your feelings with us, and how you managed and felt it in that beautiful heart of yours. It has been a big journey for you, we do know this and are here for you right now. We are always here beside you, supporting you. Keep writing every day and connecting with us.

Remember your times with us and we will help you access and heal that heart. This is your journey of love.

Dearest, the way you always gave your whole heart to me was the most magical time of all. You never held back. I could feel it all surrounding me with great joy and bliss. You also experienced sad times, and that was when I would give you so much love and healing that you may not have been aware of.

Debra: Yes, I felt your love Mandy, it was what made me feel better when I was sad at times. Such joy when I was with you and talking with you. I always enjoyed those times. And the training, I was so sorry for the discipline I used on you, but I wasn't really conscious enough to see what I was doing until later, when I was shown and became more conscious of my actions.

Mandy: Dearest, it's all part of the learning you have to do here on earth, and if you keep becoming more conscious you're on track with your journey, which you are, of course. I do not hold any grief for those times. Dearest, it is in the past and a different journey with you, helping to see and learn how different a journey can be with us souls who come to be other species' bodies. You need to share this.

Debra: I have, in my first book.

Mandy: Yes, you need to put it in this book too, so people will not miss the importance of this lesson. All the lessons you have had need to be included, how they made you feel and what you did about it. All this is going to help others find their way with their furry companions, as you found it on your own, dearest. They will want to hear from you how you did this, making it easier for them to be more conscious with their dear furry friends.

We all come to learn the lessons and we share them to help others who travel on their journeys. That is how you have learnt also, from others who may have been on the journey before you. We take others with us on our journeys by sharing our lessons, it helps so many. Writing it down in words will affect the hearts of many on an emotional level. It is a grand time on your earth to take the hand of others with you to become more conscious.

We can help you along the way, but you must write it in your own heartfelt words. This will keep the book in a powerful state, so when others read it they'll also feel the healing from your heartfelt words.

Debra: Mandy, how I missed you! I am just remembering how devastated I was when you left me after the accident, how I could not eat and lost interest in being alive. You left a big hole in my heart at that time. I was so sure you had not died, and I had guilt that we may have buried you alive. That caused me terrible nightmares, feeling you around me. And no one in my family understood my feelings. My heart was empty when you left, it felt wrenched from my chest. Oh, I feel some discomfort now in my chest area. Maybe that healing is rising to be released?

It was a big time in my life to experience your death, to have such a special friend in my life who gave me so much love and joy in my heart be taken away. My boyfriend at the time could not even fill the void I experienced. I guess the worst is no one understood. I was totally confused about why I felt you had been buried alive.

Now I know you were still around me and had just changed form. I am so happy to hear you are still here with me even now, after all those earthly years apart. That makes me so happy, with tears of joy, to know that you are with me and have been all these years, supporting me in ways I did not consciously know.

I feel so blessed to have found you, and for all the great times we had together with your very gentle, loving heart. I have so much gratitude for your love, healing and affection you shared with me over those short years to help me keep my heart open and warm with love. But to feel that discomfort was one of my very painful experiences in life and I do not wish to go through that ever again, it was so harsh on my heart.

The death of my father was another grief challenge, but I have come through that as well and healed my heart from that painful time. I hope not to go through anymore before I return to my star home. I do have Harley with me here now and I know his days are numbered. He is not a young cat any longer and is showing signs of age. He tells me he does not have much longer with me. I believe that will be a test for me to work through, as I have had him on earth with me for many years now, he is eighteen years old. I do not want to think about what I might feel in my heart when he leaves me. I hope now being more conscious on death, it will be less traumatic for my heart.

Charles was another sad loss as I was not with him. However, it was made so much easier because he came to talk with me and shared he was leaving the earth realm. That was such a blessing, and a time for me to realise I can talk with my furry companions, and how they come to be with us in great ways to support us on our earthly journey.

9
Mandy: Releasing Wounds

When I started writing this book, I felt the pain in my heart release as I thought about all the soul companions I have lost and felt grief for over the years. It was challenging to feel those wounds again, but when released, my heart felt lighter and expanded to feel more love. I now know they have been my ancestors' souls visiting me, and I can feel them energetically all around me as they come to help and support my heart healing with their wisdom. They are also around me as light beings in the spirit world, making themselves known to me across the veil of illusion.

That was quite a big first lesson—learning that our furry companions can be our soul relations who know us and come to us as teachers, as other species in different body forms. After all those years believing she was gone, knowing Mandy is still around me has made me so happy. Tears of joy well up in my eyes to know this, and I communicated with her regularly whilst writing this book.

2019: Communication with Mandy.
Subject: Releasing Trauma.

Debra: I feel so much healing in my heart right now. It feels so painful and tight. I will allow it to rise from the deep, but it is very uncomfortable. I can hardly write with what has arisen. Please help me release it. Thank you everyone for your help, it is difficult to be grounded when this pain arises. I guess I have to keep letting it go if I want to complete this book.

Mandy: Yes, dearest one, you know it is healing you and it will heal others. It needs to rise from your heart to be released and healed by your wisdom. You must convey the importance to others, or show them how it feels when they feel these things. They cannot keep blocking this pain out, it's destroying your beautiful planet with all their distractions they keep doing, instead of feeling the suffering on the planet.

It is time for them all to awaken to the pain inside their beautiful hearts and heal so the planet can feel this love once more. The love you once knew is still there. It is hidden behind the clouds of pain and suffering that humanity carries in the consciousness and energetic field. It needs to be released, or it will keep happening and be passed on to the next generations for more pain to be experienced and more animals' souls to be abused and exploited.

It needs to stop now! This planet cannot take any more of this pain humans keep giving her with their hardened and dark hearts, it needs to be released for a peaceful place on Mother Earth. Like when you are ill, you hold toxic chemicals in your body that need to be released, so it is when you hold toxic energy in your hearts. Now it needs to be released, or it will keep humanity in pain and suffering.

Mother Earth does not want this any longer. She is raising her vibration for us all to live in peace and harmony once more. Can your people not see this, dear one? You need to tell them.

Debra: Yes, I am writing my books to share this.

Mandy: Dearest, you need to keep healing that pain in your heart to keep this momentum going.

Debra: It is quite painful to access. I cannot believe how much is in there.

Mandy: This is how damaging it is, dear one. It goes deep into the energetic field as pieces disconnected from your heart. Little bubbles of energy float around, but you cannot access them when you have the pain and distorted energy in your heart. It needs to be released to really get the connection back so you can feel that peaceful place and the energy will be in resonance with your true heart and soul frequency. It's a big journey you have undertaken and we commend you for your commitment. We are all here sending you love, dearest one.

Debra: The pain is so intense! I look forward to the breaks in-between. How extraordinary that we hold the pain in our own hearts. There is so much to learn about the human body! I feel it is amazing our vehicle holds such distorted energies so deep in the energetics of our body.

Mandy: You know this, as you have experienced this in your Vipassana meditation training. Have you forgotten how that arose for you, dearest one?

Debra: Yes, it took me to a place of absolute bliss and joy to find that freedom in my heart. I do remember. I will not forget that experience.

Mandy: Well, dear one, this is always that type of journey, only you'll be sharing this with many so they may also feel and know what that can feel like in a meditative state if they write their own life stories. This is so valuable to share with others, that they can experience release by writing their books from a very sacred space and be healed to find the joy and love that awaits them, as you've found, dearest one. There are many paths to heal the heart, this is just another one of those paths many can take. If they use a sacred technique of meditation and connection with their divine author, it will all unfold for them too.

Debra: I know my work can also help many to heal their hearts, and they can take the hands of others with them to heal and find a way to the place of joy and peace we all crave in this life. We know it, but we cannot access it with all this distorted energy in our bodies and hearts, as I am learning, and how it blocks our path when it is clouded by such distortion. I feel this pain, I know how it affects me. Wow, it is still happening. I feel a little less stressed with it now, it feels so much like physical pain.

Mandy: Dearest, this is energetic pain, as you know from Vipassana. It presents physically, but when released it does not have any physical repercussions because it is released before it causes you disease and more pain. That is why it is so important to be releasing it so the body can find its balance and peace place energetically. This will prevent the disease that comes from distorted energy in your bodies and energetic fields. Keep remembering the Vipassana experience, where you released so much, and the bliss you felt at the time.

Debra: Yes, I remember. I am trying to hold that in my mind so I can keep going with this. Is my being overweight part of this distortion?

Mandy: Yes, this is why you need to detox energetically and physically, dearest one, or you'll be sick with disease in your body. It is overloaded and needs to release, just as mother is overloaded at present with all the toxic chemicals and actions of humans on the planet distorting her energetic field.

2019: Communication with Mandy.
Subject: Pain on this Planet.

Debra: Mandy, what would you like to share with me today?

Mandy: You came to be the voice for the voiceless, dear one. Do you not remember it is the voiceless you are helping here? That is why you came. You were so sensitive as a child in the garden, and felt the pain of all your animal companions, because this is your path—to feel their pain and know it is your pain, as you are not separate from them.

We are all here sending you love, dearest one. We bless you, in return, this will make your journey so much easier as you acknowledge your ancestors and spiritual family. So much love and light to you, dearest. We await the day you will be returned to us and we can shower you with the love you so deserve, beyond the 3D reality which is so dense.

Debra: This pain in my body, will it continue?

Mandy: Dearest one, you just need to do the healing to access some of the joy you've buried deep down, below all the toxic negative energy that's been pushed down on top of your heart from when you were very young. Much of it is yours, but much you have picked up along the way from others. You have absorbed other beings' pain and suffering, as you naively did not understand energy then and how it works, so were unable to protect yourself.

But that is all part of the journey, dearest one, to learn how to be in your own power without taking on the pain of others, even the other species that you have spent so much time with. It is important to be aware of how you collected this pain from others with your empathetic heart. Dearest one, pain will cloud the real heart of light that is buried deep down in you.

It is certainly a big journey for us all to keep detoxing and healing ourselves, but I know it will help this beautiful earth if we all do our little part towards this healing on the planet. One person at a time, we will help Mother Earth feel once more the beautiful resonance she had on this planet before pain and suffering was produced by unaware, unconscious beings living on this planet.

It is our journey to keep this planet in love too, and to heal ourselves and evolve for our spiritual growth. We need to be more conscious of how we affect the energetic field of Mother Earth, and others, with our own suffering from the pain we cause to others. If we do not, it will be returned to us and held in our energetic and physical bodies, needing to be healed at a later time when our soul decides it's time. The time is now for all of us to find heart healing—it is crucial to humanity's survival at this time on the planet.

2019: Communication with Mandy.
Subject: Healing is Supported.

Debra: How to deal with the pain when it arises, so intense.

Mandy: Dearest one, just stay focused on the journey of healing and allow it to rise. Observe what happens and how you feel along the way. You can share in your book with many others to feel their own pain rising, so they will understand what they are feeling and not to be fearful when this happens. It is all part of the bigger plan here on earth for each human.

The other species are here to help you humans heal, but many are not listening or are ignoring these beautiful souls at this time. They are missing out on so much magic from these souls who agreed to come and be teachers and companions for the humans.

Debra: I feel so much needs to be shared for the earth to heal humanity right now.

Mandy: It will be your greatest mission yet, and then you will be home with us all again. Just keep remembering and feeling us all around you, dearest. We do not leave your side ever, we are here with you, as one with you. We certainly know you have had a big journey. You're on the home run, dearest, and it will be worth your pain, as it will all be rewarded with such love within you and around you, and by the many who will see your light shining.

Many have no idea of your light, dearest. Do not

dampen your light, it is coming through the cracks, as you say in your book. We can see it shining out already. The cracks will be released and your whole body will be such a strong light to many you'll not need to talk, it will heal just by being who you are and what you've accomplished—they will feel the light from you affecting them.

Open that wounded heart, dearest, keep connected to your soul and it will guide you, as it has always done, for your life and beyond other lives. Know who you are. Remember the light that once shone out and feel it coming through those old cracks that can now be opened to let your real light shine through. It is in there. We can feel it here, others will feel it too. You will feel it from the bliss you will access when this happens.

Debra: I know this is my mission and service to humanity, why I came to earth—to feel and share the healing, to encourage others to know if healed it will take them to a place of bliss and peace they all deeply look for. Even if they're not awakened enough to know this, it's the human journey to find the bliss and grow from the pain that's felt on this planet, to return to the light and love as an evolved spiritual being after a life journey here on earth school, yes?

10
Mandy: Remembering Wisdom

Many years after Mandy's death, my shamanic training taught me to telepathically tune into the energy frequencies around me in a more consciously aware state. This opened me to receive my first message from Mandy to say she was sorry I suffered so much when she passed over, and that she had come to help me open and heal my heart as a young adult because I had been traumatized and my heart was beginning to shut down to love.

Communication with Mandy.
Subject: Remembering My Wisdom.

Debra: Hello Mandy, what is our subject today?
Mandy: Many past lives ago we were together on the planet, travelling as souls. The planet was going through a great change, as it is today. We felt this together and assisted humanity to the point of evolution, but it was not successful because the planet was destroyed with life.
Debra: When was this? Around Atlantis was it?
Mandy: We were very young together as souls and spent much time together.

Debra: Were we spiritually on a journey, like I am today?

Mandy: Yes, but you knew your power and remembered your wisdom in those times, so you could really make some big differences.

Debra: Does that mean because I do not remember many things, I cannot make such a difference?

Mandy: No, it just means you are holding back on your wisdom, dearest. You have so much to share, and so many need to hear your wisdom. I am here to help you remember what that is. Try to remember your past. We are here to help you remember so it can be shared.

You were a great leader of spirituality many lifetimes ago. Do you not remember this?

Debra: I try to, but I only get very small pieces of memory, not confident to share at this time.

Mandy: What do you remember?

Debra: I remember a lifetime in Atlantis when I lived around large, beautiful white temples and buildings. It was peaceful and my heart felt free and loving towards everything, including the other species.

Mandy: Can you keep trying to remember?

Debra: I had a closeness and could hear many animals speak to me quite often as they shared their wisdom and life with me.

Mandy: How does that feel?

Debra: Yes, I feel my heart opening now to this time, but it is still very cloudy. Occasionally something reminds me of past times on the planet when everything was peaceful and we cared about the animals with respect, something that sadly, does not happen now. I am so sad to see how so many humans exploit the animals.

I feel so many tears, and pain in my heart, wishing for those times to return. But there is so much pain here on earth, this brings so many tears to my heart to feel so much disrespect and killing of our beautiful other species who are here to help us grow and evolve.

I keep feeling the emotion, it is still rising. I feel so sensitive to this pain inside of me the keyboard is getting wet with my tears. How can I convey these times to people to remember, and how can they do this again?

Mandy: Healing their hearts, dear one. Just as you have done, they need to heal so they will feel the sensitivity to other species as you do.

Debra: It makes me so sad to see what happens on this planet towards other species.

Mandy: Yes, we know dear heart, you are a very sensitive soul who has come with a message to the many to heal their hearts and to feel them again, and this will change the situation on earth for everyone. So many do not know this.

Debra: I feel it is so important, and time is running out on this planet for us to care more for the other species, our relations.

11
Mandy: Divine Union

Mandy surprised me this year whilst writing my book. Twin flame is a term I have heard a great deal in new age spiritual networks, but I never felt the need to research it more, believing I had a basic understanding of what it meant. Then I had the following communication with Mandy, and this triggered my curious nature to know more.

So, what is a twin flame? A twin flame relationship is a divine union with a divine purpose. These souls are literally the other half of your soul. You only have one twin soul, ever! There are magnetic pulls between the two souls that keep them together once they have appeared in each other's lives.

2020: Communication with Mandy.
Subject: Twin Flame and Soul Guidance.

Debra: Mandy, what would you like to share today?

Mandy: I have much to share with you, and not sure if you are up for all I have. Let us begin with how we know one another.

Debra: Yes, in Atlantis.

Mandy: Yes dearest, but there is so much more to our connection.

Debra: What do you mean?

Mandy: We were family, sisters of another time.

Debra: Yes, what time?

Mandy: We had many siblings in that time, and you were the one who connected with me. We were rarely apart.

Debra: Were we twins?

Mandy: Yes, spiritually twin flames.

Debra: What is a twin flame, anyway?

Mandy: Two souls who split off from one another, same spark, but you go into different forms. One goes into a physical bodysuit and the other in the spiritual form, but you are always together.

Debra: On my 40th birthday, I received a gift from my sister, a spiritual drawing of my soul guide known as 'Kara Tan', with a long channelled message received through the spiritual artist from my soul guide. I had trouble with my logical mind believing the information was true, but when I held it to my heart, without a doubt my heart knew it was true. I became very emotional, making me cry at feeling so loved. Now Mandy, I am feeling intuitively and wondering was that you—my soul guide, aka Kara Tan?

Mandy: Yes. I was so happy you took the information on board, even if it was extraordinary for you to read.

Debra: Wow! I would not have guessed this connection, thank you for sharing. I feel so loved and supported by the souls who visit me.

Now I write this book, twenty-two years after receiving that drawing, I have no doubts. So much has unfolded to confirm what I was given in that soul guide channelled message on my 40th Birth Year. I have held it dear to my heart as a prized possession that helps me remember who I really am and why I am here. Apparently, when we incarnate in the human bodysuit our soul self stays in another realm, meaning half of the flame is in the human bodysuit and is supported by the other half of the flame who acts as a soul guide. This goes on through lifetimes, supporting one another to exchange places and body forms as we choose.

That was a surprise, and an enormously powerful message to receive twenty-two years ago! It blew my heart open. Now I find Kara Tan (aka Mandy) is part of me, and that is why she has always been with me. Her picture has travelled with me to many homes. I rarely keep items for long as I move about a great deal, but her picture struck a big chord for my heart and I knew it was important to keep with me. Right now, her picture is up on my wall beside me, watching over me as I write.

It has made me so happy to know she is still around me after all those years of thinking we were apart. Tears of joy well up in my eyes to know this as I now communicate with her whilst writing this book.

Death does not mean permanently gone, just a transformation into another form to live in another realm of existence.

12
Sabastian: Finding Joy

Some months after Mandy's death, my partner was so upset for me she surprised me with another furry companion. Sabastian, a white Labrador puppy of only two months old, was like a little teddy bear, white and fluffy, and I loved him. I still had to get over Mandy and he really helped me. A very different personality, he was extroverted, friendly and happy with everyone, liked everyone he met, was enthusiastic, and loved adventures with me. In fact, I might have said his personality was not too different to my own.

I had a wonderful time teaching him language with hand signs. He loved it too, so we always had lots of fun doing the lessons. I never used treats, as I believed if I showed him love and praise he would be willing to learn. I was right—we were the best team in our dog training class. I prefer to call it people training class! He learnt fast as I was very clear with my requests.

There was another side he did show which surprised me. He was very protective of me around men, particularly in the evening if I was walking him, barking at males he was not sure of. Any other time you would not believe he had an aggressive bone in his happy body. When he was six months old, I took him to a large park with ducks and geese swimming in the lake. Sabastian decided to swim with the birds, but it backfired when the largest goose in the flock saw him as a threat and kept jumping on his head to drown him. As I stood on the foreshore my heart told me I had better go save him from drowning, so I took my shoes off and rushed into the lake. He appeared quite shaken up after that event. It was his life-changing moment, as he learnt to keep his distance after that.

We had many adventures together, and he also gave me some truly embarrassing moments to navigate, particularly when he cocked his leg on a gentleman's leg at the traffic lights! Thank goodness the man's pants were loose and he did not feel the wetness! When the traffic lights changed, Sabastian and I ran across the road and down to the park quickly before the man noticed his trousers. That worked, phew! Saved me a confrontation and a cleaning bill. I'd have been about eighteen years old and wasn't confident with confrontation or strangers.

Another time he peed on a lady's basket at the beach—a tricky situation! Luckily, she liked dogs and his friendly nature won her heart, so she forgave him and me. When I was out on my surf mat, Sabastian liked to go into the ocean with me and take the waves in. In another embarrassing moment, he must have thought, *there's a human, I can ride his back and take that wave in a little faster.*

And he did—riding a wave in on a body surfer's back! I cracked up laughing, until the man pushed Sabastian off his back when he landed on the foreshore and his body language appeared to be angry as he looked for the carer of Sabastian. I stayed out in the waves so Sabastian would not come to me and highlight who I was to the man. That worked, I was saved from another bad-mannered moment with my cheeky soul companion.

My message from Sabastian was to remember the joy hidden inside of me, and to feel love in my heart once again so I could receive more love from other beings.

Sabastian was another soul who returned years later with a message for me.

Communication with Sabastian (short version).

I came to help heal your heart after Mandy left the earth, and to remind you of the love and joy you have inside of you. Remember your past lives with the dolphins in Atlantis. We had lots of fun and many adventures together. I was sad to leave you so early, but you were ready for a new journey I could not go on, living and travelling overseas.

13
Sabastian: Recalling Wisdom

Sabastian came to me in a joyful dog's bodysuit to help heal my heart and remember my past life as another species after I experienced tremendous grief from losing Mandy. He showed me the joy of life, and his love healed my heart to let go of the grief I had been carrying, to move on in life to my next journey. The joy and adventures we experienced reminded me of the joy of dolphins. Interesting that I intuitively felt that without knowing it was already in my soul memory—working with dolphins in my past life, working on the energy grids of the planet in joyful ways. Now Sabastian has come to support me with writing this book for all the voiceless species.

2019: Communication with Sabastian.
Subject: Our Past Life.

Debra: How was your life with me as a dog, Sabastian?
Sabastian: Lots of fun. I remember we had many adventures together. I was sad to leave you so early. You were ready for a new journey and I could not come with you, a long journey away overseas.
Debra: Yes, that is true, and at twenty-one years old it changed my life to do that journey. But I did miss you too, because we had a lot of laughs with all your

embarrassing actions with other humans. You kept me entertained, and sometimes a little stressed, not knowing what would happen. It is wonderful to talk with you Sabastian, as I have not had that pleasure before now.

Sabastian: I did not have anything to say before, but now you are writing this book it is time for me to share too.

Debra: Oh yes, do share with me. I would like to know what you have to say!

Sabastian: It goes something like this ... you, me and Jason all knew one another in a past life.

Debra: Did we?

Sabastian: Oh yes, we loved to hang out together.

Debra: What did we do in the past life?

Sabastian: Are you ready for this?

Debra: Yes.

Sabastian: We were all dolphins.

Debra: Oh, I see. When was this?

Sabastian: Before Atlantis fell.

Debra: What did we do as dolphins?

Sabastian: We worked with the energetic grids of the earth.

Debra: How did we do this?

Sabastian: We sounded, as you do now, this is not new for you. The dolphins in Western Australia remembered you from the past, that did not just happen. You were known to them, that is why they came to see you, to help you remember.

Debra: Wow. That sure does explain my joyful fun side. I like to have fun and find where there is joy.

Sabastian: Yes. Your book is very apt for your journey of looking for joy. That is your dolphin memory rising.

Debra: Have I been other species in my lifetimes, not just a human?

Sabastian: Yes, we all have. If you have been to earth as many times as yourself, you have been many species.

That is why you know the connection to all things on your planet. It is in your memory banks of your soul. It's why you have such a beautiful rapport with other species and they feel it.

You have a very open heart to all species, that's what your book is for—to tell others it's time to open their hearts to commune with other species and more.

Debra: Yes, I guess. Well, this is a surprise to me. I can see why I have to keep connecting with you all every day, there is much for me to remember and share. I had no idea. How can I get confirmation I am not making this up, that it is you talking to me Sabastian, before I mention it in my book? That is, if I use it in my book.

Sabastian: Yes, do use it in your book.

Debra: I feel I need confirmation, to know it is not my mind of illusion. Can I feel you in my heart, please? Yes. I am feeling tension in my heart, right side now, as I so often do when I sit here healing and writing this book. Keep healing and releasing, yes? I guess I am starting to see I have had a bigger life than I first thought.

Now I am finding out what that has entailed, so I can help heal others on this planet ... and help others know they have bigger lives than they remember and believe possible. We have so much to heal and remember from our past.

Sabastian, do you have anything else to share with me right now?

Sabastian: Yes, there is so much more you need to know. But I will allow you to take that on board before we go into many other things for you to remember.

Debra: This is very surreal, yet intriguing for me to know more. I will have to keep talking with you more often.

After this message was received from Sabastian, I shared with my beloved husband that one of my past life embodiments was another species, a dolphin. I immediately felt goose bumps, my sign from my soul to say that it is my truth. Thank you for that, Sabastian.

Would your heart be open enough to receive wisdom from your support team of ancestors if they came to you in another form?

The more I learn, the more I realise how little I know, exciting my soul to explore more.

Living With My Companions

14

Unconditional Love

The unconditional love of our furry soul companions and other species can take us back to feeling the divine force of God within us—if we can let them into our hearts. This is so precious, and why I love to have them so close to my heart, reminding me of the feeling of being bathed in God's divine love. My heart feels like it is exploding as I remember what unconditional love feels like when this happens.

Harley kitten and Charles shared a bed basket together, their choice, because they were so happy together with Kara and I in our loving home. I remember how much joy and peace I felt sitting with all my furry companions, such a happy place for me to be with my partner at that time, Kara. We were happy, and so too were all our furry companions, three cats and one dog. Thinking of those times makes me feel great warmth and joy in my heart, taking me to tears right now at the thought of this memory.

The joy of sharing my life with other species really opens my heart to feel so much unconditional love for all my furry family. It was all returned to me in those moments one-hundred-fold. I feel to share this now for you if you have not recognized or experienced this feeling when being present with your furry companions. It is beautiful to feel the heart expansion of peace and joy from them all in a moment in time. It felt like true unconditional love, for no one expected anything from anyone else in those moments. Even my novice musical abilities of playing guitar and practicing songs never made any difference to my furry companions, we all enjoyed that moment in time together with the music with no judgment.

For some time, I have had a vision, maybe a past life memory presenting to me. It is a scene with many animal species from all levels of the food chain, including a lion, all sitting with a human in the forest, peacefully resting together. It feels like it is the future, and it will come to be one day. Imagine the human, lion, lamb and the deer all sitting peacefully, no victims, no fears nor predators hunting one another. It is all about the inner peace they all hold with an evolved human. When our planet has shifted from the abuse energy of the victim and predator consciousness, I believe we will all have the peace and joy that we seek deep inside us as humans.

I have sat with my furry companions and my loving partner in our living room and felt the unconditional love in the room and this vision of all species peacefully resting. I can only wish for this to be for the earth mother. One day it will come to be after much healing is done by the human race. Am I dreaming here? Yes, but dreams are where a new reality can be seeded to manifest in the 3D world to physically materialise. We need to have the dream and start to visualise this peaceful scene for all species in our minds so it will be what we create for the future. I so hope it is soon, but there is divine timing, and humans need to keep evolving as Mother Earth is evolving quickly towards a peaceful and joyful planet. We need to keep up.

> *Human evolution is through the heart of healing our wounds, so we are not inflicting pain and suffering on other species and causing that abusive energy to be held in the energetic field of the earth mother as toxic memory. It will be a happy time for all other species when we can do this healing for ourselves as a human race.*

Have you seen those heart-warming videos on social media of many other species living and communing together in harmonious ways? The most unexpected species of animals are living in harmony together in some facilities, and the loving carers are posting on social media for all to see what's possible. Some female species are feeding orphans of other totally different species (sometimes due to the acts of human hunters). These evolved souls show us it can be done. They are trying to help us see and learn this. We see these videos as entertaining, but there is so much more behind what these other species are trying to teach humanity. We are not the wisest or most conscious of all the species. Due to their wounded hearts, many lack the awareness that we are all connected.

I remember with a smile when Charles would sit on the sofa with me. He was such a large furry companion for the small sofa, but he'd squeeze in and make himself fit into the space with me. So funny, it was quite a comical sight, Charles on my lap and his long legs dangling over onto the floor. I so loved that feeling of hanging out with Charles and Harley kitten. I remember being cuddled up together on the sofa with Harley sitting on my shoulder, smooching with me as he liked to do while I played the harmonica. He was such a funny boy.

So much love in our little two-bedroom older style apartment with our furry family. They were all so well behaved we never had to worry about the apartment being damaged, they seemed to be as chilled as we were and simply hung out with us all day. They did have to entertain themselves when we were at work, but they seemed to be happy together, chasing one another or sleeping together.

We would take Charles for rides in the car to great parklands or bush tracks for beautiful long walks in nature. He loved that as much as I did. He never left my side as he was so loyal to me from the first day when I took him home from the pound. I believe dogs taken to new homes from the dog pound really appreciate and know they're being saved, and they just want to please you and thank you for saving their lives and giving them love. It must be so upsetting for them to see dogs taken to the area where they euthanase them. Being sensitive and aware of the terrified soul leaving its body, as they are aware of other realms of existence and sensitive to the energies of others, they would know every time another dog was killed.

How appalling to put our furry companions through that type of experience when they love unconditionally and just want to be with us, give us love, perhaps protect us, and help us learn about ourselves to evolve. They choose to come and help us evolve. Every dog or cat has its own reason to be with us. If we can allow them to be who they are, and love them in return, it would make such a difference to our planet with the peace and joy that could be felt by all species. The high levels of disrespect cause pain and suffering, inflicted by unconscious humans who also suffer from pain in their hearts. That is why we all need to heal our hearts and be present with other species, so we can then feel real love around us.

If we have pain within our hearts, we miss out on all the love that's around us and our experience on this planet becomes dulled. We have an opportunity to experience so much more with open, healed hearts. I know, I've felt the difference and seen what it did for me when I healed my heart and became more conscious and sensitive in my life by waking up to what was in and around me at a deeper level. Believe me, there is so much magic waiting for us at every moment if we can expand our hearts and open up to what's around us, instead of being closed down, insensitive and feeling numb to our environment, unconsciously walking around with heavy and blocked hearts.

That is what the Indigenous people call the 'walking dead'—humans not feeling what is all around them. Disconnected and insensitive, they feel separate to nature and other species, possibly other humans too. I have heard this mentioned in a Buddhist tradition—they call it the 'hungry ghost' (ones with empty hearts). Such a sad place to be. I know this, for when my grief of losing my father took me to a dark place of separating from everything in the world around me, I experienced that feeling of being dead inside. A very dark place, I would not want to experience that again in this life. When I healed my grieving heart, I no longer felt separated from everything on the planet. To this day, I continue to feel supported by other beings and Mother Earth.

When Kara and I moved home with Charles to live in a coastal regional area, many miles from the old address, the new home had no fences, so we had to trust he would stay home while we were at work all day. Apparently, he took himself on a walk to the beach each day, dropping in to a couple of shops to say hello. Unbeknown to me, one of the real estate agents was my husband-to-be. When I returned home at 6pm each day, Charles would be at the front porch waiting for me. The neighbours told me later that Charles wandered off on adventures to the beach all day while I worked, returning within ten minutes of my arriving home. How did he always know the right time to come home when I returned home at different times?

When I finally met my husband-to-be months later, he came to my house and met Charles.

"I know this boy," he said, "he comes to say hello every day on his way to the beach. I pat him and give him a drink of water when he passes each day." You never know where your soul companions will find friends for you! I thought it quite funny that Charles knew my partner before I met him! Was he up to mischief, matchmaking maybe? I had thought he was on the veranda all day waiting for me—how wrong I was!

15

Sharing Our Wounds

Healing our hearts will get us connected to magical realms of existence with other species. When we hold pain deep in the heart there is no space for anything else, as it limits our ability to feel energetically the love of others trying to connect with us. We also become consumed by our own pain and suffering. You cannot hide from it, for it controls you, and your actions towards others will be based on the pain and suffering you are uncomfortably feeling, so it can become your shadow.

Even if you cannot see it, other species can—from your actions. They can also feel it energetically, even though they may not know what it is you are suffering. We share our pain and suffering with others; we never keep it within ourselves. Every action is shared outwardly with others, consciously or unconsciously, as the energetic field will shift with the emotions we feel. That is the phenomena of how pain works: It distorts your energy field and body balance, sometimes so much it can cause you dis-eases when not released to heal it.

Harley has triggered me in the past with his loud baby crying sounds to gain my attention, to the point I have felt agitated. When not in my best peaceful mood, or feeling a little frail and stressed, this has triggered me to tell him to be quiet, something that would happen to me as a child when I unintentionally agitated my parents and they felt triggered. I would be told to be quiet, and so my voice was not heard. I learnt recently that a baby's cry is a sound a human finds difficult to ignore. As I had no children, I found this fact of great interest for my evolution to be triggered to heal. When Harley triggers me, I now use it as my barometer of how balanced I think I am—this is my reality check. Our companions are teachers!

How our wounds are triggered gets passed down from one generation to another, and before we know it is shared with our companions, the other species. Often Harley is trying to alert us to something outside, such as another cat in the vicinity of our property. Harley is of Burmese breeding, which is historically a temple cat temperament, so his nature is to protect the property that is his temple (our home), becoming quite anxious in response to an invasion of energy. I always feel safe knowing he is doing his energetic guarding of our property. When I received the first communication from Harley, he advised me he would be the master of energy in our home and he was to be treated as an equal, and that I needed to research the cats of Egypt and how they were revered for their knowledge. Should I forget this message at any time, Harley is quick to remind me with his loud, commanding sound. He has also never tolerated any other species in our home, so he has never had to share his attention with others.

Living with older Harley, we have been learning the physical needs of our furry companion through his language. It is like communicating with our own human family to discover what they need. Harley has been the most vocal furry companion I have ever lived with, constantly letting us know all his needs. Every meow has a unique tonal value, so we've been able to intuitively know what he is telling us—there is a cat outside on our property, I would like my food now, come and sit with me, where are you, I want to go to bed now, come say goodnight to me, I've just used the kitty litter, etc. He makes awesome sounds in his throat in response to our talking to him or when pleased to see or be held by us. This has made a big difference over the years, allowing him to feel heard. I swear one day he is going to speak a word to me, and I will not be surprised.

Sometimes he will raise his voice for food or attention, especially when I am working on the computer and time gets away from me. I forget to eat, so Harley reminds me it is time to get off the computer and have a break and eat every few hours. I found that frustrating at first, but now I understand he is keeping me well and safe when using technology. So I stop, and we both have lunch outside in nature on the grass with the birds and flowers. Felines are one of the only land species who hear and vocalise the hum and rhythm of the planet. The purring is not only a vocal sound of pleasure, but is actually the audible rhythm of the earth's pulse, which they hear. How extraordinary these beautiful feline species are!

I have a sensitivity to EMF and Wi-Fi devices, so only use them for short periods of time now, taking breaks to go and earth myself in the backyard. I do have an earthing mat, but there is nothing more powerful than going to Mother Earth and feeling her body directly on my skin with my bare feet and hands. There is so much to share on this subject! Our animal companions need to be earthed with their paws on Mother Earth to receive her energy for their health too. Mother Earth's big organic bio-battery is powered every day by the sun. She stores the energy in her body, and we can access it to energise ourselves, as we are made of the same organic composition. This reduces inflammation in the body that causes many dis-eases. There is plenty on the Internet on earthing if you wish to know more.

16

Travelling and Companions

I commune through the heart intelligence, which bypasses the mind of chatter, so I can have a clear connection soul-to-soul.

All species, including our furry companions, read the energetic field we radiate, so know what we are trying to convey if we use our hearts to talk with them. I realised after Harley cat first arrived at our home that he had anxiety issues when I left home without him, and soon learnt to communicate with him that I would be returning. He sees my bag being packed and becomes anxious, so I share with him that I am going away for so many moons and I will return, and that he will have a carer or is going to the cat resort, and that always settles him.

Connecting with him when I go away on travels has been a great learning for me. Harley has taught me we need to communicate any change in routine, because he feels safe knowing what is to come. We can also connect energetically with our companions before and whilst we are on holidays and are physically separated. Whilst away, I connect with Harley heart-to-heart before I go to sleep at night to acknowledge him with some kind words and let him know I will be back soon so he knows I am not gone forever.

In the past, I have used a small toy cat representing Harley to assist me to connect before retiring at night whilst on holiday. Holding it against my heart and visualising him, I can see him remotely, saying his name and talking with him. My heart feels warm when I feel I have connected to his soul. The key is to be fully present in my heart for him to receive my message. Even if I am saying it verbally, I need to share it through the heart frequency. Such a simple practice to do when we travel to communicate with our companions energetically. I see it like an organic telephone line, allowing us to talk to a family member or friend who is missing us and feeling separated.

Harley's holiday carer has commented he is much calmer now when I am away. I have found this very helpful on those longer holidays when he cannot be with me. When I get home he is happy to see me, but not anxious, because he knew I would be returning for him. Before I started doing this, he would become anxious, pine and not eat his food for the first couple of days and I noticed he had lost weight whilst I was away. Now, at that same cat resort, he shows no anxiety signs or weight loss when I am away on holidays. For Harley, not eating is a sign he is seriously unwell or unhappy. A big cat, he loves his food and tells me several times each day when it is time to serve it up, raising the roof with his loud meow sounds if I do not comply within a short time. We love his big personality and affectionate, loving nature.

It is interesting how we can easily overlook the anxiety we may cause our furry companions when we are busy-minded packing and preparing for a holiday. They need to know when there is a change in their daily routine. Remember we are their only source of food, shelter and love. A routine for all their basic needs at home makes them feel safe. They rely on us to give them that, and they so deserve it, as they love us unconditionally and come to support our evolution in whatever way we need to learn.

17

Compassion and Ageing

Now I am learning to live with a companion who has aged ahead of me. At seventeen-plus years of age in human terms, in feline years Harley is now over 119 years old. Watching him as a fearless, wise cat ruling our home, I now see a frail and courageous wise companion sleeping most of the day, living with arthritis, one eye to see out of and poor hearing. I feel he is really holding on to be here with us. At times, this is very upsetting to witness in my sensitive heart. Some days he shows ageing signs worse than others. I want to be sure he is comfortable, not suffering in his ageing years. He looks remarkably well for all his health issues. When I ask if he is comfortable, he replies, "You know what I need is your love, it gives me comfort."

I hope the day does not come where I feel it is time to ask him if wants medical intervention to help him leave, due to his body's frailty. I will respect his decision and will let him make that decision without my interference. But I have to say, it's heart-wrenching to watch my companion slow down and sleep all day, feeling his spirit slipping from his little body that was once so vibrant and full of life, letting us know of his requests. Now it is strangely quiet at times, as he is only awake for limited hours.

I do catch glimpses of eye-to-eye contact with him, the special moments when we look into one another's eyes to see the souls we really are. Harley has shown me so much and helped keep me on track. I've so much gratitude for his soul coming to be with me here on earth, but it is very painful to see him spending so much time on the other side of the veil, in other realms in Dreamtime, "Preparing to leave," he has told me.

When I hug Harley for those short moments in a day when he is active and rises to be seen, heard, and to eat, I hug him gently, with care for his precious, frail little body. Knowing his days are coming to an end feels so painful in my heart. I do not want to keep him here if he is too uncomfortable, but I have seen some big changes in him over the past months and weeks, it's becoming obvious he is getting ready to leave.

Harley has been with me since 2007, when he was four years old. He weathered many storms before he found me, literally living in a shopping centre carpark with flooding rains for many weeks. I knew it was a match, but I did need to travel. Luckily, he has been very accommodating in accepting the cat resort, winning the hearts of every owner who ran that resort. He even won my brother-in-law's heart when we were guided to go and live in the central desert for a year. My sister wanted to take Harley and care for him, while her husband wanted a dog, but Harley broke his heart open, and he was sad to see Harley return to us. Now he has his own cat to love, and his heart has warmed to that little girl. I love how animals open our hearts and get inside.

Harley is a magician! When people meet him, they love him. I do not believe Harley starved in that carpark before meeting us, as he won the hearts of the chicken shop staff and they fed him. He also won the heart of a neighbour living near the carpark who fed him every day. Even though she had many cats, she quickly realized Harley was not like the others, as he would not socialize with them or tolerate them. I know he has always behaved like he is superior, like my companion Charles, who felt different to all other dogs and called himself a dog person.

I might call Harley the cat person, but he would not like that. He has a certain knowing about him, a wise one, somehow different to my other cats. I feel he has been on a mission and that has been evident to me from our first meeting, and from finding our souls knew one another and we were once again together, as also happened with Charles and Mandy. Such joy to meet up!

Knowing Harley has discomfort and is suffering in that tired old body, I do believe we are keeping him comfortable. He appears to be happy enough and has told me he is very well cared for, but I do feel his body discomforts as he moves around. It is all new for me to be looking after an older companion, I have never had that caring opportunity as my other furry companions all left me before they aged. I feel his heart so strong with mine when we hug, but I also feel his pain and wonder if he is trying to stay with me. I do not want him to suffer any more than he deems he can deal with. I would hate to think he sacrificed himself to stay here longer with me. I so wish him comfort in what are likely his last months on earth, as he is showing signs of kidney failure now. He has been such a wonderful teacher, entertaining, cheeky and loving companion and dear friend, part of our family, and I believe he knows this.

However, we have had our moments over the years too, when Harley has been demanding what he wants. I feel his wonderful heart and how he has forgiven me for being triggered, as I have also forgiven him in our first year together when he would nip me on occasion to let me know what he wanted, trying to teach me communication when I was not listening. We love one another unconditionally, so we have accepted our frustrations over those initial months with one another.

Master Harley still sees himself as the guardian of our home, getting upset when another cat is on the property. Now he has less energy to be as concerned however, but will still try to assert himself with a loud-sounding pitch if he senses energetically another cat outside. His hearing sense might be poor these days, but his conscious awareness energetically is exceptional. He is definitely a master of energy in our home.

I feel tremendous gratitude for Harley coming to be my soul companion all these years, as my teacher. Harley helped me to see my way clear when my life was changing. He has always been there for me, communing, with our hearts always connected in love. I feel he has loved me as much as I love him. How I will miss him when he decides it is time! I know we have had our disagreements, but that is all part of our unconditional loving relationship and learning. I know Harley has had his own soul learning journey here on the planet, sometimes he thinks this is Egyptian times.

Teacher Harley has shown me to be graceful, to be aware and more sensitive of energy around me, to take my time and be more conscious of what is happening in my energy field. To have had Harley with me for all these years has been such a blessing and a joy, knowing he is there every day with me and loving me, looking for me when I've been out.

Keeping Harley healthy, I have firstly tried to use vibrational remedies such as homeopathy and aromatherapy. Be aware that many essential oils are toxic to cats, even when used in steamers, so do check before you use any oil. Cats have a very high vibrational frequency and respond well to vibrational and natural remedies. Their kidneys are particularly sensitive to heavy chemicals, like some cleaning products, medical drugs, food additives and environmental factors such as EMFs and Wi-Fi. Many cats can die early from kidney problems from some food choices such as dried biscuits/kibble. Cats need fresh food for best health.

In one of Harley's early messages to me, he shared if I gave him fresh food he would have a long and healthy life with me. Moving towards eighteen years of age now, he has proved this to be true. His vet visits in earlier years have only ever been because he caused himself an accidental injury. As he ages, particularly in relation to his arthritis, I have asked Harley did he want any medications. He refuses chemicals, only wanting organic natural products. I managed to find him a natural oil for cats, and he appears to be showing signs of more flexibility and comfort.

Harley enjoys his massage each day, and on occasion in the warm bath, and this gives him great comfort. Strange some may think for a cat, but he has always loved a bath in the summer months. Perhaps the massage helps him chill. On heatwave summer days, he loves to have water sprayed around his neck and along his back. As I massage the moisture into his fur coat, he melts onto the floor purring. This is not an activity my other cats would have tolerated. Learning to gauge Harley's pain level, I have learnt from Harley over the years when he licks his lower leg in a particular location with fast strokes he is feeling uncomfortable pain, and this licking appears to soothe him. However, I will also ask if he would like a massage or to have some herbal drops for his pain (he does not always accept drops).

We can ask and learn what each companion loves. Cats being so sensitive to energy, Harley will come to me and ask me for energetic healing, I intuitively know, and he will push his back up against my hand. If you know what Reiki healing is, it would be similar but not the same, as I have my own intuitive approach to healing with animals.

Letting you know here—you can trust your own inner guidance. Harley loves this healing as long as he initiates it. He has taught me not to initiate it, because he will not consent and walks away. This has been my lesson on learning free will and respect with other species.

I have had so many great moments with my cat companions. They remind me to be consciously aware of what I am doing as I witness them purposefully moving around a space, consciously alert and graceful. They teach me to be conscious and patient, to be aware of the divine timing of all there is, and to feel the energy as I move in space around me. When I hear that purr, I feel their joy and peace within me too. As I pat them with affection, they return unconditional love to me. I feel pain in my heart when they are hurting, alerting me to find what it is that is troublesome.

More than anything, Harley has taught me how to connect through the heart space from one species to another. It is our telephone line, available to us anytime. He is such a wonder cat! I know he has much wisdom that I may not have been conscious of at times, and he has tried hard to let me know what I needed to do. I've not always received the message, because I have not always been momentarily present enough to feel or hear what he has shared, but I do know he has tried, and there is still so much more I can learn from him, to practice my communication skills.

How do I live with my furry companions with respect? I try to let them know what I want of them by talking to them. I believe they read my energy field, so they do not have to know my language. We are all connected energetically, and other species are consciously aware of the energetic field around us all, so they can read what is shared with them energetically.

2020: Communication with Harley when I was concerned for his body comfort.

Debra: Harley are you comfortable in that body? Can I do more to help you?

Harley: My older body is now so tired, as you know, I have so much going on. You know what I love?

> Cuddles, and lots of love. I have it all, and I do not need anything except your hugs. They give me great relief when I'm feeling the pains in my body, and good fresh food is keeping my body happy. I sleep a great deal, and that also helps me as I'm now doing a lot of energetic work with our soul family on the other side of the veil, in other realms, in preparation for me to leave the earth plane. Our soul family have told you this before, yes?

I try to do the things he loves, including singing to him. I make up songs, and I believe he picks up on the rhythm and finds it soothing. Cuddles are really what he loves most, and being stroked under his neck. Harley has several locations he has chosen to be comfortable, and we provide soft bedding off the floor for each one—near a sunny bay window he loves in the day, the living room if too warm and he needs to be cooler, and his favourite, the purpose-built cosy bed with a ramp where he feels safe and warm. He loves that bed with his hot water bottle on colder nights. Harley also loves routine, and tells us when he is ready to go to his bed every night so we can fuss over him and say our goodnights. This sets his purring off and he falls to sleep happy.

Even though Harley is sleeping a lot more now, I try to encourage him to go outside in the day to earth his paws and walk to bring balance back to his body from all the toxic technology in modern-day homes. He has a lovely sunny place he loves to sleep outside too. His eyes need regular cleaning, as he does not clean them as often, and his eyesight is not as good as it was, which can make him nervous outside, so I make sure I go with him to help him feel safe.

Constipation has been ongoing for Harley, so I keep a little exercise book to record his bowel actions. This helps us know when to make changes to his diet to help him use his bowels. A couple of times he had to go to the vet for an enema. We check in with him if he is comfortable, always remembering the respect of asking before we give anything. We also have a foot stool for him to get on and off the sofa to sit in his favourite sunny place.

Last of all, we talk with him a great deal. Harley needs that communication. He has always been a talker, so we keep him happy by communing with him. At times, I feel I'm back being a nurse in the hospital checking on my patient's body health, but it is all with love and it's not difficult to be vigilant for his comfort. Considering our companions give us unconditional love every day for many years, keeping them comfortable during their last stage of life on earth is the least we can do, don't you think? We love him, and feel his big love returned to us every day. I feel his discomforts and feel helpless sometimes when I see his vulnerability, then I look into his eyes and see his soul smiling back at me with love. Bless that soul!

18
Companion Behaviours

Whilst not all my animal companions have given me the same powerful, deep heartfelt messages, supporting my soul's journey on earth, without a doubt they have all given me unconditional love. This helped my heart to feel joy and love for them all. I remember how my companions found me, or I chose them because they needed a home. Some I tried to stop from going to a shelter to be euthanased by taking them into my home, offering love and earthly pleasures for them to thrive. Whilst these were joyful and loving relationships, they were not the same experiences as the soul companions I have known from my past lives.

How do we know the difference for each companion we meet?

I can only share it as I have experienced. They were all chosen by my heart calling at a deeper level. I felt I knew them without logically knowing why. When I am centred in my heart space, fully beyond the mind of chatter and judgment, I believe my heart opens to become a gateway to my soul.

My soul sends an energetic message to my heart, letting me know when I meet a kindred soul from my past life.

Finding Charles in the animal shelter—I knew he was there, but had to search for him with my heart. Mandy was on the road, but I knew she was to go home with me when my heart engaged with hers. I persevered with my family to keep her because the knowing was so strong, even though I could not explain it to them. It was my soul telling my heart *she has to be with me, I know her.* Beautiful Harley, my heart felt his soul immediately. There was no doubt my soul knew his, thus my heart was guided to follow that feeling.

> *It is about knowing your own heart's*
> *message from your soul.*

What I have observed with my soul companions Charles, Harley, Mandy and Sabastian living with me, is that they were rarely interested in other members of their same species. They were focused to be with me on their life journey, and after passing have come back to offer messages to help me remember who I am and my past lives, to help me remember my gifts in this life journey and my purpose, why I came here to earth. They have kept me on track.

My childhood animal companion friend, Bruno, was chosen by my father as our family companion, but I probably spent the most time with him. Bruno helped me learn a great deal about my sensitivity that allows me to feel other species' pain, and that I could be heard by other species without judgment and would always be loved unconditionally by them. The love and attention my companions gave me was healing, allowing me to feel hope for a new day after feeling painful emotions from my family's dysfunctional and abusive behaviors.

One of the animal companions I saved from the death needle was Jack, the soul in a collie-cross-spaniel dog bodysuit. He was in a shelter and I thought he would be a great friend for Charles. Wrong! Charles ignored him and growled at him when he became too crazy or disturbed his peace. When Jack was in trouble with another dog, Charles, as the wiser and superior dog, would discipline him, at least that is how it appeared to me. I observed Charles was the boss and the wiser one by his actions, and Jack took notice.

Jack was a highly reactive and spontaneous personality at times, causing himself to get into trouble. Once he accidently bit Kara's hand (my ex) when she was trying to separate him from fighting another dog. Kara had to go to hospital to get the wound treated. Unfortunately, when I split up with Kara, I left Jack. Twelve months later, Jack landed at the vets to be euthanased because he had attacked the neighbour's cat, killing it horribly, so I was told later. If I had been able to communicate with him, maybe I could have found out why that happened and helped him.

With what I know now, I may have saved his life if I'd had the opportunity at that time to commune with him. He had been living with two cats and never bothered them, although they did not really tolerate him, which they showed with a swipe across the nose on occasion. He was not of the same energetic frequency as the other companions in our home, so he did disturb the peace at times, until Charles intervened by growling at him.

Living with Jack and witnessing his reactions and effects on others, I did receive insight on how our reactions affect others around us and how we can disturb their peace. We can always learn from all species. Even if we're not consciously communing with them, we can be the witness and observe interactions. I believe every species can be our teachers.

Another of my animal companions, Troy kitten, was being taken to an animal shelter after he was found in a park. I stepped in to offer him a home with myself and my housemate's companion dog, Jessie. He arrived in the home and immediately connected with Jessie, myself and my partner. He was not an affectionate cat looking for hugs, preferring to be outside most of the time. That was all okay until he kept bringing home dead prey he had caught. I would look outside the kitchen door and there he would be, devouring a rat, head-to-tail, or he would leave a half-eaten small animal. This was a little confronting, but he was a cat, and I thought *that is what they do, isn't it?* He was well fed, but continued to bring his prey home for us to see. Not having learnt animal communication at that point, I never communed with him at a deeper level beyond the physical level.

> *My insight from Troy was that I had to accept who he was, and that I could not change him, even though I did not feel good in my heart with him eating all the little animals.*

In the fourteen years we have been together, my soul companion Harley, in his cat bodysuit, has never chased or delivered any prey to our home.

In fact, I have seen Harley sit for hours observing with great interest lizards, birds or small marsupials in our native bush backyard, without ever chasing them. If he walked around the yard near their tree the birds would chase him. He has a few wound scars on his head from birds pecking him to show for it. I've never seen him in a tree chasing birds. One bird was in our native garden for many months with a deformed wing and appeared to not fly. He would pass by Harley on the ground, searching for seeds, and Harley never tried to catch him.

I wondered if this represented Harley's highly evolved soul wisdom. Mandy and Charles also did not mix with other species, or even their own species—they were always only interested in being with me. It did show me that our companions all resonate at different frequencies, which determines who they may connect with at an energetic level, such as when our souls know one another.

My Family of Light

19
Ancestors, Soul Star Family and Past Lives

We live on a planet that is evolving at great speed in order to raise the vibration of her body in synchronicity with the expansion of this universe. This is an auspicious time on Mother Earth for our spirits to be embodying human bodysuits for our souls to evolve. Mother Earth is a school for our souls to learn and evolve. We come to learn the lessons we chose before arriving to raise our vibrational frequencies.

It is a privilege to be here now, at such a crucial time in the evolution of our universe and this planet's expansion. If we can be more conscious and awake on earth, we have the opportunity to evolve many lifetimes in one life. We have a great support team to do this. Our ancestors from our soul star family groups, other species, Mother Earth and nature are all here to support our evolution. The only catch is we need to remember we are connected to everything, we are not separate from any other species, nature, our ancestors or Mother Earth. We're all here to support one another to evolve.

Ancestors of the past, future and now, we are all those returning from the past, the future, and we sit in the now. When we respect and honour the present moment of Now, we are one with all our history and future. We can tap into the well of wisdom to guide us on our journey in this life, then we can feel supported and loved unconditionally. The road is then made easier in oneness of spirit with all souls beyond all time and space.

This is my journey with my ancestors, beyond the 3D realm of existence, back to my original soul star family that I came from, in the

Galaxy of Andromeda, before I arrived on earth to have this human bodysuit experience for my soul to evolve and raise my frequency. We are all vibrating frequencies who change form when we go to another realm of existence, such as when we arrive on earth. When we die on earth, we return to our star homes to be with our soul star families in other realms of existence. These destinations will be different for all of us, as we are all unique and come from many locations across the universe and galaxies.

Most of us are aliens, from many star systems in the cosmos, and have now become interrelated while living on the earth over many lifetimes. Our souls arrived with free will to decide our own life journeys here on earth school, our mission, and in what body form we would like to experience our lessons. Most of the older humans arrived with less than 3-5% of our conscious memories of who we really are and why we came to earth, or what our mission was and what we need to learn. Many children arriving in recent years have a higher percentage of conscious memories of their past lives and know who they are and why they are here. If you believe in reincarnation, this will probably make sense for you. If you do not, I suggest you open your heart, be curious, and come on an adventure with me here.

Reincarnation is more about us moving realities than actually dying, for on death we just change form. After death, our organic human bodysuit returns to the earth once our spirit force is released. Free, our spirit force changes form to be part of another reality of existence, returning to our soul star galactic families. Many other species are also souls just like us and can be from our soul families, our past life teachers, or souls we have travelled with in past lives.

Since writing my first book, so much more has unfolded for me to better understand and put the puzzle together for my life journey, and how so many of my ancestors have been supporting me at times, even though I was not conscious of this help until later. This is why I feel it is so important to share this with you, so you can also look deeper into your relationships with other species. This learning has emphasized to me that we are all related, and All One. As vibrating frequencies of love, we are sparks from the great ocean of love that our universe is held together by.

From the moment I arrived on the earth I was very sensitive, open and communed with nature, Mother Earth and my ancestors. I have some memory, as it all felt like one to me. When I was a child someone tried to kidnap me, which had a tremendously traumatic effect on my heart, and I started to feel alone and separate from my magical world of nature and ancestors. I was already noticing all the pain, suffering and sadness on the planet from witnessing injustice and disrespect toward other species who did not have a voice, which really upset me. I questioned why there was so much pain and unhappiness in my family and in the wider world. Experiencing abusive behaviours in my own family and taking on their pains, I felt I did not have a voice at home, so began to close my heart down.

Feeling separate in my heart, unbeknown to me, anger and frustration were being stored in my body. Thus, not only was I taking on the pain of other species and my family, but I also started to make my own karma. Bruno, our family furry companion, kept me from giving up by giving me endless love and listening to me. By the time I reached age sixteen, I had stored a lot of anger in my body and my heart was shutting down. My first soul companion, Mandy, came to help me feel love again in my heart. Her death devastated me, largely because I could still feel her around me, so believed I had buried her alive. When I started my shamanic practices many years later, Mandy returned to me in spirit with a message on our past life together, and has been communicating with me ever since.

> *Our ancestors, and all species, are waiting patiently for us to commune with them so they can share their wisdom, support us, and help us heal our hearts so we can find the magic that awaits us here on earth.*

Communication with Sabastian, a past life soul who knows me.

Sabastian: Dearest, we were dolphins you and me. We have been together in many lifetimes. Do you not remember?

Debra: I feel this lightness within me, but I feel no one else relates to it. So many humans feel heavy with worry and I just want to be light.

Sabastian: Do not be taken to the shadows by others, you know what you need to do. You spent your life on this path of staying light. That is because you carry the dolphin energy. You want to stay light because you are light, dearest.

You and I have been dolphins in many past lives. We also had many other jobs, not just that.

Debra: Yes, what was that?

Sabastian: We cared for the temples and the energy they sat on.

Debra: What temples?

Sabastian: In Atlantis, dearest.

Debra: And were they under water?

Sabastian: Yes dearest, they were, and you were one of the keepers of the energy that took care of them. Back then your dolphin role was a big one, more than you are remembering.

It is the dolphin souls who are caring for the energies here on the earth at present with the whales, do you realise that, dearest?

Debra: Yes, I thought so.

Sabastian: Do add that into your book too, it would be good for humans to know what dolphins do and how it can help humanity, the importance of their work. You will already know this.

Debra: Yes, I feel their important jobs. And the whales, is this the same?

Sabastian: No, they are looking after the song lines, also energy grids, but they work in different ways. The two work together. Yes, you saw them working together on your whale trip.

Debra: Yes, I did, and I was amazed at how they team up. The whales are so big, and the dolphins look so small, weaving in and out of one another in patterns.

Sabastian: That is how they work together in the oceans and water ways. The song lines are important to keep balance on the planet with the magnetics, and the dolphins work the grids as the energy is held on the earth.

Debra: What do you mean held on the earth?

Sabastian: They are constantly moving about, re-adjusting the energetic fields of the earth, as you may already know or remember.

Debra: I vaguely remember this work. It certainly does not sound strange to me, or unfamiliar. I have a knowing intuitively of this work.

Sabastian: Yes, we have our past life memories stored in our soul's DNA memory.

Debra: Sabastian, out of curiosity, what is your other spiritual name?

Sabastian: Imogen.

Debra: What does that mean?

Sabastian: The one of light and joy.

Debra: That is so you! We have had so much fun together in our past lives, have we not?

Sabastian: Yes, we sure did!

The many light beings, souls who have come to be with me as my support team, are ancestors of my soul star family. They come from another galaxy, Andromeda, where I came from and will return to. They all know me well and what I am capable of, as they have been with me for many lifetimes. Now they are here to help me remember who I really am. As you now know, from some of the messages you have already read, they came to open my heart to remind me of my gifts, what my mission is here on earth, and how I can help here with my past life knowledge of crystals and to work with the light beings to heal Mother Earth.

When I started to write this book, many of my soul family connected with me. They have shared many messages of encouragement, supporting my writing by answering my questions for my book, and they heal my energetic body. I find it quite awesome to be getting healing from my soul star family! I was also told my writing is the way I will find to be enlightened before returning to the light of my home, Andromeda, where we do not have physical bodies. We come to earth to feel the polarities of light and dark, to have emotional lessons needed to evolve.

I share some of the healing that has taken place, so you get an idea of what is possible with your ancestors' soul star family.

This book is attracting all my ancestors to come and support me to write it, but they all share that I need to heal my heart more to release my wisdom that is locked away. Every time I write they are healing me. Sometimes I go on a spiritual journey to healing temples in other realms of existence I have visited in past lives, such as Atlantis or Lemuria. What follows is one of those sessions and what took place.

2019: Communication with my ancestors' soul star family, whilst receiving healing.

Debra: Soul family, is there anything you would like to share in my book today?

Ancestors: Maybe, yes, mention your ancestors' soul star family.

Debra: I feel like a car going to the garage for maintenance.

Ancestors: Yes, dearest. That is funny, you are right, you are getting maintenance (healing) from your ancestors. Maybe you could use that in your book.

Debra: Yes, I stop into the garage, which is my computer chair, while I receive healing and write my book. That is so true.

How have these connections with my ancestors and messages helped me?

These light beings are part of my soul star family, and know what my earthly mission was agreed upon before I came to earth—my contract to support this planet's evolution to expand with the galaxy. As we all forget when we arrive on earth, they support us, maybe with a question to remember our past life. If I feel challenged with painful memories arising when I am writing, the ancestors help me release the block by sharing unconditional love with me and I can begin to feel healing within. This opens my heart to deeper levels of my wisdom to remember my gifts, to share and support the earth's evolution, reminding me of my soul's mission here on this planet and giving me guidance for my book's focus.

Sometimes it can be overwhelming to have so many journeys to write about. I have so many words running around in my head, all wanting to come out onto the page. I do not suffer from writer's block, quite the opposite! Much of the time I cannot stop writing. I have to say, with regards to a theme for this book, I have been told I still have several more to be written on new themes.

The support of my ancestors' soul star family has also supported me to evolve, as I raise my frequency more as parts of the puzzle of my life begin to become clearer. Writing has helped me put the puzzle together, and leads me into reflection on my life. So many experiences stored in my memory banks I had actually forgotten until I started to write and reflect. I feel blessed to have had this opportunity to live this life on earth with all my ancestors' soul star family as my support team walking with me. How awesome life is when we can commune beyond the limited physical 3D world and open to other realities of existence.

Did you know you have a support team? Have you communicated with them too?

20

My Support Team

(Ancestors' soul star galactic family.)

Could there be realms of existence we can access to give us a deeper meaning, to understand why our companions come to us as souls we may already know, as our support team?

We have a support team of ancestors from our soul star galactic family who come to us as other species, such as animals, as soul companions to support us. They can work with us across the veil of illusion of the 3D realm of existence if we are open, awake and consciously walk on earth. Because we have free will, they need to wait for us to ask for help before they can help us heal.

It is hard to feel the love around us when we are suffering with painful, wounded and heavy hearts, which is why we need to be healing our hearts. Doing so can change what is happening at this time in our troubled world, supporting Mother Earth's expansion to a higher vibration and humanity's evolution to find peace and joy on this planet.

Our Soul Companions Take Our Pain

There are so many ways our soul companions come to help us heal. When I started learning animal communication practices, many requests came from carers who had soul companions suffering with ailments. So often, I found the soul companion had taken on the dis-ease of the carer, without the carer being aware of what was happening. The carer knew their soul companion was unwell, but did not know to feel deeper into the experience to understand their beautiful friend had taken on their dis-ease to help them. This kept happening, and while I found it very honorable of the soul companion, it was also disturbing that the companion was not being acknowledged for what they had taken on for the carer.

Companion animals will take on the stress of the family too. Most people do not realise how sensitive their companions are, especially if you have a very evolved soul who has come to be with you in a dog or cat body form. That is what happened to me with Charles. I was profoundly ill and had no idea he was working to keep me alive during my depression and suicidal thoughts, or that it was wearing on him too. He shared with me later how it was a big job to keep my heart open, which he did by showering me in love so I could heal my body and want to stay on the planet, as I was so unwell I just wanted to leave my body.

Charles would not leave my side. He sat with me every minute of the day. He would come to help me, that was his mission. I had only found him at the dog shelter two years before I became unwell, yet he knew why he was with me from a pup. He was such a loyal companion I never needed a lead, as he was always by my side, watching over me silently. When I became seriously ill, he sat by my bed, day in and day out, until I started to recover. It was very healing knowing that when I was in bed resting and sleeping all day, trying to recover, he was there. I would wake to go to the bathroom and his little head would pop up over the edge of the bed and look at me with those loving eyes of adoration he held for me.

What an extraordinary being. I feel so much gratitude for that beautiful soul. He was on a mission and he saved my life. The unconditional love he showed was way beyond what you would expect from a loving companion. Such blessings I have had with my soul companions who have come to help me on my mission in this life. If only more humans could see how they are privileged to have a soul come to be with them and help them on the evolving path on earth.

≈

Our soul companions and soul family can open our hearts with so much love it can heal us. Being sensitive to all species, during the horrific bushfires in Australia through the summer of 2019/2020 I held tremendous sadness in my heart. Oddly, you might think, I was not aware I was holding on to it until Harley helped me heal. I had been concerned with an eye injury he had sustained that was taking a long time to heal. Feeling into his discomfort, I felt uncontrollable heart sadness and crying as I tried to commune with him, feeling helpless in my efforts to find any solutions to help him. Such a powerful feeling, my love for Harley triggered my heart to release and let go of the sadness I had been feeling for the many species of wildlife caught up and burnt in the bushfires over the past weeks. (Many more were still being found in that week.)

When I did my usual morning meditation/yoga practice, a vision presented to me of what I needed to create as art therapy. I could not ignore it and began immediately. An incredible creation of the wildlife consumed me, compelling me to paint, colour and draw my vision. My heart called me to do this creation all day, until the end. I did. Initially I had some doubt for my artistic skills—could I really draw the vision?

Sometimes I get so frustrated by not being able to reproduce my visions, but not that day—I chose art as therapy and it healed my heart. I love art therapy because you do not have to be a trained artist, you just need to listen to your own inner guidance and let it flow symbolically. As it flowed, I drew so many wildlife species without needing a rubber for corrections. They just kept presenting on the page, and the arms of Divine Love held them. At the base of the picture I had massive, passionate flames and fire, representing the burning of bushland and trees. The message I received was, "The wildlife souls passed over are in the hands of Divine Love now." That was very reassuring to me.

I always find conscious dance as therapy wonderful for releasing deep emotions that are wanting to be heard and seen, and had attended my regular conscious dance class the day before this emotional release. A reflective session, my mind and heart kept focusing on the wildlife who had not made it out of the intense fires, their souls unable to pass over. As I find so often in my life, my heart guided me to that healing and release through my dance. The next day, I wrote with tears after feeling triggered by Harley. How sad my heart feels on this planet at these times.

The picture I created was so powerful I shared it on my personal

Facebook page, and within a minute the comments and reactions rolled down the page, people sharing how this picture had affected them, and their friends. In that moment I realised the importance of sharing my artwork—I drew to heal my heart, and helped heal many other hearts. I was blown away. I generally would not share my art therapy, as it is usually a highly personal process, but that day I had to go beyond my fear of others' judgments and follow the strong pull in my heart to share it with friends. How extraordinary life is when we follow our heart guidance and keep the logical mind quiet for a moment.

I feel so happy now my heart has had a big healing, and I share for others to have healing too. The point I would like to make here is how our soul companions can heal us. When we are close to them and let them into our hearts, they can open our hearts to all sorts of healing and feelings that another human is not able to. Our soul companions are so unconditionally loving and do not judge us, I believe that makes them so special in our lives and allows us to feel safe to let them into our hearts. When one heart meets another in the unconditional space of love, it will expand our heart to feel more love, and this allows healing to take place.

I've many experiences to share with you on how my soul companions have healed and saved me in my life by giving me so much unconditional love it made a difference to my life journey. You cannot overestimate the power they bring to heal us and open our hearts to such expanded states when we feel let down or unable to feel our hearts due to the pain. Another species can just get to that deep place and open my heart so easily when I am with them. It is quite extraordinary. Knowing what I know now, it is such a blessing that these souls choose to come be with us in our life, to support us to heal our hearts to find our way when we feel like giving up.

I never knew what was underlying my relationships with my animal companions, but I felt the power of their love in my heart, and that was all I needed for it to make a difference when I so needed love for my painful heart. Whether grief, or just sadness about something else in my life, they have always been with me and made a difference, uplifting me and opening my heart up again to receive love when no other human could do this for me. Just the sounds birds make give my heart a lovely warm feeling and expands it to really feel myself and the beauty this planet has to offer. If you have an opportunity to allow another species into your heart and life, you would be amazed by how much they can change your life and help you grow and trust life more.

It puzzles me how people can hurt other species. I believe many just have not opened their hearts enough to feel what is possible, because if they had, they could not possibly want to hurt another species. I hear many people say they know We Are All One and do not intentionally hurt other species, but I see them with broken hearts—for if they had released their painful hearts to become more sensitive, they could not eat other species, nor support any activity that exploits another species, because they would feel the pain of others strongly in their own hearts.

So many people can justify eating other species without honouring a life, but this supports the exploitation. I believe we feel guilty, and justifying is the way to get beyond what our hearts are telling us to feel at a deeper level. We need courage to open and heal our heart of trauma and the pain we experience in this life and our past lives. I guess many do not have the strength or courage just yet to do this, and there is no judgment here. We all find our own divine timing for changes. However, these choices people make do not support the We Are All One here on earth, and they are missing out on going really deep into the truly beautiful, sensitive heart space of compassion and peace that comes when we can start to heal our hearts.

I can share this from my own experience of walking the path of heart healing. As I continue to open my heart to deeper levels of compassion, I receive greater love and more magical interactions with other species. We live on such an awesome planet and can grow and evolve to be so much greater than we can even comprehend to be possible with our limited 3D thinking mind.

The magic I have unveiled on this planet takes my breath away, showing me what is possible to experience and feel with other species and our companions. There is so much more to our physical world. We can go beyond this reality. If we can open our hearts this becomes obvious to us. Other species and beings of the other realms of existence, such as the ancestors, are just waiting for us to wake up and evolve, because they want to help us. I have written my stories with their support, encouraging me to go deep and share from my heart experiences.

My companions have given me so much love! I cannot believe I even deserve that much love at times. The healing that has come from my companions and other species is such a gift to behold and feel in my heart. When my heart has been broken, they have come to me. I open my heart to them and am rewarded with so much more love returned to me. It is all so magical, what I receive from the universe. I am often heard saying I feel like I am riding a magic carpet in my life. I keep healing my heart and then I open to more extraordinary experiences happening for me.

Such joy comes from those experiences that they are hard to share, because I feel them so deeply in my heart and they do not feel of this world. My heart knows the special feeling of knowing I am communing with a very special soul, and my interactions are at a deeper or higher level, however you look at it. Every time, my heart actually melts into a warm vessel of love and I just want to pour my love out around the environment I am in. When I do, the experience deepens even further and I feel the oneness that is around me in nature. Other species, flora and fauna all become part of my energetic field. A gift to behold, joy becomes bliss in those moments.

This does not always happen, which I guess is why it is so special when it does. It is also unexpected, for you cannot plan for these encounters. You just need to trust your heart, then the universe opens up with the gifts of magic and feelings that make you very aware of being connected in a real metaphysical and physical sense. I do not find it so easy in my everyday activities when I am busy doing and not present to the moment in time to allow an opening to happen.

That is the secret—being open to the moment that is and leaving space for whatever wants to commune with you, knowing it can because you left a space for it.

21
Healing Across Realms of Existence

> *"We are interdimensional beings, existing simultaneously in parallel worlds. The best gift we have as human beings is our ability to consciously move through all these dimensions, effortlessly transcending time and space."*
>
> *Puma F.Q. Singona*
> *(Shaman, Peru)*

After I experienced very deep healings with my ancestors this year, continuing to open my heart while completing my book, my ancestors thought it was time to share more about human connections with other species and soul star families. I share here something Charles shared with me only this year—that he is definitely from my soul family and is my spiritual mentor.

Ready for this? Charles was my grandfather in a human bodysuit in this life!

He has protected me all these years—since he passed away when I was four years old. I knew he was around me when I was twelve. I remember questioning my mother, but she fobbed it off as me being silly. I never understood why he was not in his bed when I visited one day, or ever again, for death did not make sense to a four-year-old.

Now here he is, sharing that he has always protected me and is the grandfather soul I was so close to as a child. That blew my mind just a little! His soul was my grandfather in the human bodysuit, then Charles in the dog bodysuit, and my spiritual teacher in past lives—that was a lot to take on board!

He asked did I notice how protective he was as my dog, Charles? Yes, that always stood out for me, and his all knowingness. The thing that upset me was when I left Kara, I left him with her. I knew she loved him too, and I could not take him with me travelling. Had I known he was Grandfather I would probably have changed my plans in some way to accommodate him going with me. You just never know who your soul companion could be! If I had been consciously communing with Charles at that time, I would not have left him behind. Would that have changed my journey? I will never know.

Leaving my partner and Charles caused me a great deal of heartache, I did not make the decision lightly. Charles also shared how he had missed me, and how the love in the house was missing with my ex-partner's new relationship, because the new partner did not have the same compassion for other species. That made my heart sink with sadness, but Charles assured me it was all part of our soul's journeys and I did what I had to, following my soul's guidance. He had his own journey to learn humility.

A friend shared with me recently that she swears her mother who passed over has come back as her cat and is very protective of her daughter, just as she was in her previous life as her grandmother. She shared many strange events that kept intuitively telling her the cat soul is her mum. I found this very interesting. I wonder how many other people have acknowledged a companion animal feels to be a soul of a close relative?

2020: Communication with Charles, Spiritual Teacher and Paternal Grandfather.

Debra: Who am I talking with here?

Charles/Grandfather: Yes, we are the same ancestor soul. I was not sure which to tell you, dearest.

Debra: Well, now I know, can you tell me something in our past to convince me I am not making this up?

My heart accepts this, however my mind is needing to process it.

Charles/Grandfather: Yes, dearest. I have always looked over you, and when I was your companion Charles, I was always by your side. Yes, that is because I was looking over you on earth and wanted to help you with your healing.

Debra: I am so sorry you had to leave painfully as a dog, you did not deserve that. I was so happy and had so much gratitude for what you did to send me healing in my heart. I so love you, Grandfather. I remember when you left the planet when I was a child. I found it confusing as you were no longer there at the house, but later I felt you around me.

I knew it was you when I was around twelve years old, even though my mother said, "Don't be silly, he died many years ago."

Charles/Grandfather: This book is so important to share that humans need to respect other species because they are so connected to us, they may even be our soul family.

Debra: Should I mention that you were my grandfather as well as Charles, the spiritual teacher?

Charles/Grandfather: Yes dearest, if you can find a place for it.

Debra: I had so much guilt leaving you behind with Kara, now I know why, even more so. I always said I would never leave my companions behind or give them away. I justified it by saying Kara was your carer too. Please forgive me Grandfather/Charles.

This sure is quite a lot to take in here. Could I ask for healing from my soul family while I am resting?

Charles/Grandfather: Dearest, you must not be hard on yourself. This is why your book is so important to get out, so others know they have souls of family members who come to help them. Humans are never alone, because we are all connected on both sides of the veil. We are not separated, your ancestors are right behind you, dearest.

Debra: Thank you for talking with me tonight, and I realise how important it is to keep talking with you all every day. Much gratitude, I feel I need to go rest after this news and let my guilt be released for being so unaware of this fact. I suddenly feel very tired. Goodnight Grandfather, love you so much and miss you, but I'm so happy to be able to talk with you here now.

At this point I want to share what the healing is like whilst I am being supported to write my book. Every time I connect with my ancestors' soul star family, I receive healing. They have made a contract with me that when I connect with them, they will help me heal. This is only one example of what can take place. Every session is different, it depends on what I need or have processed since the last session with them.

March 2020: Excerpt from a healing session conversation with my soul family.

Debra: What is it you are showing me right now?
Grandfather: A temple.
Debra: Yes. It is large and white, reminds me of Atlantis from my memories. Yes? Are you taking me inside for healing?
Grandfather: Yes, dearest one. Your soul family are all here with you, including Mandy, your twin flame.

I became drowsy, then twenty minutes later I awoke, slumped over my computer, to see writing on the computer screen. Apparently, I relaxed so deeply my hands let go and I hit some letters on the keyboard unintentionally. I felt very drowsy and ungrounded, similar to that feeling of coming out of a deep meditative state. This feeling continued for quite a few minutes in human time, maybe twenty minutes.

Debra: Wow Mandy, it felt like I went into a deep meditation to receive this healing?

Mandy: Yes dearest, we took you to the temple that you helped design and build, the Temple of Unconditional Love.

Debra: Mandy, I feel tired again, is this the healing taking effect here?

Mandy: Yes, possibly what you are feeling now.

Debra: I am very drowsy. Is there anything I need to know right now? Am I being helped by compassionate beings here?

Mandy: Yes, yes, yes dearest! We are your soul family. We are helping you.

Debra: I just had some doubt come over me and had to double check. So much is going on and on so many levels, I feel I need to check in.

Mandy: Yes. Do understand this—it is good you are on alert to be empowered. Your heart will not let you down dearest, as long it is what you feel to be right.

Debra: Yes, I feel that in my heart to be true. There is so much confusion here on this planet right now, and so much deception.

Mandy: Yes dearest, you are right. There is, and it will all be revealed for the masses to change this very soon.

Debra: This planet is on such a big journey right now with all humans being taken along, consciously or unconsciously. It is a big transformation time on earth. Many of us are feeling what we have waited for over many years, but it presented in a surprising way. Thank you for my healing here. I feel I need to go and rest now. Do you have anything else for me to know about tonight?

Mandy: No dearest, it is best you go and take rest.

These healings have taken me on some big journeys since writing my book. If you can go into a sacred space to write your book, the ancestors of your soul star family will come and support you to heal. They want to help us at this time in our evolution. We are so blessed to have this opportunity. I am always in gratitude for what I receive.

I speak to them all regularly, like I am talking to my human family here on earth. I have some jokes with them, but most of all I am continually surprised at what we in human body form are not aware of because we come without our memories of our past lives. I have known this fact, and remember being told by a spiritual mentor long ago *if you knew who you really were it would be a surprise to you all.* I did not know how much of a difference that could make to our lives! It has taken me to so many magical and awe-inspiring places metaphysically, and to feel so supported by all my star family coming to help me in different body forms makes me feel great gratitude for what's possible beyond our small, egoic minds. I really get that death is just changing my form, because I am only energy, I guess you could say part of the matrix of light and love of the divine source (not the 3D famous movie version of the matrix with polarity and darkness).

2020: Communication received from my paternal grandfather.
Subject: Where I Came From.

Debra: Hello, is this my soul family here?
Grandfather: Yes, dearest one, we are here as always. We do not leave your side; we travel with you.
Debra: Would anyone like to talk with me now?
Grandfather: Yes dearest, we are all here.
Debra: Who am I talking with here?
Grandfather: Dearest, it is your Grandfather here!
Debra: What would you like to share with me today?
Grandfather: You are an alien!
Debra: Yes, I know I am from another star system, yes?
Grandfather: Yes dearest, and that is just the beginning.

Debra: Do share what you mean, I need to know more.

Grandfather: Your DNA is slightly different to many on your planet, that is why you've had so much trauma. Your sensitive heart has felt so much over the years. You have tried to block this with your warrior spirit.

Debra: Yes, possibly.

Grandfather: That is why we need to be healing you now, so much has been taken on from others on your planet. You need to stop doing this, it will make you unwell if you keep doing this.

Please know we're helping you, but you must also try to keep alert to what you're feeling and taking inside of your body by reacting to so much that's presented on your media, etcetera.

Be alert and aware of this coming from many places you may not even be aware of just now. We will help you keep alert. Beware of your media, which is the worst of all for your sensitive heart. You felt all this as a child.

Debra: Yes, I remember not being able to watch scary stuff or others being injured on TV.

Grandfather: Yes, that is what we are meaning. You are to keep vigilant and avoid this type of entertainment, which you often do, we know. But do keep working on this or it will affect you energetically and make you unwell.

Debra: Okay, I have taken that onboard, thank you Grandfather. Is there any further sharing or healing for me today?

Grandfather: Oh yes, we have much to share with you, and you will, as always, receive healing. That is our way to support you, dearest. We are here for you to keep going with your book writing.

Debra: Ok. I am so grateful for this experience and to have you with me. Just wondering here, are you one of the family I met when I went onto the lightship, the spacecraft twenty-one years ago?

Grandfather: Yes. That was your soul star family. We were so happy to have you with us on that day.

Debra: I was overwhelmed to be there. I kept thinking I was making it all up, but from sharing our stories afterwards I discovered everyone else I travelled with had a similar experience, so that really helped me acknowledge it as my truth.

Grandfather: You need not have doubted, your guidance is exceptional, dearest one, it has helped you so often and brought you to where you are right here and now.

Debra: Are you doing healing work with me here now? I ask because I feel tingling in my feet.

Grandfather: Yes, we work on your healing every time you connect with us. That was our contract to help you, dearest, as our family member. We will be here for you and look forward to meeting you again soon. But you must complete your books.

Debra: How many more do I have to write?

Grandfather: Four.

Debra: Ok, so what is my next book?

Grandfather: You will be sharing on how to be in a zone of meditation. It is so important people realise they need to be able to do this. You are very experienced and have many past lives of this knowledge to share.

Debra: Ok, now back to this book, is my editing going ok?

Grandfather: Yes dearest, you have found the thread. The editor will be able to help you tidy it up soon.

Debra: So, I am on the right path here with it?

Grandfather: Yes, yes dearest, you are doing so well, just a few more add-ons here and you are there.

Debra: What would you like me to add on?

Grandfather: Your story as a sensitive with us.

Debra: You mean all that we have been talking about?

Grandfather: Yes dearest, they need to know how

you were supported to do this. Many others will then want to be doing this too. You can help them learn this.

Debra: You mean I run workshops to help them, like I have done, connecting with all my ancestors?

Grandfather: We need more people doing this work. You are such a great candidate for the job—you have the experience and the stories to share on this. You know what it takes and how to do it now.

Debra: Interesting, I did wonder recently if I would be doing workshops somewhere down the track, because I have had some readers ask if I will be offering them soon. That was not my intention when I started this. I was just trying to get my message out first, before I become distracted with workshops.

Grandfather: Many hearts will need to be healed to do this, yes? And if they connect with their soul families, they will be able to heal those hearts as you have done. You see where I am going with this?

Debra: Yes, I do, an empowered way to get people healing themselves and trusting their guidance.

Grandfather: Yes dearest, you have it. Yes, they will be empowered, as you have found it to be.

Debra: I am so keen to help empower others. That has been my passion for my soulful journey workshops in past years. This will be done in a new way?

Grandfather: That is what you do, inspire, is it not?

Debra: Yes, it is! I had not considered it quite like that, but now you mention it, I can approach it that way. I am coming to that in my editing at this point. I am so glad you have come to mention this for the add-on and how I can approach it. Thank you, Grandfather, blessings and much love I send you.

Sound

22
Magical Sound with Other Species

Sound is a way to move between realms of existence, to heal us and Mother Earth. It is a universal language to commune with other species beyond all realities of existence.

Sound is one of my most magical forms of communing in nature, when I feel consciously connected to Mother Earth through my feet and expanded heart space, with deep reverence of love for all around me. My mind is in a deep state of stillness beyond the chatter, and I can open to my soul's connection as energy flows like a river through my being from the earth. I begin by using my own unique sound and feel it changing the frequency of the space all around. I become aware of a vibrational hum. My awareness becomes even more expanded to be conscious and sensitive to other realms of existence, where everything is alive with colour, sensation, and moves with me in oneness. What happens next is never predictable, and that is what makes it magical when other species come to me in this expanded state of consciousness and we can commune across realms through sound vibration, soul-to-soul. This requires me to be in a deep meditative space beyond the chatting mind of the 3D world.

Feeling in to sound in spontaneous ways as a child, I thought this was my special gift with my dog companions as I played in the yard with them. Apparently, my family did not think so, as they would promptly tell me, "Stop that noise and come inside!" They may have had good reason, if they were concerned with what the neighbours might say about the noise! I would be sitting outside chatting to my dog, then I would intuitively feel to make this almighty howling type of sound. It was a joyful call, and always called all the neighbourhood dogs to join in without delay.

To explain the type of sound, it was similar to what you hear dogs sound as a high-pitched howling when a siren passes nearby. At the time, I lived in a terrace house in an inner-city suburb, so our home was attached to the neighbours' walls. Our yards were a good size to have a small companion animal, and all our neighbours had dogs, so the noise could be quite deafening when I called and they all responded. This memory, perhaps a sign of what was to come for me in later years, came to me when I wrote this book. I had forgotten these special times.

In my adult years, the soulful force of sound presented to me as a spontaneous spiritual awakening as I sat in nature one night, admiring a beautiful full moon that made me feel I had to meditate. While meditating I felt a vibration under my feet, then it moved up through my body, a strong force that spontaneously presented out of my mouth as the sound 'AAA'. It kept coming out of my throat as my heart kept expanding. It felt like a force of nature flowing through my body, coming up from Mother Earth and into my feet, moving up into my body. I felt I had no control. It lasted for a significant amount of time without me taking a breath.

That was the first time I experienced the powerful 'AAA' sound from my body. It felt like I shifted into another realm of existence. I was totally present in that state of being. I felt fully connected mind, body and soul to all of nature around me, including the wildlife who kept presenting. "We Are All One" are the only words that come to mind, and that lived experience gave me a whole new understanding of those powerful words.

It was surreal. Wildlife kept coming out of the bush to sit beside me while I made the sound from my body. It was as if I had called them to me and they knew the sound and were responding to my call. I remember rabbits, a wombat with its young and some smaller marsupials all sitting there listening to me while this was unfolding, for quite a few minutes. Nigel had to alert me to what was taking place at first, because my eyes were closed in meditation. When I opened them, wow!

The magic of that moment expanded my heart even further, feeling like it might explode. Life changed for me with wildlife and many species after that event. I had found a new way to commune with other species and nature through sounding. Something had awoken inside me, and I felt the freedom to open and connect with everything around me, taking me into other realms of existence while being fully present in the moment. I felt oneness, bliss and joy. Did Mother Earth give me a gift of healing my heart to expand?

Travelling and living in many parts of Australia, I have had many beautiful and incredible encounters with other species that made my heart glow with warmth. I would feel so much love coming from them! They appeared to always be ready to communicate with humans if we open our hearts consciously to the universal language of love and believe all species can commune with us. Whenever my heart is expanded, feeling joyful moments in nature and being fully present in the moment, I have extraordinary encounters communing with other species open to using sound.

In January 1999, for no logical reason, only an intuitive calling, my husband and I packed up house and left the east coast of NSW to move to the west coast of Australia. We had no address or idea where we would land, it was just a strong heart calling we had to follow.

After travelling across the country for ten days, we eventually stopped at a small regional town by the ocean, where we connected with local wild dolphins who visited the town's beach and the estuary every day. We felt them calling us to stay in a small oceanside town. We had not considered staying, as we were only passing through on our way to explore the Margaret River region, further south along the coast.

After that first encounter, we travelled south to Margaret River and set up camp at a beautiful beach, but we kept feeling the call of those joyful dolphins to go back and stay in Bunbury, and we kept talking about them and thinking about them. Decision made, we headed back to that small seaside town and this became a life-changing decision.

We found a house to live in overlooking the estuary, and purchased a cheap little runabout boat to explore the waterways and meet the dolphins each day to commune with them. They would come and greet us even when they were nowhere to be seen, just turning up beside our little runabout boat. I sounded to them in my language of the heart,

AAA, and they would become quite excited, dancing in the water and circling our runabout. We were graced with the mums and younger dolphins. What a treat to see them playing and interacting with us.

It was tempting, but we never dived in to swim with them. We respected them as wild dolphins and did not need to be in their space, touching them with our human germs we carry with us. In return, we saw them whenever we were out in the estuary or on the beach. My sounding sent them into a frenzy of excitement, so I knew we were communing and interacting with them in magical ways. I could hear them sound and play as they jumped out of the water and dived back in, joyfully circling our boat. Such a beautiful memory to recall communing with them at that time in my life.

Message received from the dolphin souls.

They were calling me to stay in Bunbury because they wanted to commune with me. They remembered me from past lives and were helping me to remember my gift of communing with other species.

Another encounter with wild dolphins called us to explore the north coast region of Western Australia, so we packed our camping gear and drove north along the coast road to Kalbari. We were keen to walk in one of the national parks recommended to us by some locals for their beautiful red rock formations. On the way, we stopped for lunch on the ocean front of a small town. We found the perfect place—a park with a beautiful picnic area above red rock cliffs, overlooking the ocean about 100 feet below the coastal rocks.

Called to sit on the grassy edge of the cliff, I felt such gratitude for the life we were living and the beauty we kept finding as we travelled. As I sat in awe of the beauty of the ocean, my heart felt so expanded I had to do my AAA sounding out loud. Within a few minutes, dolphins appeared below the cliffs. They swam from the ocean towards the rocks below me, dancing around together, diving and swimming around in circles. My heart went into a crazy flutter of excitement. How stunningly delightful was this? They heard my call!

Nigel alerted me to the black sea birds circling above my head. It was one of those magical moments in time. I really did feel I was communing with nature at the highest level, from the heart space of unconditional love, and I had shifted into another dimension. My heart kept expanding, exploding with feeling as I continued the AAA sounding. I was surprised to see so many dolphins. More than thirty from several pods played together. When I eventually had to stop, they all swam off down the coast. The birds also left, flying down to the ocean looking for food, I guessed.

What a moment! I could not believe it at first. I will definitely never forget it! I took a breath and felt it all in my heart. Yes, that really did just happen! How unexpected! We were only going to eat a picnic lunch at the cliff top, then I spontaneously felt to meditate with the AAA sounding with nature. When it comes, I cannot stop it coming through my body, and I never know what will happen. I felt very blessed to have had such a strong encounter communing with two species at one time, and happy no one else was at the carpark when we were there. Life was really getting to be exciting on our adventure in Western Australia.

Interesting to note that when it ended about five tourist cars and caravans arrived to park for a lunch break. I have noticed on my travels that when I have these experiences in nature there are no other tourists around until it ends. Are we in the universal flow of life when this happens, allowing space for magic to present? Or perhaps another realm of existence? I did not know at the time, but I felt I must be in the flow of life, not in control and enjoying the spontaneity of whatever we were gifted. We then walked the national park at Kalbari with such open hearts and with tremendous gratitude for what we had just experienced.

Message received from the dolphin souls.

> They came to help me to remember my past life gift of communing with other species, and that if I can call them, they will come to me.

Our human understanding of dolphins is that they are graceful, artful, love to play and have a strong sense of family and community. Dolphins communicate through sonar, a complex system of sounds and frequencies that have taught humans (the military) about the use of sound to navigate. Research studies have confirmed their ability to help humans heal from brain damage, or if severely compromised, by recalibrating their sonar pulse. Highly intelligent, dolphins have large brains that are capable of many functions humans have not yet found, for we still do not know all they can do. Their extensive range of acute senses are multi-dimensional and have been proven. They have special gifts of understanding and consciousness for our human race. Are they a gift to our human race?

Etched into my mind is a beautiful romantic holiday on Lord Howe Island in 1998 with Nigel, when we experienced a full moon night with the whales nearby and heard them singing. We sat on the cliff, and as I sounded AAA it felt like we had shifted inter-dimensionally into another realm of existence. With the full moon shining out across the ocean in front of us, we could feel something extraordinary was happening around us.

I felt a powerful energy from the earth move up into my feet, feeling it in my body, and finally in my heart. As this powerful energy travelled through my body, I was overcome with a strong urge to sound AAA—it exploded out of my mouth. Not the first time this had happened out in nature, it had started occurring more frequently.

While I sounded AAA, eyes closed, my husband was taking it all in and noticed many black sea birds flying in a spiral above our heads, which he alerted me to when I opened my eyes. While the birds were flying above, we could both feel the ground beneath our feet vibrating, which was new for us. We heard whale sounds in the distance. We could not see them, but we could definitely hear their song calls in the ocean in front of us.

We asked was there a message for us. Yes. We were told this was Lemuria and we had shifted space and time. This was a gift to show us how we were once connected with all species and communed with them in our past lives, and to remind us of our abilities so we would remember how to do this again in service to Mother Earth.

A powerful message, we both felt it in our bodies and my soul gave me the goose bump feeling I get when I know it is my truth. After we received the message, the whales stopped calling and we continued along the clifftop trail and down the hill. Strangely, the black sea birds continued to travel above our heads in spirals, going up and down. They travelled with us all the way to the bottom and left as we moved into lights of the small town. It was like they were guiding us to where we needed to go. A magic moment to behold with gratitude, receiving messages and connecting with all our relations.

What an evening! Nigel and I were on our first holiday together after meeting and love was in the air, our hearts full and expanded. That was over twenty-three years ago, and it has continued to be magical as we commune with other species on our journeys, wherever we feel called to go. We have only ever been guided by our hearts, which at times has not made sense logically, yet we trusted.

Being called to journey to a place or destination and never knowing why, that trusting was a great decision many times, over and over. For years those explorations called us, opening us to find magic awaiting. I often say our life together has been like a magic carpet ride. After travelling so many years together, we trust, and know our hearts will guide us to where we are meant to be for some bigger purpose for our souls' growth, a new experience to open us to other realms, or meeting new friends on our path who invite us to take part in an environment project to support Mother Earth.

That has been the magic of communing from the heart, sharing the language of love by intuitively sounding AAA. I did not know that at the time, I simply felt a strong urge to use the sound. Many years later, I have learnt it is the sound of the heart connection and healing. I am really blown away when listening to my heart—it has guided me to magical experiences and helped me to remember my past lives with other species. The best part has been that when I use this universal language of love and stay present in my heart space, I feel it return to me one hundred times over from other species. These joyful experiences have felt very healing, expanding my heart to new levels of love. I cannot help wondering, what else is possible?

Message I received from the whale souls.

They were reminding me of my past life communing with other species in Lemuria, an ancient lost civilisation that existed prior to the time of Atlantis.

23

Shifting Realities at Power Sites

Egypt called me to travel with our spiritual group and a leader who channelled many of the ancient masters and beings of Egypt. We travelled with a like-minded local guide who took us to many places regular tourists would not visit. I was not expecting a journey of sounding! As we moved in and out of the temples we were singing, or I would be sounding, and we all felt transported to other realms and received channelled messages.

One of the most significant temples was the King's Chamber at the top of the Great Pyramid in Giza. We were booked to go to the top chamber at sunrise to experience the energy. What happened we did not expect! We had the first hour at dawn and were preparing to leave when the guard arrived and said we could stay another hour because the Japanese group booked after us were not coming—their fear had stopped them entering the tiny tunnels that led to the top chamber.

One empty initiation sarcophagus sat in the middle of the chamber. We had already climbed in and out, so we all sat and meditated in the space. Standing up, I was pulled like a magnet to the walls of the chamber. I started to sound AAA. It vibrated my whole body, and apparently everyone else's too. I was in a sweat with the power that flowed through me, then everyone in the group started to sound their own unique vibration.

After a few minutes, the whole room transformed into a liquid state and we could not feel our bodies—we had shifted our consciousness. It was a portal to other dimensions, we all confirmed later, after our discussions. Many were joyfully crying with the sound, and later shared they had never used sound before, nor had they felt that vibrational force in their bodies. Our sounding came to a natural energy downturn and it was our time to end the bliss.

The next group, German tourists, arrived in the chamber and asked, "Did you meet some angels up here? Your voices sounded angelic. What songs were you singing?" My group looked stunned. How interesting, for we did not sing songs. Our voices had synchronised with all our unique sounds and our bodies had experienced an inter-dimensional shift. There was a lot of talk after that event on our last day in Egypt. All had felt the strong force of the portal through those stones and the earth taking us to another realm, where we felt the strong forces of peace and calm in our hearts. We all believe we had a huge heart healing. But hey, doesn't this happen to everyone who visits Egypt, healing their past lives and connections?

This is a gift to humanity that the ancestors have left us, this legacy at sacred sites to heal our hearts and get powered up to evolve quicker and remember who we really are. That is how I experience these sites around the planet.

Yardi Creek—the Magic Power of the Land

I had a powerful experience with nature and Mother Earth while my partner and I were trekking along a dry creek bed, high cliffs all around us, in a remote location in a very dry, arid part of Australia. We stopped for a rest, and I immediately felt the energy from the rock I sat on move into my body.

Spontaneously, I sounded AAA. As my heart expanded, we both felt the bushes and rocks around us become liquid—that is the only word I can use to describe it.

I believe we tapped into another reality of the unified field of everything around us. We did not feel separate from nature. The vibration that surrounded us was subtle and made everything look sparkling with vibrant colours. Such beauty! It did not look like this in the 3D physical world. Everything was luminous in colour, even the dry creek bed.

Over the years I have had many experiences with mother nature, and writing this book reminds me of how blessed I have been to be presented with so many gifts of magical moments. I believe it happened because my husband and I have always trusted and followed our own heart's guidance, and I love to explore new areas. Australia has a very magical, powerful landscape. From many years of consciously connecting with the land, I believe it can also be the place that mirrors something you need to know about yourself, which can be very challenging, particularly a shadow, if it rises up inside of you to be seen and healed when travelling in remote areas.

Dancing Connects Our Mind, Body and Spirit to the Land

Living in Western Australia in 2001, I spotted a small advertisement in the newspaper for a weekend workshop with a sound therapist who I did not know, yet I felt intuitively called to go out of curiosity. Little did I know we would also be working with an Aboriginal elder from Uluru, Uncle B (name withheld for cultural respect), twenty years before he passed away, sadly. I had no idea of his notoriety until many years later, when I lived in the central desert and read his life story and learnt of the great work he did with such humility. He was a gentle soul with a great sense of humour, and passionate about sharing his culture with us. We played music together at the workshop, and I had no idea of his life. He never shared with us that he was a community leader, helping his people's culture be better understood through his music, books and movies.

The workshop took place on a large property, inland in Western Australia, and for one of the sessions we were taken on a walkabout with Uncle B across the paddocks where sheep once grazed. We arrived at a small crop of rocks stacked up organically, probably the size of a tennis court in area. They appeared to have been there untouched for many generations, by how they presented to us. We were asked to find a location amongst the rocks and tune into them and the surrounding landscape in meditation. Uncle B left us to sit in silence and within a few minutes an Aboriginal family of about twenty members presented

The Power of Love with Animals

to me in spirit. They appeared so sad! This was so clear in my meditation and I could feel the sad energy around the rocks.

I felt to use the AAA sound and the vision became stronger. The message I received was that they had been massacred by white settlers. This was so upsetting to feel and see with my spirit eyes. I struggled to believe this. We were not ready for it, and Uncle B had not given any indication of what was to come. We were not expecting this type of walkabout tour, to feel the ancestors of the land come to us so strongly. Uncle B shared later that the massacre did happen, and the families have been energetically imprinted into the surrounding rocks where the massacre took place 150 years prior. This is the power of what happens when suffering occurs as a being of any species leaves the earth—it is imprinted into the earth and other species. Such a sad story. We did some healing on the landscape.

Uncle B also shared with us the importance of dancing on the earth with joy, in celebration, and to be welcomed to land. In the Indigenous culture they do not learn history from the intellectual logical thinking, they embody learning. Uncle B's culture shared a powerful technique to learn their history experientially, through the body and mind with the story, the dance, and the song, and then it is practiced until it is remembered. We were not allowed to write or keep any notes, it was all taken orally, and we had to keep focused using our body's intelligence and wisdom to remember. It was a special experience to have learning in the traditional way. Uncle B taught us three different stories with dance and song, and we had to agree to share them wherever we go, far and wide, to remember to honour Mother Earth and to be welcomed to the land. The three stories, dances and songs took us three days to learn.

I kept the promise and have shared these stories with groups across the world, in other lands at shamanic celebration gatherings, and in Australia when appropriate. With respect, I have always asked Mother Earth and the spirits of the lands of other nations if it is appropriate to welcome us to land. When Nigel and I were married some years later, we performed one of the dances and sang one of the stories in the Aboriginal language at our celebration for our family and friends. They were all a little surprised, but they did enjoy our sharing as they all smiled, and I believe the sharing was received powerfully, going by their responses.

Healing with Other Species Inter-Dimensionally

One time, I participated in a day-long women's only workshop to heal the divine feminine archetypal energy grids inter-dimensionally. This was one of the most beautiful and extraordinary journeys with other species. It began in this 3D realm and took us across many dimensions of time and realities, healing abuses of this life and past lives for all women.

Our facilitator, Kali, took us on a very deep journey with our bodies, through our wombs, to connect with spirits of other species to support us. She called in all the ancestors across realms of existence and the ancient whales' spirits to come and support our journey of healing. Before starting the journey, Kali explained how we would be going into deep meditative state to work inter-dimensionally to clear many energy lines. When she called in the ancient Grandmothers, we could feel them fill the room, those wise women. Some could see them with our spirit eyes.

Kali continued to call in other souls, and we noticed one very vocal white cockatoo perched on the railing of the balcony outside, watching Kali and making eye contact. When we commented on the intensity of the cockatoo's gaze, Kali shared that White Cockatoo was her totem and would come to her when she was doing deep and powerful healing. The spirits of the cockatoo kept arriving. The front yard of the house soon filled with white cockatoos, all talking and looking in the window, some hanging off the roof and in the trees. They were not going anywhere, but stayed focused on our room. We honoured and acknowledged them for coming as our guardians to support our healing journey. They gave us a sense of feeling protected, and to open deeper into the practice. It was so reassuring and exciting to know all these souls had come to support our journey.

Next, Kali called the whale spirits. We were overwhelmed by the incredibly powerful energy that filled the room. Working in pairs, we were guided to start using sound into the location of our partner's wombs, setting up a powerful resonance across the room. Within a few minutes, the sounds of whales bellowed from the vocal cords of all the women, such powerful sounds, and songs of the ocean—all clearly audible in the 3D realm of existence. We were all surprised, as none of us had ever made those whale song sounds before, yet they were vibrating through our bodies as strong frequencies as we worked with the ancestral souls in the forms of other species.

Cockatoos represented illumination through our personal messages, while the powerful sound healing that crossed dimensions of time to meet us from the ancestral whale spirits decoded distortions in the DNA to heal genetic weakness. This was in 1995, and I had never consciously used these sounds before in this way. I could hardly believe what we were experiencing, it was so powerful, I could not help wondering if this was in this 3D reality or in another realm of existence.

When the whales' spirits left the room, we worked in circle with the ancient wise grandmothers in ceremony, also in another realm. I had to blink to check if I was in the 3D world while the ceremony of celebration took place. One of my own ancestors arrived to guide me in the healing. Was I really in another realm of existence? It felt like a reality we could touch physically, so surreal.

The healing from that day changed my life to feel empowered from the whale spirits' healing and the Ancient Wise Grandmothers who reside with the earth in another realm of existence. There are so many ways to experience other species. I felt this was important to share with you to show how supported we are by other species. They are all here waiting for us to call on them, not only in the 3D realm. So much magic awaits us when we open our minds and hearts.

Have you ever used sound to heal and commune with other species?

Sound reminds me we are multi-dimensional beings of the cosmos, with a rhythm that connects us to all realms of existence beyond our limited 3D bodysuits. It is a language of light, a higher frequency that knows no boundaries. We can connect to everything at any time when consciously sharing our own unique soul sound—our soul knows the frequency, as oneness with divine consciousness.

24

Hearing the Call

A beautiful memory I have is exploring the northern region of Western Australia (WA) in springtime, admiring all the stunning varieties of wildflowers along roadsides and in paddocks. The exquisite array of colours, shapes, sizes and varieties of flowers as far as the eye could see inspired Nigel and I to stay longer in the region. I said to him, "This feels like God's garden in heaven we're driving through."

Eventually, we arrived home from the wildflower adventure and my sister rang from the east coast of Australia to say, "I had this dream last night. I need to come over to where you are in Western Australia to find special wildflowers and a cave. I don't know how to get there. Would you and Nigel be able to help me find this place I had in my dream?"

How is that for synchronicity!

"Yes, sure, we'd love to. We have just returned from up north, checking all the wildflowers near the town you are describing. We'll meet you with our 4WD and take you there to see if we can locate it from the details you have from the dream."

Five days later we met up in a local town for an overnight stay. We woke early in the morning for a country drive to find the wildflower region Kim had pictured in her mind from the dream. She had never been to WA before and had no idea what to expect, but she did know it was important to her healing work to find a particular flower for her vibrational remedies to heal clients. Her message, *it was for the next level of ascension healing needed for humans with new energies coming to the planet in 2001.*

Up before daybreak and on the road, we found some of the flowers by the side of an isolated road that led to backtracks. I am not sure how we found them, but we had been exploring, and after feeling into our hearts we felt guided to search for them along a dry creek bed. At one of the stops, I was sitting on the side of the road, looking across at the farm paddocks but not seeing any animals. My sister was madly collecting her essences in containers of water, just as the sun was rising. Feeling very relaxed, my heart open with the expansive beauty all around me at daybreak, I closed my eyes and allowed my AAAA sound to come spontaneously up through my body, heart, and out my mouth.

Suddenly, I heard a thundering—a stampede of cattle were racing down the hill towards me! The paddock was huge, so the hill was way out in the distance from where we were and wow, we could hear them and see the dust from them charging. As they gained ground, becoming larger as they neared us, they showed no sign of slowing down. I continued sounding AAAA and they kept charging towards me, on the other side of the fence. When they hit the fence between me and them, I mean *hit* the fence with a force, they were falling over one another, ten cows deep up against the wire fence. I was forced to stop sounding to protect them from pushing the fence down.

I patted some of them over the fence and chatted to them. They appeared to settle down, watching me curiously, then began to graze around the fence before slowly making their way back to the other side of the paddock, over the hill to where they had come from. An unexpected event, I was not sure what to do with them all, so I thanked them for their friendly greeting. They were so happy for the call out to commune with me. What a moment that was, to see them all climbing over one another to get to me. My sister and her travelling companion were dumbfounded by what they had witnessed.

I was a little less surprised, as this was becoming a common occurrence for me after living in Western Australia over the past few years. Earlier that year I had experienced an encounter with sheep wanting to greet me at fences when I sounded. How blessed I felt to start a stampede of cattle to come and greet me with such friendly, joyful and excited behaviours. This was one of those exciting moments in time that you cannot quite believe, especially when there were no cows to be seen in the paddock, then out of nowhere they heard the sound and came charging over the hill to greet me. A magical moment in nature for me, communing with love and receiving love back from the cows.

Message received from the cows.

They want to commune with humans and to help us feel great love and compassion. They also have a mission to help Mother Earth and want the exploitations by humans of their species to be stopped, can I tell my people.

Nigel and I spent our honeymoon in 2005 travelling South America. Trekking for four days on the challenging Machu Picchu trail, we experienced the majestic scenery of the Andes Mountains on our way to the ruins. Arriving at the Sun Gate opening to enter the Machu Picchu ruins, along with our group of ten, our hearts wide open, I became emotional and burst into tears of joy. Walking the site and feeling the energy of the ruins was incredibly emotional, as it was one of the places I knew in my heart as a child I wanted to visit. To feel my dream manifest as a reality was overwhelming.

Exploring all levels of the ruins and buildings, I had a strong urge to sit on one of the many stone terraces up on the highest level to take in the magnificent view while no tourists were around. It was early in the morning, so our small trekking group had the site to ourselves. I sat in awe of the massive mountains surrounding us.

Looking below to the ruins I felt to meditate. As soon as I closed my eyes an awesome AAA sound came bellowing out of my mouth, vibrating my whole body as it came up from the ground where I sat. I was in bliss. Everything became lighter and brighter, like I had shifted reality. Then Nigel called, "Open your eyes and look down."

Alpacas were rushing to the wall below me, trying to get onto the next terrace where I was sitting on the wall. Wow! That was incredible! I sat and kept with the sound, then stopped and watched them. I felt I was communing with them inter-dimensionally through my heart. No words could describe the feeling in my heart and body and what had just taken place, it was sheer magic, and they responded with such enthusiasm to be with me. I believe the AAA sound was calling them. A condor was spotted circling above me as I sounded out into the mountains.

This has happened to me many times in nature with animals. It is not planned, but comes spontaneously from the earth up into my body. I do not think my throat even felt the sound. It came from my body and my heart vibrating with the sound, and felt like I had shifted realities in an altered state. When I stopped and observed the alpacas, they stood looking up at me. I had their full attention in communing with them, before they slowly walked down the mountain, returning to where they came from, turning back to check on me as they left. That was incredibly special and magical to experience.

The next day I went up to the ruins again. I did not see one alpaca, nor had I before my sounding the previous day. Only when I sounded did they appear, coming enthusiastically up from the base of the mountain. *What a blessed life I have* is all I could feel, along with tremendous gratitude to have an energetic exchange with those awesome alpacas. Continuing our tour with the group, I felt a special rapport with alpacas after that experience, glad that I had made a deep connection with another species. I felt the energy in my heart as it expanded on each meeting as we walked past them, contained behind fences on farms.

> We humans can have so many extraordinary experiences on this planet when we have an open heart and stay present, to feel with all our love and gratitude. Then the magic that is already here flows to us for an awesome encounter.

It was similar to my first unexpected encounter in Australia in 1997 with the wildlife, wombats and rabbits under the full moon, when a spontaneous AAA sounding came from Mother Earth up into my body. At that time, I also experienced an altered state of being with a blissful heart that opened and expanded in gratitude for my life and what I had been experiencing on my journeys, spontaneously communing with other species. So much magic finds us when our hearts are open and we are consciously walking on earth.

My message.

All species really want humans to commune with them. They want to be heard and seen. The alpacas shared and showed me how happy they were to feel and hear the sound of love coming from a human communing with them from the higher frequency that they knew as the language of love.

Travelling more consciously across the planet and honouring Mother Earth using sound vibration has opened me up to shift into other realms of existence, giving me a multidimensional life. This has helped me heal and expand my heart even more to commune at a deeper level with other species and Mother Earth. In my early travel years, I was not consciously aware this was available to me as a human.

25
Seven Days of Whale Play

Whilst living in Brisbane in 2004, a friend highly recommended we take part in a whale research trip with a beautiful couple, Wally and Trish, who loved whales and dedicated their lives to care for them. They lived in Byron Bay and travelled to Hervey Bay, along the east coast of Australia, for six months each year to live on a catamaran and do research on humpback whales. They knew them like their family, with great respect, and those whales knew them as family in return.

Landing in Hervey Bay, ready to go on a research adventure with the whales, we had no idea we would return 'not the same' as we had arrived. We had limited knowledge on the lives of whales until we spent seven days interacting and travelling with them in the waters of beautiful Hervey Bay, where the humpbacks from the Antarctic region migrate to each year with their young. A huge bay, it offered plenty of food for the whales and safety for the younger ones from the ocean, so it was quite busy.

Wally and Trish had been doing these research trips since the 1980s and were funded by tourists like us paying to be onboard the large catamaran to have a real-life encounter with the whales. Trish took photos of all the whales' flukes (the tails) and had them all categorised, as each had unique markings to identify them. She knew all the babies, and older ones who she had seen for many years, and they all had names. Every year she knew when a new whale had arrived. The catamaran (called Moon Dancer) held ten of us comfortably for the week. We shared the cooking and eco research work, which consisted of taking turns to go to the bridge to write our observations on interactions, and collecting DNA samples when they flapped their flukes and left skin on the surface of the water, from where we collected it in a little hand net.

Trish was on the bridge every day, taking photos and documenting what she had seen and the interactions of pods. Her real gift was when the mother whales were around with the babies. Trish always knew when to tell Wally (the captain) to move the boat on if there were intimate moments between mum and baby. She appeared to be in the same resonance with the whales, communing with them. We never looked for the whales, they would follow us and play around us, with dolphins playing and diving in-between the majestic whales. As the whales chased one another, I often wondered if the dolphins would get crushed, being much smaller, but they never did. It was an awesome sight to witness so close-up.

There was literally never a dull moment, 24/7, and it did not stop at night. We had a member onboard who played the didgeridoo in the afternoons, over the bow of the boat. The whales would all go crazy, they so loved that earthy didgeridoo sound. It was like they made sounds with the humming sound, extraordinary to witness. As the catamaran had two hulls, there was a trampoline between the two where we could sleep in swags at night to be under the stars. We also found a great location to hear songs in the four cabins below water level. As the whale songs echoed, we fell asleep in bed. However, I was very keen to see the stars too, whilst falling asleep listening to whale songs, with those wise ones of the sea all around us. The magical songs of the whales sounding would continue throughout the night. One of those goose bump moments you never forget.

Life really is magical when you have these encounters reminding you of the wonderful planet we inhabit. I did go on a few day trips to see whales in other regions of Australia, but none ever filled my heart like the one in Hervey Bay—seven nights of pure bliss hearing whale sounds around us. Wally and Trish were such beautiful hearts who really loved, respected and cared for the whales. Pioneers in humpback eco research, they were known and respected worldwide for their extraordinary knowledge which they so passionately shared with us. I believe those whales knew that, as we never had to go find them. They were around us all day and night. How healing that was to experience!

How grand life can be when we interact with another species with great respect and in a consciously aware state. They also want to commune with us. I believe if you can be patient, present to the moment, and observe with your heart expanded the trust happens and other species will do the most profound things to connect with you. We were on the boat one time and someone yelled from the bridge, "Look! Mother and calf feeding." Apparently, that was an unusual thing for a whale to do with people around. There she was, upside down in the water, fluke straight up and vertical with the calf under the water coming in horizontally to feed on her milk. I even captured it on my camera. (Calves drink thousands of litres of milk from the mother over the first couple of years of growth.) Such a magical moment to capture so close-up, and unexpectedly, in front of our catamaran.

So much went on around us living on that catamaran, as we lived in close proximity to them in the water. We never went swimming with them as Wally and Trish did not encourage that. The whales had always felt safe around the boat; swimming with them was seen as invading their personal space. I believe Trish was concerned we would change their natural behaviour if we interacted in the water with them, taking our germs and whatever else we had to share, unconsciously causing them to be harmed, as humans do when they start to interact closely with other species. Trish was keen for them to be truly wild around us, not to be concerned about us being in their personal space.

To be honest, I do not think we missed anything by being above the water with them. They were very natural and had some wild events going on with the young males playing at speed. You would not want to be in the water then, as it could have been risky. One was called Horn Blower, a young male who stirred all the other juvenile male whales. They played tag! It was awesome to watch so many big mammals playing and jumping over one another, like dolphins do, but the dolphins also took part. I was anxious at times, wondering if the little dolphins were safe jumping and weaving around those huge mammals at great speed. Just another day on the boat for us very privileged tourists with the researchers, I thought.

At night, we had slide shows and information talks on the whales. Sadly, Wally and Trish have now retired from the research trips to Hervey Bay. After many years doing the pilgrimage and gathering so much information they have a wealth of knowledge, which I believe they now share with the world in books. What a wonderful, worthwhile life—supporting the whales to be understood and saving them from heading towards extinction. The mighty elephants of the sea with such wisdom and knowledge. If you have ever eyeballed a whale you know what I mean—it is indescribable how they connect with your soul.

2019: A brief, powerful message I received from Dolphin souls.

From a metaphysical multi-dimensional aspect, it is the dolphins and whales who are caring for the energies on the earth at present. They use their sounds and sonar to balance out the earth grids and magnetic field that surround the planet.

Whales are looking after the song lines and energy grids differently to the dolphins. They work in different ways, but as a team, together. The song lines are especially important to keep balance on the planet with the magnetics, and the dolphins work the grids as the energy is held on the earth. That is why we see them constantly moving about, re-adjusting the energetic fields of the earth in the oceans.

They have important work to do in all the joy that humans observe. To lock up another species without consent is going against free will and causes more karma on this planet.

The other important reason to not be locking them up in captivity is that treating them as entertainment for humans is detrimental to the earth's energetic field's ability to be balanced, for humans and other species to live here in relatively harmonious ways.

> The balance is held by other species in ways you humans still do not know. For example, the dolphins can calibrate their sonar pulse for different purposes that only dolphins can understand.

This message resonated for me after spending time closely observing the interaction between whales and dolphins. The dolphins dived in between the whales in patterns across the water in front of us, as we witnessed with curiosity for hours. Had we been witnessing the magnetic grid work they all do for earth? I was amazed at how they team up, such large whales and the dolphins looking so small while weaving in and out of the whale pod, working together in the oceans and waterways. This made so much sense when I received the message explaining what I had seen.

I received a message in September 2020, at the time of the spring equinox when 500 whales were stranded on beaches in Tasmania. This broke my heart, so I remotely visited them in spirit and communicated with them. Following is the actual message I received from them.

> Whales and dolphins are calling humans to stand up now and be counted, to send them light to hold the energy grids for the earth, as they are working hard to keep the light strong on these energy lines as they collapse and need to be recalibrated. They need human relations to connect with them every day, sharing our light and love, metaphysically, to support them to hold the light on these important energy grid lines.
>
> It has been the dolphins and whales who have been caring for the energies on the earth for eons of time. They have worked in different ways, but as a team.

They ask all humans to please support them, it is time. Many can help them, but they feel so many humans are being distracted. They share it is very important work that is being done right now and they need their human relations to hold the light, wherever they are. It is crucial for us all to work together now—beyond species. We have moved into a new realm of consciousness—of no separation between species. It is not seen yet in the physical by humans, but if we connect to the dolphins and whales we will feel it has already happened. They suggest humans just need to tune in to the whales and dolphins at this time to feel the new consciousness that is already available to all.

I asked if whales and dolphins have any messages for the ones who will do metaphysical practices, such as meditation.

Yes, keep connecting with us every day with their beautiful light hearts, and remember us and their past lives working with all species as one, with no separation. The more humans that can do this will make so much of a difference to the other species. Even the trees work with the whales and dolphins from the land, working the grids. This is something many humans do not realise—when they chop trees they are affecting the grids of the earth. Every tree has a part to play in the grid system with the whales and dolphins. Dearest, you know this, but many do not please. Please share with your people. This is important."

We will have strength with the human species helping us. We have done this for many lifetimes, but the human species have not been conscious enough to help us. Your Indigenous people know this work well. They have been holding the dream of the new earth for many lifetimes and are fully aware of these times as the timelines are collapsing for the new earth to be configured.

All humans are here to help be of service in this time of change, but so many have heavy hearts and cannot believe this or know this. They are needing to heal their hearts, then they will remember all that is within them and that the frequency of the earth will be raised quickly with great strength.

Please remind your people this is the service they came to do—to support the earth mother and all humanity to evolve and hold the energy lines on earth, as the channels of light and love that they already are, if they can stay in love and joy. They now need to be practicing this as humans, for every species relies on every other species. This is not the time to be living in separation. We all need to be working together for the good of all, and of course Mother Earth, as the galaxy expands and the earth raises her vibration to a new frequency for all to move towards love, peace and joy for all species.

Humans need to acknowledge there is no separation from other species. We all have to work together with all species, otherwise it is going to be very difficult for us all on the planet going through these earth shifts.

Crystals and Rocks

26
Hearing Crystals and Rocks

Crystals and rocks have intelligence and wisdom, holding the records of all time on this earth. Most humans are not listening to them or asking questions of them.
I have experienced healing and learning when communicating with crystals and rocks.

The healing energy of crystals and rocks has been known for thousands of years, and now helps us with technology. Ancient cultures, including the Mayans, built sacred sites and structures such as temples, the pyramids and entire cities on grids, aligning with energy fields and power spots on the earth.

My spiritual awakening occurred in 1992. A life-changing experience, I had an epiphany state of bliss. Sensitive and connected in my heart, I became consciously aware of the unified field of source consciousness that surrounds us all. Completely unexpected, I was out in nature when I consciously felt a powerful force of connection flow through my body and heart, connecting me to feel Mother Earth and the natural world with heightened sensitivity, on another energetic frequency. I felt at one with everything in nature, and witnessed my personal vibration affecting the natural world around me as my emotional state changed.

I sat in that expanded state of consciousness, totally present in that moment of being, and it lasted many weeks. I realized I had tapped into another realm of consciousness that was familiar to me as a very young child and in my past life, but due to emotional and physical trauma, my wounded heart had shut down part of this portal of sensitivity to feel this high energetic frequency consciously.

After ten days of silent meditation retreat, I had started to heal my body. As my heart began to expand from the shadows I had released, I remembered this expanded state of feeling oneness, being sensitive to all the world around me. I felt I had once again tapped into other realms of a more subtle vibration of love that I had forgotten. This epiphany transformed my life dramatically. I began to see the world through new eyes—the curious child once again able to commune with other realms of existence, with other beings, and with many species on earth. Previously, I had enjoyed extensive travels across the planet from a physical 3D perspective, unconsciously aware of the other realms that could be available to me if I became a more aware and conscious human being. And so, the magic began!

I had always communed with crystals and rocks at various levels, but after my epiphany, communing became a whole new level of vibrational conscious communication. My soul companions remind me I have had many other lifetimes communing with crystals, rocks and sounding. I hope to inspire you to remember your past life connections to crystals and rocks.

What I find most upsetting now is how many humans have forgotten how to commune and are not respecting Mother Earth or other species, for it is so important to help heal Mother Earth and humans. We need to start respecting all species who inhabit the earth with us.

Crystals, rocks and other species have a wisdom and intelligence that needs to be considered. We take them from their locations to use as toys and decorations, but they all have a mission to help this planet. I have been reminded of this from all the gifts they have given me to help me remember my past lives working with the rock and crystal families. Many humans have forgotten these connections from past lives.

We need to listen to them, commune with them and ask what they would like, for they have their own wisdom and intelligence that needs to be respected by humans. I see they are so disrespected by so many humans and not used with sacredness or honour. They are being used for decorations and toys to play with and adorn our houses. Asking respectfully points towards a healed heart, healed enough to hear the whispers of the voiceless.

I believe it is my calling to inspire others to remember their connections with the earth and the voiceless species. Crystals can heal humans if they are treated with respect by asking for their wisdom. So much confusion, anger and pain around our planet from what humans are unconsciously doing to other species, and to ourselves. We humans are all creating more karma and pain from unconscious actions of disrespect.

Do you ask crystals if they want to come with you before you pick them up and take them away?

Crystals Calling for Help

This is still a vivid memory for me, and very emotional, as I felt the pain and suffering of these crystal rocks. Visiting my sister interstate for Christmas in 2000, she was excited to take me to a huge warehouse in Sydney to see some great specimens of crystal caves and smaller crystals.

Walking into the warehouse, I was overwhelmed and taken aback by the sounds of many crystal caves calling out to me to help them. What was happening? All I could hear was, "Can you help us? We miss our families. We were taken away and are so sad now, missing our families a long way away."

It was deafening! I could hardly think, so rushed outside, tears running down my face. My heart was so heavy and sad for those beautiful souls. They were some of the biggest crystal caves I had ever seen. The huge warehouse had shelving all the way up to the tall ceiling, all filled with large crystal caves. I suspect people were buying them for their homes, or as ornaments to be left somewhere, without much thought on how they had been taken from Mother Earth or what they needed.

My sister came out to see what was happening. I shared that all the crystal caves were talking and calling out to me to take them back home. They were so sad because they had been dug up harshly and ripped from the soil to be transported to many parts of the world. Taken from their families, they felt alone. They so wanted to be with their families!

While I felt their pain in my heart strongly, with such sadness it was palpable for me, everyone else was buying those crystals without any thought to what the crystals felt or had experienced. Every time I tried to go back into the shop, I heard them all calling out to me. It was terrible. I could not stay. What could I do for them? They were not mine, and they had hefty price tags on them.

I left that shop with an extremely heavy heart, and the realisation they are being disrespectfully taken from the ground and their families. I had started out very happy to go to the shop, but it was a sad day for me. From that moment, I understood it was not respectful to take them without asking first if they are to come.

This is another example of the disrespect humans have for other species, and how our ignorance and separation from them causes great pain and suffering. Our separation comes from hearts that are not healed or sensitive enough to feel the connection to everything around us. Something the Indigenous peoples understand well is to respect all species who share the earth with them. If they eat a species they use respectful practices, with ceremony before and after hunting their prey, and a sacred ritual blessing to allow the spirit of the animal to be freed before they process them for consumption.

Western culture needs to practice respect for all species and not assume we can take what we like without asking permission or doing a ritual to commune and release the soul. For example, when cutting trees we can connect with them first and let them know they will be removed soon. That way it prepares all species to leave the tree and the tree spirit to free itself from the earthly plane by moving into another realm, instead of our heavy-handed approach of taking them down and leaving their spirit confused and locked into the earthly plane. As for a human who dies unexpectedly, maybe murdered, their spirit becomes confused when they leave their physical human body unexpectedly, thus they can become stuck between realities, such as the astral plane on the earth. This is where psychics see spirits who are lost.

Is your heart healed enough to hear the whispers from other species?

A Journey Guided by a Crystal

A beautiful memory is the day I met a large crystal rock, owned by a psychic friend. I was admiring it when she said, "I feel this crystal wants to be with you for a while." I agreed, and borrowed the crystal. I placed it in my bedroom and it talked to me all night! I could not sleep, so moved it away from my head to the other side of the room. Nigel and I had planned a big walking trek to the Blue Mountains National Park the next day with an early morning start, so I needed my sleep.

As we were packing our backpacks the next morning, the crystal called out to me.

"Take me! Take me! I want to go with you!" I packed it into my bag. A large, heavy star mica and quartz crystal, maybe two kilograms in weight, it made my load much heavier. But it wanted to go, so I took it with me.

We drove a couple of hours before arriving at a remote area of the national park, somewhere near where the ancient Wollemi Pines were found many years ago. I do not know exactly where, as it was kept secret to keep them alive, but from the documentary I saw it looked like the remote area where we liked to walk alone. We rarely met other walkers on those trips. It was stunning scenery with steep rock walls, and mountains and valleys below. Funny how I always had this feeling around Peru at that location, even before I visited Peru.

On arriving, I heard the crystal talking to me in spirit, giving me guidance at the beginning of the track we already knew. Listening further, it guided us to another track, down to the valley opposite to where we were planning to walk along the ridge. I trusted in my heart it would take us to a great location, so off we tramped down some steep tracks to the base of the valley, passing beautiful waterfalls and running creeks. We had never been to this location before and it was gloriously beautiful. I hoped we would find our way back.

The crystal kept us on track. We passed a few landmarks, then we were following the creek until I heard directions to take the crystal out of my backpack and place it in the water. I placed it exactly where I was instructed in the shallow running rapids. Nigel and I sat on the ground beside the water's edge, watching the crystal. It was incredible! The crystal started releasing sparkles—like stars from the water. So strange to try and explain. I guess you could compare it to the little light sparks released from sparkler sticks you burn at birthday parties.

We had no idea what was taking place, but we were given a magical show. I did not know how long to leave it in the water, so I waited and allowed the crystal to commune with me. We sat and watched for quite a while before the crystal guided me to remove it from the creek water and I placed it gently on the ground to dry off in the sun.

The crystal was so glistening and happy! I could hear the joy and gratitude for the light it received—loudly—and I heard it thanking me for what we had respectfully done. We headed home and I knew my time with the crystal was over, so when we met up with our friend the following week, I handed it back to her.

My friend felt her crystal light being and said, "Wow, what did you do to this crystal?"

"We took it on a bushwalk and it guided us to exactly where it needed to go," I shared. My friend could really feel the change in the crystal.

She shared that it had, "...so much more clarity and looked like an amazing jewel, it glistened so much." I always knew that crystal was not for me to keep, it simply had a job to do with me. We had a resonance with one another, so I could hear its guidance and what it needed. I felt we were rewarded with the beautiful show in the water, and we had been shown another beautiful location in the national park that we may never otherwise have found. It was such a magical experience to commune with that crystal being.

Nigel also felt how powerful it was to be taken on a journey with another species. We trusted, and were rewarded by a beautiful journey and learning. That was a new experience for me, a kindred spirit in crystal form that I resonated with so deeply I could hear its voice to know what it needed. We connect with other species in relation to our own personal frequency or resonance we vibrate. I have not communed with all crystals in this same way. This was one of my early experiences of communing with a crystal and finding a journey of joy and magic awaiting me. I learnt that when we deeply listen without judgment, staying open-minded, spontaneous and alert to what unfolds in the moment of being present, many gifts can be offered to us. That treasured journey is held in my memory as a strong emotional experience and adventure communing with another species.

Communing with and listening to other species has given my life more depth of meaning, providing many magical experiences we would have missed without the interaction. Every species has a spirit for us to connect with. It is up to us to heal our hearts and open our minds to see, feel and listen so we may find the hidden gems that other species want to share with us. Mostly, we humans are too busy in our heads to hear anything but our own thoughts rushing past, and get easily distracted by what we need to do in the future.

Soulful moments will be revealed when we stay present moment to moment.

Crystals and the Desert Rains

We were living in the central desert of Australia, where the big rains had not touched the earth for twenty years. The Aboriginal people were so excited to know the rains would come—all because a lone pelican had shown up on the road in the community. It was a sign to them. In two weeks, we had so much rain we were flooded. The community was surrounded by water, for the town had been built on a sandhill mound. We were on a dry island but surrounded by water, so we could not leave the town.

We were isolated for a few days before the rain was absorbed back into the sandy soil. When the water receded, we had to make a visit to head office. Living 500 kilometres west of Uluru, it was a big day's journey through the central desert of Australia on the clay roads into Alice Springs as the roads were drying out. We had taken that journey many times and thought we knew the road very well. That day, driving past one of the remote towns, we saw a white-looking shiny material just off the road. Curious, we parked on the side of the track and walked over to the area. It was covered in smoky quartz crystals! Wow! We had never seen that before on our regular drives—where did it come from? We suspected it was unveiled by the flooding.

Walking closer, I heard voices.

"Take me!" the voices called.

I found their calls overwhelming, so had to stop and clear my head. Those awesome crystals were a white glow, very strange for a desert scene. They looked like snow or hail from the road, catching our attention and calling us to explore. I could not believe so many of the crystal rocks were asking me to take them. It was a strange thing to hear. In the past, I would have arrived and asked if any of the rocks wanted to come with me. On this occasion they were all asking, "Can we go with you?"

I intuitively selected a couple of pieces of smoky quartz, even though I was not looking to take any with me. Before arriving at my desert home location, I had received a communication message from Charles to take double terminator crystals with me to bury in the desert. I had done so, all buried before I found the smoky quartz crystals, so believed my mission was complete. I don't know why, but I just trusted the guidance of the crystals. Later, my light being family shared with me that this mission was to support their lightship activities in healing the earth mother.

When I departed my desert home, the smoky quartz crystals went with me on my next journey, to be included in ceremony practices. There is still one quartz with me as I have not been guided intuitively to leave it anywhere. Maybe it is meant to be with me for a while longer. Since leaving my desert home, I have been guided to bury double terminator crystals in a grid around each home I have lived in. When departing each home, they are left buried. I have not been guided to take them with me.

This is just one of many experiences I have had with crystals being heard. When the voice is heard and received through the higher heart frequency, I hear their whispers. So many crystals have come into my life, then leave as and when they guide me to release them. Many I have left in locations across Australia, and in other countries across the world when I have travelled, as guided by them, and asking them what they would like me to do.

This may be quite right brain for some, but it is my truth and shows the many realms of existence interspecies communication can tap into, such as light beings from other dimensions—my galactic soul star family.

Have you communed with crystals and found them supporting your life journey?

My early experiences with crystals and rocks were in meditation. I have found them helpful in magnifying my communications with other beings across other realms of existence, to receive messages for myself with greater clarity. In particular, I feel strong connections with clear quartz, rose quartz and amethyst crystals. Crystals can also support human healing. When I experience body discomfort or pain, I use them on my body to heal (after I program them). One time, I was regularly waking up in the mornings with a stiff back and could not even move out of bed to organize a massage with a therapist. I started receiving messages and guidance to use my quartz crystals along my spine, so I did. Lying on my back in bed for half an hour was enough for me to shift the energetic discomfort, then sit up and walk around. I felt healed, no other treatment required. I remember to have gratitude and thank another species for whatever I receive.

Being a sensitive, I believe my energetic field needed to be re-aligned slightly. I feel out of balance often when energies are affecting the planet, such as strong weather patterns or solar flares hitting the earth.

I always ask crystals before taking them. They are not all on earth for human healing, some have a mission to hold the energies for the earth and have supporting families around them to do this. Use your intuition and higher heart intelligence to connect and go beyond the mind. Using meditation to start, this will help you get into that space of bypassing the mind. Feel the crystals intuitively before you work with them. Ask *is this crystal in resonance with my own vibration?* If not, the crystal's assistance in healing may not be possible.

2019: My channelled communication message from the Crystal Oversoul (Devas) sharing their wisdom.

Debra: Would you like to share your wisdom for my book?

Crystal oversoul: Yes dearest, we would like to be heard too. We are the wise ones. We hold the records of all time and we are being exploited and treated very poorly.

We have many answers to many questions about the earth.

We hold the energies to heal the earth, but humankind do not honour our place and keep moving us from one location to another. This disrupts the energy field of the planet.

We all have a mission and purpose to be doing this work, just as you humans have on this earth. Could you please tell the humans to please ask us before they take crystals from one place to another? It's a big problem. Some are exceptionally large crystals that are being taken and sold for gold. This is so disrespectful, like selling humans in a slave trade. These humans need to know they are being disrespectful.

We have a consciousness that has to be honoured, as the trees and stones and animals do. We all come to earth to be part of the big plan to heal and assist the evolution of all species and humans. We can heal you humans if you would just ask us. We can tell you which crystals will heal and which ones need to be left for the energetic grid of the planet, it's imperative for this to happen. It is getting exceedingly difficult to heal the earth and humans when they keep disrespectfully moving us without asking us what we are meant to be doing for the earth.

We all have different missions here on earth. Many are not for healing humans, and many are. You need to ask us, and we will be more than happy to help you know. We would love to be healing humans when that is our mission. For others, they would prefer not to be healing humans, but to be holding the energy for the planetary balance that is so needed right now as Mother Earth is going through this birthing phase. We are all needed.

Tell the people to heal their hearts. We can help them, and then they will hear our voices just as you do, dearest. You can hear us. It is time for so many to know this. It is time for respect on all levels and realms of this earth.

Many will be surprised to read this, but this is the real story that many do not know. And we are so happy you are now sharing it for us, the voiceless. Please share your experiences, as you have had so many and you know the magic that happens when you commune with us in other realms with respect. It is quite a magical journey we can take you on. And we can help with the

The Power of Love with Animals

humans' questions. Yes, we have much knowledge from times before you arrived on this planet.

Your conscious state needs to be expanded to hear us, the voiceless. It is time to be with us and listen to us, it is so time for this to be. It is all part of the healing plan on planet earth to respect other species. We know that you have been very disrespectful to your own race, and we ask that you heal those hearts from all the abuse that has occurred on this planet. We can help you do that if you ask us when you meet us. If it is our mission to be with you, we will help you.

Please know that we all have a unique resonance and not every crystal or stone will resonate with all of you. As with humans, some will be comfortable towards you and others will feel a little less comfortable and less healing for you. Please know that this is the case with us crystals. We have certain resonances and vibration frequencies that allow us to work with you. As you resonate with different frequencies, so do we, as crystals. Like a radio station, we find the station that we can hear and use that station. Then we find we need to move to another station as we evolve, needing new information to be shared, and we find a new resonance to share with another, as some healers who are humans will have a resonance for some and not for others.

If you follow your heart calling this will become clear to you, dear humans. Your heart knows so much more than you give it credit for. Many hearts are overshadowed by pain and suffering. Keep healing those hearts to know what is your guidance, as this soul here has been doing, and you'll also be able to hear us as you heal that heart and forgive all who have hurt you.

It is unconscious acts and thinking that cause pain onto others. Become more conscious with your thoughts and actions, which will happen automatically when you heal your heart. You will not need to do anything. You'll feel the strong urge of what calls you, as you have done, following your heart guidance, and now your heart is being healed to hear us again, as you have done for many lifetimes.

This is our message: Please reconsider your actions towards us. We are not toys or decorations. We need to be programmed and honoured, and asked if we have anything to share with you. This soul has many examples of how to listen to us and the stones. She has been doing this and shares these experiences with you. We hope you can be inspired to also follow these paths of respect and listening.

We need to heal so much abuse on this planet, and humans can make a huge difference, instead of making more pain and suffering. You can change the vibration just by being respectful and considering all species have a purpose, and there are many more realities to the earth than many know.

The physical 3D world is quite limiting for a human. When you begin to access other realms of existence you may find it quite magical and exciting to be playing with us, as this soul has done in the past. She shares her experiences to give you a taste of what can be possible, to give you a much deeper experience of life when communing with many realms of existence.

27
Meeting Ancestral Land Spirits

In 1997, someone left a youth hostel magazine on my front porch with an article on a safari adventure in the Northern Territory. I never found out who left it there, but I was excited to adventure into central Arnhem Land and stay on a safari camp on Aboriginal reserved land with an Aboriginal tracker to explore sacred ceremony sites and learn about the culture, food and initiations. This became a memorable adventure in nature with Aboriginal people, an ancient culture on their land, sleeping under the stars and learning Dreamtime stories.

One night we slept in a dry gorge with one-hundred-foot-high walls all around us where the summer wet season rains rush through. It was the end of the dry season, so mother nature was not ready to flush the gorge yet. The humidity and heat were intense as we explored the region with the Aboriginal tracker. A group of eight, we travelled across the land walking through waterways with freshwater crocodiles, which we did not know about until the night the tracker shone his torch over the waterway we had walked through that afternoon. There in front of us were many red eyes of the freshwater crocodiles looking up at us as we sat in our swags in the dry gorge bed. The tracker laughed and we were shocked, because we had been swimming with those crocodiles all day!

When we got over the shock and settled into our swags under the stars, lots of insects sang along with the rhythm of the tracker's voice as he shared stories of the Dreamtime, of the ancestors of the land, and rocks in the region. I heard whispers above us. Looking up, I was surprised to find dark figures, tall and skinny with their long legs dangling over the cliffs of the gorge walls. I checked in with Nigel, "Can you see and hear what I see above us?" "Yes," he responded. We also shared how we both had heard the whispers all day while trekking through the bush and had thought they were insect sounds. They were the ancestors of the land communing with us all. Magic! The land was showing us how alive it was with life of all forms and on many realms of existence.

Our journey continued day by day, painting ourselves with ochre, learning how to forage for bushfoods for lunch, and meeting the local wildlife (buffalo). This was the build-up season of storms before the wet season arrived. With no rain and high humidity, temperatures around some of the rock locations were as high as fifty degrees Celsius, so hot we could feel it through the soles of our walking boots.

Our tracker walked barefoot over the boulders and rocks without reacting to the heat. I travelled closely behind him and noticed he was not moving the loose rocks when he stepped on them, not like me rolling around them. He travelled so lightly on the earth he did not touch the ground, rather, he appeared to glide gracefully over each rock. I felt uplifted by his big energy, astounding to feel and experience. This became an insight for me on how this ancient Aboriginal culture is so connected to the land. They do not have the separation from the land as Westerners experience. They do not feel different to landscape—it is part of them.

I was really getting a sense of how alive the land is in the Northern Territory of Australia. I felt it was different and magical, but I could not really explain how. I do know it was alive in response to the Aboriginal people respectfully using ceremony to honour ancestors, elements and the land by communing with all species, and Mother Earth was responding in her vibrance and magic.

I could not ignore that the Northern Territory land spoke and communed with my soul. Arriving home to the east coast, I could feel the difference of a land missing, less vivid, lacking spiritual activity. It felt 'not alive' compared to the aliveness I had experienced with the ancestral spirits and other species in Arnhem Land. My intuition was telling me the difference was respectful ceremonies to honour Mother Earth are not practiced in the Western culture, who mostly occupy the coastal strips of Australia. I questioned, was

Mother Earth depleted of energy without honouring practices to energize her through ceremony, song and dance? Is Mother Earth's body depleted of energy, unable to give back the magic and aliveness to these coastal regions missing respectful practices?

I was learning that Mother Earth and nature can mirror messages to our soul for us to learn and commune in magical ways with the natural world around us. This insight became clear to me as we travelled across the land on this adventure in Australia.

Arriving at Uluru for the first time, we felt the intense power of the monolith as we drove up to it, so much that Nigel became dizzy and cloudy headed. We decided to stop to walk around the base trail. We never intended to climb it because we knew how sacred it was to the Aboriginal people, it would be disrespectful, like climbing over a Western Christian cathedral. Not acceptable. The circuit around the base was a nine-kilometre walk, and it was beautiful. We took in all the rock formations and the many sacred areas that still receive honouring ceremony when the tourists are gone. I do know that happens after living out in the desert.

Meditation Message received on my first visit to Uluru.

> Your people, white man, will never understand the Aboriginal culture, because they are from the earth and you are from the stars. Your people must be in acceptance of the differences and learn from this.

Every day we communed with the land and received magical interactions and messages about the ancient, powerful land we inhabit. I felt blessed that the Indigenous people are the caretakers and practice ceremony to honour ancestors, elements and Mother Earth for all species to benefit from the power of land that's respected. I hope many others feel the difference when visiting, that it is alive. I remember meeting German tourists at Uluru and asked them why they only visited that region. Their response was, "We don't know, we felt called to just come, and we did." They were driving back to Darwin to return to Europe after a few days at Uluru.

My own mother shared that when she visited with a friend, she could not believe how powerful it was. She said it changed her in some way, but could not explain how. The local tourist office told us that when tourists visit and take rocks, many times the rocks are later returned to Uluru by mail. The pulsating power of that big rock Uluru?

I believe there are many secrets around Uluru that the Aboriginal people have not shared yet with us Westerners, and maybe they never will. Who could blame them, with how we have treated them and their culture historically, disrespecting them as the custodians of the earth? I have been told many stories about Uluru having tunnels and crystal caves, with galactic activity, but we may never be told. However, we can have our own experiences to confirm.

The magic and power of the land in the Northern Territory was shared with me by a friend who failed to fall pregnant for many years on the IVF program. Fed up, she ditched IVF and went on a solo adventure to the Northern Territory, with her tent but without her husband. She stayed in the national parks, connecting to mother nature and camping alone and communing with the land over two weeks. She fell pregnant within one month of returning home.

I do not believe that is an isolated story, as I have heard many stories of communing with the powerful land in the Northern Territory. I believe that is what is possible when Mother Earth is respected as the divine feminine and celebrated with ceremony; she keeps giving to nourish the soul of all beings on this planet. We owe so much gratitude to the original custodians, the Aboriginal people of this region, for continuing their sacred ceremonies for thousands of years. The oldest continued race on the planet, their culture holds great wisdom.

Do you think this ancient Aboriginal culture deserves respect, to be heard and acknowledged for their great wisdom of living and honouring the earth mother?

28

Rock Families

Rock families, the cousins to crystals, are often not seen to be as glamorous as crystals by humans.

The Karlu Karlu rocks (aka Devil's Marbles) are a stunning example of the spirits who live within rocks. Nigel and I were travelling along the main highway from Darwin to Alice Springs when we spotted beautiful big red boulders stacked up on top of one another off the side of the road. I was curious to see what they were. It was also a tourist viewing area, so in we drove.

Approaching the boulders, they felt eerie, like an uneasy spiritual presence was around them. Getting out of the car to look closer, we felt like someone was watching us. You know that feeling—when you feel an energy around you, but you cannot see anything? You have a *knowing* in your gut. An intuitive feeling told us *it is important to feel our way around this location.* These were exceptionally large boulders, each the size of a garden shed, stacked precariously on top of one another over about three levels.

I observed a couple of gaps that did not look natural, where rocks may have been in the past. It was dusk, so we pulled over to the carpark to stay the night. On the other side of the carpark was a van, and a caravan towed by a 4WD. The harsh desert terrain, mostly rocky ground surrounded by dry spinifex grass, was not an exciting place for our little tent to be pitched. As we set up a campfire to keep warm and cook some food, we noticed how beautiful the night sky was and felt we could almost touch the stars, they felt so close and bright!

Sitting in our camp chairs, we suddenly heard the noise of a pup. It was not a full moon, so looking into the darkness we could not really see anything... then out of the darkness walked a mother dingo, her four pups trailing behind her. They walked between us and the campfire, which we thought strange as they never come that close to humans. The dingo mother did not even acknowledge us. It was like we weren't even in her radar. The pups, scurrying to keep up with Mum, did not see us either. That was a beautiful encounter!

In the sky above us we noticed strange lights moving in right angles across the sky and into the distance. In the outback, away from the light pollution from streetlights and cities, the sky is very bright with lights. We watched for a while before going to our tent to rest up, ready for the early start we had planned for the morning. After being in our sleeping bags ten minutes the wind began to blow, circling outside the tent. I guess you might think of it as a willy willy wind, spinning and throwing debris up from the ground and all around.

Our tent shook violently. This wind was fixed on our tent—was that even possible? A strange feeling, it gave us goosebumps. After some time, we both agreed we were not going to get any sleep with the tent shaking and vibrating, and intuitively did not feel safe. Time to get out and sleep in the car. The wind followed us to the car and shook the car! That was spooky! We tried to ignore it and get some sleep, huddled in the car seats. Eventually it left and moved around the carpark, picking up debris and throwing it around. We did finally fall asleep.

We woke in the morning to a beautiful, clear blue sunny day. We waved to the couple across the carpark, who had camped in the caravan overnight, then noticed the woman from the campervan step out of the caravan. There were three of them in the caravan overnight? All looked very tired and upset. We started up a conversation, asking if they felt the wind last night.

"It was so scary and eerie, I had to ask the caravan owners if I could stay in their van for the night. I was so shaken up by the wind and scary feelings. I've travelled alone for some time, and I've never felt so scared as last night," the campervan woman shared with us.

The caravan couple also said they were very shaken and upset, scared by the rocking of the van with all the wind and the intensity it held. We all noticed it had spiralled around the van and cars in the carpark for several hours before disappearing out of range at daybreak.

Those campers could not wait to leave! All had made a new friend, but there was no excitement in that as it was under such scary conditions. We packed up and drove off down the road too, wondering what that night was all about and unable to make much sense of the event. We had no doubt something was happening on another realm of existence—those winds felt so eerie and that site had strange, supernatural activity.

Moving the clock forward five years, we were living in the Northern Territory and happened to see a documentary of a ceremony to return some rock boulders that had been taken from an Aboriginal sacred site and used for a memorial site early last century. An Indigenous woman was crying with joy and relief that her sacred site was being restored to its former glory with the return of the big boulders to their original location.

Where was that? The Devil's Marbles... oh no! That was where we'd camped that night with all that disturbing activity and the strange meeting with dingoes. The woman shared that the spirits of the rocks were very upset, unhappy they had been taken disrespectfully and they had to be returned and kept there. By this time, the carpark had closed and there were absolutely no overnight stops allowed at the site any longer. Well, that explained it! We had stayed at a site with angry rock spirits and they were trying to tell us or move us on. It worked—we never went back! I wonder if anyone else had strange experiences as we did?

Background.

The name Karlu Karlu, given by the Aboriginal people of that region, translates to round boulders. The Karlu Karlu are culturally and spiritually significant to the land's traditional Aboriginal owners, both men and women. The name Devil's Marbles was given by white explorers in 1870. I wonder why?

Have you ever heard a rock or stone calling you?

Travelling in a remote region in North Western Australia, Nigel and I were driving away from Karajini national park when I heard a call from the side of the road from a group of very red rocks, to an area off the main road. My heart was excited to go and investigate why the rocks called me. Happy to stop, even though he did not know why I wanted to go onto a dirt track to stop in front of a large collection of rocks, Nigel made a cup of tea while I communed with the rock family consciously, through my heart.

They were all so beautiful, many shapes and sizes, and spread across an area the size of a house, positioned on top of one another to a height of about twenty feet. To some people they may have looked inviting to climb all over, but I did not feel I needed to do that and knew it was disrespectful if not asked. Instead, I enjoyed their company and the interaction with them. It was basically a very dry and arid landscape surrounding them, very little green around and no trees, just a few shrubs spread sparsely around the area, so they stood out. What a treat to be heard in such an isolated region, and the rocks happy and wanting to talk with me about their life.

"Was there anything wrong?" I asked. No, they wanted to talk with me and tell me about the rock families, how they were a family, because many people do not know they exist and do not hear them as I do. They were so happy I heard them calling me and stopped.

Were you aware that crystals and rocks come with a family around them for support?

Did you know rocks and stones store our memories and thoughts energetically?

Twenty-five years ago, I was gifted a beautiful hand-painted rock from a dear artist friend who was very respectful and tuned in to the spirits of the earth and other species to design his works. This particular rock had been decorated with Indigenous artwork, which he did mostly. I treasured this rock not only for its artistic and natural beauty, but it had another quality—I felt its power and strength.

Some years later, Nigel and I were married, and we asked our guests not to buy wedding gifts for the ceremony. We did an honouring ritual with the elements and the earth and requested gifts to be created from the heart as a song, poem, story or dance. Everyone was happy to accommodate our wishes and we were fabulously entertained for a couple of hours. After the sharing, I invited our friends and family to gift us again by placing their blessings for our future energetically into the beautiful painted rock I had been gifted and had been using on my travels for earth ceremonies. Many commented on the power they felt when holding it. Everyone was excited to take part with this part of the ritual and the rock was shared around a large circle for quite some time. I thought the guests were very generous with their blessings.

Seventeen years later, I was invited by another artist friend, a photographer doing a community project, to bring a treasured object to be photographed as I held it in my hands. I chose a beautiful crystal cluster family which was happy to go with me, and I also took my painted rock with all the blessings. When the photographer took the pictures, she commented on the light beam that was captured coming out of the rock. It had over-shadowed my crystal cluster family. Eventually, I was able to view the photo ready for the exhibition and I could not believe the white light that came out in the photo! It clearly had a powerful light with all the sacred activities it had been lovingly chosen for, and emphasized to me the importance of respect and sacred honouring of other species and how they store energetic memories.

My gifted rock is still with me today, and is certainly up for the task of whatever it has been involved in. It is one powerful rock, shining light out to all who have had the opportunity to meet its spirit. Gifted to me with love and respect, it continues to keep giving gifts, as I treasure its spirit. I share this to show how rocks can hold energetic memories, and if the earth is not receiving positive thoughts from humans, how does that affect the stored memories of rocks? They are the record keepers of the earth from eons of time, which is why we need to be more conscious of our actions. If we want to have a peaceful planet, we need to send out respectful actions towards other species for positive energetic frequencies to be stored with the record keepers (rocks) of Mother Earth.

Have you ever considered a rock as a gift that keeps giving?

Do you honour and respect the rocks you collect for sacred purposes?

≈

Did you know some rocks have families, souls, and missions to do on earth just as we do?

They choose to come into this reality as a stone with a soul. That is why we need to ask before we take any stone, rock or crystal. They also hold old souls, which can be stuck inside of rocks. I learnt this when I was in Central America on a spiritual pilgrimage to Tikal. The rocks standing alone at that sacred site had many stories to share about past humans and activities at those sites. Some held old souls locked inside who wanted to be released.

In Honduras, at a site called Copal, the lone standing stones had many messages to share on the earth's history and human souls who had come and gone. Some of the stones held a few old souls inside. I found this fascinating, as no one ever talks about or shares the wonderful history they hold energetically. Unless you are consciously communing with your heart open and can bypass the mind of chatter to hear this information, you will not receive it. So much magic opens to us when we can be more open of heart and listen with our spirit ears and see with our spirit eyes. This is what I have witnessed whenever I visit sacred sites. Not only sacred sites though—it can be a group of rocks on the side of the road. If you are consciously awake, you will hear them.

≈

Are you aware that rocks live in many realms of existence, as do many species on earth?

On one of many visits to Uluru, I was walking around the base of the rock, admiring and feeling the energy of what the Indigenous groups do in ceremony. I sat to meditate and felt a strong urge to look up to the top of the rock, probably about 200 foot up, and my spirit eyes could see as plain as day, tall blue light beings, my soul star family, looking down upon me, letting me know they were there with me.

No, I was not on drugs, and I'd had a good night's sleep and had not been drinking. I swear they were above, looking down on me. I felt like I knew them very well when I went into my heart. I was not concerned, but they did seem familiar to me, similar to the beings I'd met on the spacecraft a couple years earlier. (And yes, many years later, it was confirmed these beings were my galactic soul star family making themselves known to me again.) They shared a message that white humans come from the stars, and the First Nation people come from the earth, and we may never be able to fully understand them, but we can all accept and learn from one another. I had been visiting this site for several months as I passed it on my way to Alice Springs to the head office of the Aboriginal community I worked for at the time. So many things had happened to me on those visits, so I was not surprised to find light being aliens were also part of the region. I had also been told about secret caves in the area, and that they may be part of that system.

It was quite an experience, and assured me that we have opportunities to connect with many other beings in other realms, like alien races, if we are open to see them with our spiritual eyes or to tune in energetically in high frequencies. Other realms do exist in sacred places where the energetic fields are stronger, where gateways and thin veils exist between other realms for us to access, as I did that day.

Uluru is more than just a rock—it is a living landscape, considered sacred to the Yankunytjatjara and Pitjantjatjara people.

The spirits of the ancestral beings continue to reside in these sacred places, making the land a deeply important part of Aboriginal cultural identity.

One of the earth's great natural wonders, encountering Uluru for the first time is breathtaking. The Aboriginal name for Uluru means Great Pebble rock (the first white settlers named it Ayers Rock before handing over ownership many years ago). Kata Tjuta means 'place of many heads', a men's place energetically.

Handing the land back to the Aboriginal people has allowed regular ceremonies to honour Mother Earth, and she responds.

You can feel this when you visit, it's an incredibly magical place.

I remember the first time I visited Kata Tjuta, Northern Territory (Uluru-KataTjuta National Park). When I got out of the 4WD vehicle to go for a walk to explore the area I could feel something different, like I was in Egypt walking in the valley of the Kings. The strange part was I had never been to Egypt, yet I was receiving messages about the landscape and connections about another location across the world in North Africa. Where did that come from? The rocks? Had they stored the energetic memory? Or was it a strong energetic ley line which connected Africa with Australia? I found Kata Tjuta quite a different energy to Uluru. When you see it from the air, as I did many times flying to my desert home, it looks like a huge lizard rising from the desert.

Walking at Kata Tjuta, I felt so many ancestors watching me. One trail was called Valley of the Winds, and that's where I felt most strongly the ancestors were around us. I believe the rocks hold the imprints of the ancestors within them, as the souls were very real and alive in that area. I did eventually go to Egypt some years later, and felt the connection to that Kata Tjuta experience. In fact, we stayed on the Nile, on the opposite side to the Valley of the Kings. On the first night, my partner and I could feel ancestors calling us over to the area to come to see the tombs, etc. Egypt is an extraordinarily strong place of ancestral souls and rocks with history to share. At some of the temples I felt strongly called to sound inside when there were no other visitors.

The guards welcomed us to do so. One even took us to a place behind the temple wall to show us another cavern that had hieroglyphs inscribed on the walls but was not for the public to see. The guard thanked us for sounding and honouring his lineage in the temple, a surprise to us! He felt the energy as we did and enjoyed joining in with our sound experience.

Life is full of amazing things to experience and see when we are open with all our senses and with an open heart to feel the more subtle energies of places! Most people do not feel it because they do not take the time to stop, listen and feel what is trying to be shown to them. I always feel blessed and great gratitude for what has been shown to me. I have had so many experiences in other lands, not just Australia, where the ancestors have shown themselves to me so I may receive learning. It is such a privilege to have these experiences with what I believe are other realms of existence. My life is enriched when I go on these journeys and connect to new lands—the joy of travelling consciously.

The crystals and rocks remind me to respect all species, as they all have families in nature. The wisdom held in the natural world is all around us. An organic library of earth wisdom history and knowledge is available to us at any time within the crystal and rock families, if we open to connecting with their spirits and many other species.

Wildlife

29
Wildlife Encounters

What if all humans could commune with wildlife?
They all want to commune with us. Would you want to
commune consciously with them all?

If I sense, feel or see another species has been injured, I feel their pain in my body. Just recently, I was leaving the house after some big rain overnight. Opening the porch door, I heard a little squeak. Weird, I thought. Looking up, I saw a tiny little frog had placed himself along the door runner and his leg was caught. I was unable to dismantle the screen for fear of causing his leg to be lodged even deeper into the frame and possibly cause his death outright. Not a good outcome. My sensitive heart was heavy with the pain I had unintentionally caused the frog, and I could not release his leg. I hoped if I left the screen in place and allowed him to find the best way out, it would save him.

On checking later, my husband said, "He was moving his legs. He'll be ok, because he has moved on." We still do not know if he was okay, as we never saw him again.

Another time, I was driving to a job interview and collided with a beautiful rainbow lorikeet bird. With impeccable timing, he smacked straight into my windscreen. My heart sank. I had been rushing because I was late for the interview. What a wake-up call to slow down. I stopped the car to pick him up. He was alive, so I hoped he was just shocked and stunned. Wrapping him in a towel, I placed him on the seat beside me in my car, put gentle music on and tried to get to a vet. Sadly, he died on the way, with me holding him.

Devastated to think I was the cause of his death, my heart was heavy with sadness for him for days. I buried him, respectfully honouring his blessed life with my two young nieces taking part in our ceremony. That slowed me down when driving for some time. I kept remembering that we have lots of wildlife in our area and we need to be vigilant for them and drive slowly. A shocking number of wildlife are killed on Australian roads thanks to cars and trucks. I have heard overseas tourists express how upset they are by how often they see dead animals on our roads.

It is so sad to see a life lost on the road in this way with no respect, as many drivers do not stop. I always stop and check if they are alive. If not, I perform a little ceremony to honour their life and send a blessing to release their soul back to the light, then try to bury them nearby, or at home. I have a little box with a towel in my car for when I see a wild animal needing help. What upsets me most is that people hit them and do not stop to check them or bury them away from the road. If they have a pouch, we need to check there is no baby inside, as they can survive for some time after the mother passes.

When we consciously interact with other species through our hearts, we can expand to feel and receive unconditional love from everything around us in the natural world. Thus we become part of the web of life, not alone or separate from other species, nature or Mother Earth. We can transcend this limited, physical 3D world. We begin to see how we can change our environment by witnessing the way our unconscious actions lead us to feel separate and alone from the web of life when we are not plugged into it, and our relationships with everything change.

With many of my interactions with wildlife I have been consciously awake, at other times not so. And yet, what I found is the wildlife still tried to commune with me, continually reminding me they were present and wanted to interact with me, to share their love and offer me wisdom to remember who I am. Of course, we do not need to be fully conscious and awakened to have interactions up close and personal in joyful moments, as you will read from my encounters with other species, but we can miss the depth of love offered to us and the wisdom they have to share to support our human evolution when we're not consciously awake. So often we miss the opportunity to go beyond this limited 3D reality to find the magic that awaits us in other realms of existence with other species.

My life has always been focused on being out in nature, wanting to spend time with wildlife species. In my twenties, I was not fully consciously communing due to the pain of the wounded child I carried in my heart and needed to heal. This blocked me from consciously communing with wildlife at a deeper level. When I began to release the pain, my interactions unfolded to a whole new level, expanding my heart to receive unconditional love and to learn much more about myself and other species, taking me to other realms of existence with my ancestors—it became magical.

Have you ever experienced your soul being touched by another species' soul, leaving you feeling helpless?

Many years ago, backpacking in Indonesia on the Island of Java, I was at a zoo, a place I would not normally feel comfortable to visit. My friend wanted to see a Komodo Dragon. Giant lizards native to Indonesia, Komodo Dragons are an ancient relic dating back 900,000 years. We were told the zoo was the place to see them up close. They were so large! I found them intimidating, yet it was extraordinary to see them so close, with only a fence between us. I was glad of the fence on that occasion, even though I do not enjoy zoos. I feel the loss of freedom for all the souls locked up, such as birds. I have never understood people keeping birds in cages, I believe they need to be free to sing their songs, the sounds of the universe, weaving the landscape and bringing healing to the land.

Leaving the zoo, I noticed a cement cage with monkeys locked in behind the bars. A little monkey caught my attention. His body language said he was depressed, sitting slouched over and eyes down. My sensitive heart picked up on his sadness and intuition informed me his spirit fire was lost. Our eyes locked and I was hooked in, his emotions with mine. A loud voice in my head begged, "Help me! Please take me from here! Can you help me?"

This totally rocked me. I stood with tears of emotion, trying to figure out how I could help this poor soul. It was a zoo—how could I take a monkey home to Australia? I communicated briefly, wishing him a new home soon. That dear soul sat in my heart for the remainder of my trip. Each day I mentally tried to work out how I could take him out of there and where I would place him. My head was in overload. My friends also thought he looked sad, but I was the only one who heard him ask for help. Too much to bear, I locked it deep down inside me.

Three weeks later, I eventually arrived home. The monkey's plea continued to haunt me, but then I was distracted by life and it was pushed down deeper into my heart as another pain of sensitivity for another species. I held on to the guilt of feeling helpless and unable to save him for many years, pushing it so deeply down I had actually forgotten about it. It happened around thirty years ago.

Whilst writing this book, this memory arose to be healed as a big emotional wound, even now. I know that zoo has since closed down and I pray the monkey's soul was taken to a better place to find peace. I share this to show how, as humans, we keep blocking the pain out with distractions in our life, and it is causing suffering on this planet. We need to awaken to the pain in our beautiful hearts to heal, so Mother Earth can feel this love we once knew.

The clouds of pain and suffering that humans carry into the consciousness and energetic field, if not released, will keep happening, and will be passed on to next generations, creating more pain for the animal souls and more exploitation on this planet. Your pain goes deep into the energetic field, like little bubbles of distorted energy that float around. You cannot access love when you have distorted energy in your heart from holding onto emotional pain in your physical body. This distorted pain energy is toxic and needs to be released to get back to feeling that peaceful place, so your energy resonates with your true heart and soul frequency of love. If not released, that energy will eventually cause physical dis-ease.

Have you ever had another species heal your fear?

Many years ago, a six-foot-long adult diamond python snake helped me heal my fear of snakes. My two nieces, teenagers at the time, came to visit me in Northern Australia. We visited a large wildlife park, and they were keen to handle a diamond python snake. Both girls compassionately stroked and patted the snakes and allowed them to move all over their bodies. When one tried to go inside my niece's shorts, she lovingly and gently redirected his movements, without being fearful.

I witnessed the love of the snake and my nieces' interactions and wondered why I was so intimidated. I had no reason for this fear, and I understood that if I felt love towards snakes they would feel and know this and respond in love. I dubiously picked up the snake and tried to chill and relax into the moment, as my nieces had. As I felt the snakes' bodies moving around mine, I patted them and felt the awesomeness of their skin, soft and cool. Slowly allowing myself to feel into the movement of the snakes around my body, I started to realise there was no reason to be scared. They did not want to hurt me, or I them. In fact, it felt very calming and meditative to hold them. Observing the snakes with people, I felt sure they picked up on the energy of the person holding them.

I share here from many years ago, some of my up close and personal interactions where other species tried to commune with me, making themselves known to me, but I was not consciously aware at the time or able to commune with them at a deeper level. My loss, I feel now, however I still enjoyed my wildlife interactions even though I was limited to a more physical 3D experience.

Have you ever had those moments with uninvited wildlife that left you scratching your head? An uninvited dinner guest arrived as my partner and I were sitting at our campsite admiring the bush landscape, the sun setting as we watched the native birds returning home to the trees.

Waiting for our big pot of hearty vegetable stew to cook on the campfire in front of our little two-man tent, we watched a small kangaroo appear from the dense bush. He curiously come over to our pot of stew to check it out, sniffed the pot, and as he leant in got his foot caught on the tent guy rope. Confused, he tried to hop off and hopped straight into our small tent and onto the double mattress. Thank goodness he missed falling into the pot of stew! Quickly realising there was no back door to the tent, he made one with his strong back legs. He jumped up and slashed an opening in our tent from top to bottom, then hopped off back into the bush. Now there was a back door and we had a gaping hole in the tent.

We scratched our heads wondering how to fix the tent, then remembered we had duct tape, so we kept dry for the remainder of our camping journey. Lucky we were prepared campers! No camping trip should be without duct tape. We have used it many times to save us. Our neighbour the kangaroo just wanted some stew, but he became too spooked. Poor hungry kangaroo, he missed out on our stew.

Have you ever noticed changes in another species' behaviour, then learnt later it was a warning sign of unexpected changes to come?

Having done a lot of camping and bushwalking throughout Australia, I have seen snakes, but not normally so many up close and personal to me. One day in 2003, we were trekking up Mt Warning trail and noticed two large python snakes, around six to eight feet long, at the entry to the walking trail, lying on the rocks like guardians in the sun. Admiring them, we thought it a lovely greeting and kept walking. Later, we noticed another one pass us on the track. Reaching the top of the mountain the views were stunning, so we sat on a rock on the trail to eat our lunch. After about ten minutes, Nigel called to me.

"Just get up nice and slowly. Move over here to me. There's a large python coming your way."

I did as he suggested. Looking over, I saw the python coming for my lunch, so left it for him. He moved very gracefully past my sandwich and went straight over to where I had been sitting, then took himself gracefully back into the bush off the walking trail. That was an interesting moment. He was determined to pass exactly where I had been sitting, and was not after my food. His sheer size demanded respect.

As we stood watching, more hikers came up the trail. They also respectfully allowed him to pass as they stopped and observed. Interesting to note that only two weeks earlier a young girl, a tourist, had slept on top of that same mountain and was fatally bitten by another species of snake. I feel now these snakes were trying to commune with me, or offer a definite warning, because they kept popping up all day.

Some years later, I found this information on Mt Warning: Indigenous name Wollumbin. The summit track is a sacred place of the Bundjalung

People and was named an Aboriginal Place in 2015. Elders requested visitors avoid climbing this difficult trail to the summit, as it has great spiritual significance to the Bundjalung People. Now I understand the snakes are the guardians of Wollumbin Sacred Place.

One Christmas time many moons ago, as my partner and I lay in our tent late at night while camping in the Barossa Valley, we heard a great commotion in the attached area of the tent where we did our cooking. The room was full of possums, all caught in the act! They had splashed our Christmas cake around the floor and were busy eating it. Their big, dark glossy eyes looked at me with no fear. Others were on top of a table munching on opened packets of biscuits. They were having a hell of a party!

Those little friends must have been hungry. I thought they only ate fresh fruit, not fruit cake, or was I just naive? What message would I have received if I had been communing at a deeper, conscious level? Maybe it would have been come and join us, we are here to have some fun with you. My partner and I did laugh a lot that night with those little possums.

Camping in a national park in the Northern Territory, Nigel and I had settled into our swags for the night for a well-deserved sleep, our tent butted up against a native tree. At daybreak, we woke to the sound of pitter patter on the fly sheet of the tent and agreed it must be raining, no rush to get up just on dawn light.

When we did get up, we were shocked to see millions (and I mean millions!) of what looked like green ants covering the fly sheet. They had been eating our flysheet, leaving small pin holes. We could see daylight through the holes! Duct tape was not going to fix this tent problem! We had to live with the damage until we returned to Darwin city. It was the dry season, when the temperature rises and there is no relief from rain, so little water is around the landscape and many of the seasonal billabongs were dry, waiting for the wet season to arrive. Did we have moisture on our tent they thought would quench their thirst?

Perhaps they were telling us we had camped on their tree home, as their little ant nests hung down like small bags from the branches above our tent. I was not consciously communing, so I will never really know what they were wanting to share with us.

Have you been consciously aware of cohabitating with other species at home?

Living in Darwin many years ago, Nigel and I shared our suburban tropical garden house block with many wild species. Wildlife shared our human habitats in large numbers and reminded us every day in our backyard with tree snakes around the pool, large goanna lizards passing us, frogs in the pool, exotic birds singing in the trees, and so on. A wonderland of sounds and movement, I felt like we lived in a jungle and so loved it!

One night, we were eating outside at the BBQ area near the pool with family when we heard a big splash. We all stopped talking and looked to the pool, but could not see with the dimmed night lights. Getting up to investigate, I saw a very wet, furry possum had fallen out of a tree and landed in the water. We rushed over to save him, but he moved with such speed he appeared to be running across the water, then scrambled up the nearest tree that hung over the pool. I did not know if possums swam, but this one was not stopping to find out! Dear little soul was gone from the pool as fast as he had fallen in. That home reminded us daily how many species cohabitated with us. I so loved that we lived outside a great deal, enjoying our meals outdoors more than inside to be with all the wildlife in the tropical climate.

Another time, we were enjoying the great outdoors in a national park with crocodiles. We had been asleep for a few hours when we were awoken by heavy breathing, munching and scratching sounds circling around our little two-man tent. What was that sound? What sort of animal was moving around us? *It must be a goanna wandering around looking for food scraps on the ground,* we both thought, then tried to go back to sleep.

Suddenly, we heard a loud snorting sound very close to our heads! Nigel opened the tent's zip, torch in hand.

"Holy shit! I just spotted two big red eyes looking straight at me!"

He closed the zipper as quickly as he could and told me it was a huge wild pig! This set off all sorts of vivid visions in our minds. We had seen what dogs looked like when the hunters took them out to kill wild pigs, torn and bleeding from those big tusks. Feeling a little scared, we decided to lie still in our flimsy two-man fabric tent and wait it out.

The wild pig kept circling us for what seemed hours. In reality, I think it was more like half an hour of tension. It was very intimidating to encounter a wild pig so close with no protection around us. We tried to be still and silent, playing dead like other species do, in the hope he would not get upset with us and would eventually leave. He did! What a relief when we heard him grunting off across the park.

As we packed up the campsite in the morning, I rolled my sleeping mat up to discover a scorpion underneath. He was alive and had been there the whole night. I believe we slept together, me on top position. He scurried off, not sure why he did not want to spend another night with me? Lots of laughs. That outdoor adventure in the wild had given us many encounters up close and personal with wildlife. Beware of what you ask for!

30

Rescue

It was time for me to learn about caring for wildlife. While driving one night on a quiet country road with my sister, we heard an almighty thud against the car door. We stopped to find a possum on the road beside the car. My heart sank into my stomach. It was pitch black, and at first, we thought the possum was dead.

Picking the possum up, I held it in my arms and felt it breathing—a good sign! Its little heart nestled next to mine, pulsing faintly, we drove to the home of a friend who took in rescued wildlife. Having just moved from the city to that wildlife region, I had no experience with rescued animals, it was all new to me.

When I arrived at my friend's place with the possum in my arms, all snuggled and calm, my friend became very anxious and upset.

"You shouldn't have picked up the possum without placing her in a box for protection." Her concern was that when afraid or anxious they become dangerous with their sharp claws, so both the possum and I could have been badly injured. My friend directed me to her spare bedroom to place the possum down. After I shut the door, a loud screeching sounded—like a wild cat was loose in the bedroom! Oh, my goodness, that happened so quickly! Only two minutes before the possum was in my arms in a very calm state.

Sadly, that soul was a pregnant possum. She died six weeks later, but her baby survived the shock and was cared for in a sanctuary, to be released when he was old enough. I was a little naïve at that time and lucky I did not get injured, but I feel my loving heart helped that possum feel safe and secure until I had to let her go into that bedroom. With what I know now, I would probably have been better to place the possum in a box with a blanket to cover the box, as keeping them in the dark reduces shock and stress to wildlife. Then I could have transferred the possum to my friend's bedroom, still in the box, thus not disturbing her warm, safe environment. A novice, I did the best to my knowledge at the time. I now keep a little box and blanket in my car boot to be prepared for wildlife encounters.

Have you had that moment of feeling 'I want to learn more to help others?'

Communing with wildlife near home, and that encounter with the mother possum, prompted me to know more and become a volunteer wildlife rescuer, so I joined the group Wildlife Arc and trained in wildlife rescue. One of my first rescues, a ringtail possum who I tried to keep alive for several days, gave me one of the most profound messages I had ever received after he died. He returned to tell me that he had such gratitude for all the love he felt when he died. I was upset I could not save him, and he said:

> It is not important I did not live, more important that I felt the unconditional love of your heart, because it was enough as I passed over. It made it easier to feel at peace leaving the planet.

A magpie gave me a similar message, coming back to thank me for the love he felt when he died. Other species have shared these same messages when they pass, that they have much gratitude for the unconditional love they felt from me when they left earth, that feeling so very loved gave them peace.

Insight.

Not to be forgotten, I make sure every species has an opportunity to feel unconditional love when they are dying. If I find them on the side of the road, already deceased, I bury them with love, sacredly honouring their life and releasing their souls.

The laughing neighbours, a family of kookaburras who live in my area, fly in to greet me when I go outside. Up to four from their family will arrive, just sitting on the fence and watching me work in my yard. They come quite close and sit beside me on the garden furniture. One week I was inside a great deal for a few days, missing my outside time communing with nature. When I eventually went out, I was greeted by a kookaburra sitting on the table beside me.

"Do you have a message for me today?" I asked.

The response, "Yes, don't forget your family outside, we're all out here too." My heart melted at the reminder to go outside to commune with my other family of wildlife species.

Insight.

Remember to spend more time with my family of other species, for they notice us missing and not communing.

Enjoying a country drive with a friend, we were chatting happily when we both spotted a beautiful coloured bird in the middle of the road. Was he alive? Perhaps he had been hit by a car and was in shock?

When we stopped to pick him up, he started to breathe and moved, so appeared to be stunned. I could not see any injuries, but I knew wildlife could die from the shock, even with no injuries.

My friend drove and I held him to my chest so he could feel my heart and the warmth. When we arrived at my friend's house he appeared more awake, so I kept him in a box for a while longer, then placed him back on the ground when he looked more alert, ready to let him go. He was still a little unsteady, so I decided to keep him with me in the car and take him to a vet. I placed him in the little box beside me and kept stopping to talk with him and give him loving hugs. He would sit up and chirp at me, so I assumed he was getting better. He was all quiet, resting. Then I heard a very loud chirping, like he had a lot to say, and he closed his eyes and died.

Sadly, I felt into that moment. I believed he was thanking me for not leaving him on the road to be run over, and that he felt the love I gave him. I believe sharing our hearts is enough. They will often have such gratitude before passing, shown with a little noise. I believe it is a *thank you for caring for me* when they die. That is the message I have received time and time again, from many species.

Once, as I sat at the living room bay window, playing my drum under the full moon at midnight, a little possum appeared. Sitting on a tree branch that was against my window, he observed me and listened to my drumming. A magical encounter, we sat close to one another, enjoying the drumming rhythm and sounds. My heart was so full of love and I could feel his little heart listening to the drum rhythm. Possums are normally shy mammals who hide in the trees at night, foraging for food. I felt blessed to enjoy the encounter as he sat exposed with me, obviously feeling safe with me. I could have touched him, he was so close. When I stopped, he waited patiently, looked me in the eye, then climbed back into the heavy growth of trees. What was my message? "We are out here. You can come out at night to commune with us."

Insight.

> We always have opportunities to share and commune with another species and feel the love and peace shared together whilst connecting to the web of life.

As a wildlife rescue volunteer, I learnt the importance of not feeding wildlife our food, or any other food, unless for rehabilitation purposes. It is advised we refrain from this practice for the benefit of the wildlife. I believe this is worth sharing, as humans can wipe out species of birds through our naïve practices of giving our food. I have never fed the family of kookaburras around my home, but they always come to see me. If I put the washing out on the clothes line or fence they will come and sit beside me, getting my attention. So I have a little chat, asking them how they are today.

To be honest, I do not believe we need to feed wildlife unless we are rehabilitating them, because by doing so we interfere with their natural selection of food, which is important to a wild animal's balanced diet. They can become dependent on getting food from humans, then teach their offspring go to humans for food, like a wildlife supermarket. Often the food humans feed them is not a normal diet to them and can change the gene pool to be weakened, they may become malnourished, and the younger birds do not learn to forage for a balanced diet and do not grow strong. The other problem is that when we go on holidays or move to a new house, what happens to them being fed? Do we expect them to suddenly find food elsewhere? It is unhealthy to be interfering with their natural selection of foraging.

Have you ever travelled with wildlife on migration up close?
On safari in Tanzania, I felt privileged to be travelling so closely with herds of wild animals on their seasonal migration trail. I found it particularly interesting to learn and witness how the zebras and wildebeest travel together, supporting one another. One has good

eyesight and the other is more robust for protecting the herd from predatory lions. One eats the grass down to a certain level, leaving grass for the other species to eat the next level to the soil. They knew they were safe together. Each had a skill the other didn't to survive and keep safe.

There is so much we need to learn from other species and how they survive together. Humans are not an island. We live with many species and need to live in harmony. Although I continually hear the opposite in people's comments, we are not superior to other species. I am not even sure they know they are saying this consciously, they just haven't stopped to think about their actions and comments towards other species, or if they could be more respectful towards another species instead of thinking we know best for all. Maybe the non-human species can teach us how to live on earth together.

We do not know it all. I have to say this strongly, as my experience from other species tells me they know so much more than humans, particularly how to survive and what we need to be doing on this earth to live in harmony together. We are extremely poor at living in harmony, destroying everything within a short time—have a look at what we have done to our countries. Many species were here on earth long before humans arrived.

Did you know wildlife can give us warning signs?
While living in many regions of Australia, I have witnessed other species giving humans early warning signs of changes to come in the weather patterns long before our weather bureau alerted us. In the tropical areas of Northern Australia, one to two days before cyclones appeared, I observed the dogs became very unnerved and the birds disappeared. It can feel eerie to observe this behavior hours or days before the event happens.

Most species are guided by a primal force and know the warnings before the season arrives, so can change their migration pattern from a particular region they have visited for thousands of years. When one year they do not arrive for the seasonal breeding, the locals in the region will say, "We haven't seen those animals this year, which is strange." Their internal primal alarm system has already been alerted before humans feel it. One summer in the region I live in, we missed the rhythmic cicada sounds, a seasonal event you can count on during pre-summer months.

The devastating fires came later and destroyed large areas of habitat they would have birthed and lived in. This summer their rhythmic sound is back, deafening and beautiful, filling our trees and my heart again. Did they have a message for humans that summer?

Years ago, at another location, I observed a remote coastline region in Northern Australia where turtles had come for hundreds of years to lay their eggs on the beach. That year they did not arrive. Within weeks, a devastating cyclone season arrived and the small town near the turtle breeding beach was flattened, to the point the locals needed to rebuild their town. The turtles returned the following year. Our intuitive senses (primal guidance systems) need some practice to keep us safe. Alternatively, we can start to observe other species more closely. When I commune with other species, the message I receive is, "Watch us, the other species, we have highly tuned primal navigation systems."

Most of us are too busy and do not use what is available to us all. Children have awesome intuitive abilities, as they are also driven by the internal primal signs. As adults, we need to practice using our gut instincts and feelings to tune in to what is around us, instead of all the distractions we find. We need time away from the mundane earthly distractions to have a well-developed intuitive, primal system that alerts us. If you make time to go outside and observe other species' behaviors, and become familiar with what their movements are in and around your home, your observation of changes happening from one season to the next may save your life, and your family's, if you take notice.

It does not take much to observe nature in your day. I try to make it my priority to go outside barefooted for breakfast or lunch every day and watch curiously what goes on in my backyard community. If you live in a high-rise, which is becoming more common in Australia, you can spend time in the parks and watch what is going on in nature below and above you. I have noticed over the years how the Ibis bird, once never found in cities, is now almost over-populating in our tropical northern cities, as they know food is easily accessible.

More recently, I am noticing the water dragon lizards arriving in our parks. You would never see them in built up areas previously, only out in the less urban areas and bushlands. Now they have worked out where water and food are easy to forage. In fact, they are over-populating some parks in a tropical city in Northern Australia and are seen confidently walking around the carparks. They appear to have lost their fear of humans, approaching them even. In the past they were quite shy, but now are very bold and stand their ground, which can be dangerous in a carpark as they could be run over. I have read scientists' claims that they are so well fed and watered in the city parks now they are evolving into a much bigger species who live a good deal longer than their ancestors who occupied their natural bushlands and survived on dry, harsh terrain.

Particularly noticeable with all the droughts we have experienced in Australia over the past ten years, the strongest and smartest species are survivors and have found towns to get their food. I guess it is like us going to the supermarkets—easy access to food and water. That is just one of many ways humans have changed the landscape considerably and affected the habitats of all species.

We have so much to learn from other species. They live by the universal language of love, and they speak through our hearts. When we experience this with our own close animal companions it cannot be ignored. Our hearts are opened to feel such beautiful, unconditional love, given so freely from other species. There are so many examples, such as different species in the wild found mothering and feeding other species with their milk becoming more common to witness as people capture photos or videos and share on social media. It so warms my heart. They are showing us we can all live in harmony with other species if we can have respect.

Whilst I travelled in Africa, on safari in Kenya we camped in the national wildlife parks, with no fences protecting us from the wild animals who shared their habitats with us. We experienced some exhilaratingly memorable moments. It was the dry season, so we were on the migration circuit with the animals as we moved in a 4WD.

When the animals stopped at waterholes, I watched the respect and saw how the pecking order existed. Every species had their share of the water, even though it was extremely dry and the waterholes were becoming severely low on water. I watched predators drink near their food source of other species, but not hurt them. The chase was on for food away from the waterholes. When elephants arrived in large numbers to a small waterhole, the monkeys would sit back and wait, then large numbers of monkeys would arrive. As soon as the elephants left, they all passed one another calmly, allowing every animal to go to the only waterhole found for miles. Lions and their food source, zebras, were drinking in close proximity to one another, yet the night before we had watched a lion take a zebra down for a meal, and the lion's pride come to eat after teaching the cubs how it was done.

We had close encounters with a pride of lions living around our safari campsite and chasing prey past our tents. We camped on the foreshore of the busy wildlife river, the Masai River, where crocodiles waited for the migration of wildebeest and zebras to cross and hippos passed our tents at night. Thinking back, we were lucky to get out of that place alive. I would not have missed that journey though, as it was a magical experience and reminded us of our mortality in life, with the cycle of birth and death up close and personal every day as we moved around.

Wildlife species remind me of my wild nature as a child of the earth, and to go outdoors to be with my other relations to play and observe the magical beauty and wisdom they hold for us humans.

Can you recall moments when wildlife tried to commune with you?

Trees and Plants

31
Trees Support Me

My experiences with the trees started as a young child. They have always fascinated me, and I have always felt their strength, flexibility and love as they hug me when I feel challenged and go to them to commune in nature. They are home to me, and I feel them supporting me on my life journey.

One memorable and intensely emotional experience was in tree groves in a dense forest in a wilderness area of Australia, where I walked for seven days and slept on the trails. The trekking was getting quite challenging for myself and Nigel, and we still had a long way to go through varied terrains. My body was exhausted after walking for many hours through gale force winds to cross a plateau, before we descended into a beautiful forest with an ancient tree grove whose huge roots ran across the paths. We had to climb over them to get past.

As I climbed, I could feel them intuitively helping me every step of the way. My legs and feet were tired, but I felt I was somehow uplifted by the trees as I clambered over their roots. I wanted to sit and admire their majestic beauty, of all shapes and sizes. They looked so ancient, I felt I knew them somehow from another time and that they had lots of wisdom to share. It was a moment in time to really see them—another species whose majesty I had missed until then. They had so much moss growing on them, and looked very woody and gnarled. They seemed much older than me, looking at the size of them and how they had planted their roots so permanently into the earth.

Inspired to simply be with them and feel the calmness, I could almost feel them breathing around me as the breeze blew gently past. I believe the breeze was the ancestors communing with me. My heart knew they were doing something powerful, and I accepted what was gifted to me as my blessing.

Healing Properties of Trees

Trees are known for their invisible life force energy that can help humans to heal.

Many ancient traditions see trees as a source of emotional and physical healing and themselves as meditators, absorbing universal energies for earth's health. Bigger trees have the maximum energy, such as large pines.

Many physical healing effects can be received from trees, such as:

- Banyan trees and Bengali figs purify the heart and help eliminate moisture from our body.
- Fir trees help to absorb bruises to reduce swelling and heal bones.
- Hawthorn trees support digestion and strengthen the intestine.
- Birch trees lower body temperature and detoxify the body.
- Elm trees calm the mind and strengthen the stomach.
- Willow trees lower blood pressure and strengthen the urinary tract.

Building a relationship with trees takes longer than with humans. Visit a tree regularly and it will expect you to spiritually commune. Just like making love, it requires all your senses and tenderness. Once established, there is no need to control the communing—simply allow the tree to respond. It may or may not give guidance, your job is simply to stay open and present in the moment.

To commune with a tree respectfully:

- Ask if it wants to commune with you.
- Be in silent communion with the tree.
- Not all trees are generous, and some are too weak and ill, so may need healing from you first. Always ask them.

- Tree hugging: Always ask if the tree is ready for this practice. If you receive a 'yes', absorb the energy, then return the energy to the tree.
- Meditation: Sit with your back against the tree and sense the energy circulating around you and the tree. You might prefer to stand in front of the tree. Without touching the tree, send your energy into the ground, up into the tree, and receive it through the top of your head as it comes from the tree (setting up a circular energy system).

32

A Community and a Forest

When I moved to Western Australia, I realized how much I deeply loved and cared for trees. Nigel and I had left our home on the east coast of Australia as we felt called to move interstate. We never knew why, but our hearts had called, so we packed up our house and moved with a few personal belongings. Selling everything and filling the car, we had no idea that the trees would be a big part of our new life.

We arrived at a small coastal town, a pretty location beside the Indian Ocean on the west coast of Australia. The next day we left the camp site and spent the day riding into town on bicycles to explore and hopefully discover why the town had called us. On the way in, we cycled past a huge pile of woodchips. It looked like an industrial site we needed to pass on the track. A few minutes later, a policeman pulled us up and asked why we were in the area. He kept questioning us. We were a little perplexed, as he seemed suspicious of us for some reason.

"We were cycling into the town centre from the campground. We have just arrived from New South Wales and we're planning to live here now," I explained.

"Oh," he said, "so what are you doing here, around these woodchips?"

"What do you mean?" we asked.

"With your green jackets and bicycles you look like greenies who may cause trouble. We've had a few problems here with this wood pile, and I thought you may be part of that crowd of greenies."

"We know nothing about what you're telling us."

"Okay," he said, "on your way. I wish you a nice cycling day, the weather is certainly good for this today."

Off we cycled, totally confused about what he was saying and why he chose us. That was our introduction to the West Coast. What sort of place had we come to? A few days later, we found an advertisement to take part in the annual Women's festival. We jumped at the opportunity to make masks and take part in the pre-activities for the seasonal event, which included many artists and locals in the region each year. We had a wonderful time, and met some beautiful people who were fascinated to hear our story of being called to live in south Western Australia without knowing why.

It was a sensational festival, with all the community involved. We had lined the streets with coloured bras hanging off the buildings and posts, and we made a huge papier mache of the Hindu goddess of fire, Kali, which we burned at the end of the night's activities as an offering to celebrate.

We also joined an environmental group educating and gaining support from the local communities to save 500-year-old old growth forest trees from being cut down for Japan to use as toilet paper. The region we wanted to save was 200 kilometres south of the town, inland, and in a very out-of-the-way place. It was the only old growth forest left in Western Australia, so we were told.

On aerial photographs it did look like a large area, but Western Australia is mostly a dry and arid terrain, as much of the coastal areas had lost their trees due to white settlers cutting them down when they settled. The government of the day had told settlers if they wanted free land grants they would have to clear the land before using it for farming. Those properties had some of the hardiest trees in the country, able to survive the droughts. Now they were all gone due to the limited thinking of lawmakers of the time. Western Australia already had a dry climate, now it really suffers from the harsh, dry climate, with no trees to help hold water in the soil or provide shade for other species.

I took the opportunity to commune regularly with that ancient forest, to feel with all my senses, to see the beauty, hear the whispers and smell the fresh green undergrowth and the decayed woods being recycled. I savored the gentle aromas on the breeze that flowed between the trees, carrying the messages of the ancestors and the conscious communication the trees send to one another on the air currents, sometimes loud winds, other times soft, gentle breezes that touched my skin.

How emotional I felt in my heart to feel such joy with these extraordinary, old, wise beings of the forest, and to feel them hugging me when I sat with them. I was a child of the universe and they were my big brothers and sisters holding me, or a grand old tree holding me as a mother would hold a small child.

It was a blessing to feel this from such old growth forest, and that gave me the passion to save them from the clearing machine taking them down to be mulched for toilet paper for a Japanese company that was purchasing them from the Australian government. Many people rallied for two years to stop the clearing and felling of this ancient forest. Some of the trees were so large a busload of fifty people could stand on the stump without any effort after they were chopped down. Such big, old, wise trees, they had stood long before white man arrived in Australia.

Witnessing the destruction of the forest was horrendous. Everyone campaigning to save the forest really felt how devastating this clearing was on the land, where many animals and birds had all lived for generations in harmony. The campers patrolled to save any wildlife who were stranded or injured as the workers kept coming with machinery. Most of the campers were serious and professionals—nurses, doctors, physiotherapists, artists, chiropractors—all taking time off their busy practices or jobs to save the ancient forest region. They would rotate with other volunteers at the campsites to report back to the environment centres and try to stop the workers using the machinery.

In a 100-year-period we have razed almost all the old growth forests down to the soil. So much is lost when this happens. To feel these old growth forests is like going into a very sacred temple or place of prayer or meditation; it transports you to a place of peace and calm. Most of the people who make decisions on our forests being sold and cut down have never been to these places, they just sit in offices making decisions.

Campaign wise, we found the best results came when we took the politicians out of their offices and down to the forest. Artists of the earth set up organic art installations made of the earth's materials along a walking trail through the forest for everyone to be inspired by, and to maybe feel the magic with the trees by sitting and spending time, feeling what they offer us and many other species. That was the tipping point. After all the emails and letters that had filled politicians' inboxes, this action was the most successful. It made them rethink what we were asking them to stop destroying—such sacred areas that take hundreds of years to evolve into a forest. No amount of regrowth twenty years after clearfelling was going to give the experience of deep connection to nature that an ancient forest gives in tranquility and peace.

The politicians were then taken to a 100-year-old forest to experience a manmade forest and to feel the difference between it and the wild ancient forest. While the younger forest was beautiful, it did not have the mystical, magical feel of the old growth forest area with its thick canopies and undergrowth of decayed matter. The politicians could not deny the feelings they had experienced and the differences they had found. Then the government in power was voted out, and the new government agreed to save the old growth forest area for everyone to enjoy, to allow it to keep evolving without human intervention of clearfelling and destruction. It was a win we could not have imagined at the beginning, but when we had everyone on site it gave the politicians the experience of what we were trying to convey in words—they could not deny their senses were awakened by those beautiful places, or the peace that had touched their souls.

There was a problem though. The timber workers in the nearby towns were getting frustrated with all the distractions, unable to work and make a living. Many workers became a little heated as outsiders came to view the devastation taking place. Some wise individuals realised we needed to help the workers, as they had been doing this work over generations and needed to make a living for their families once the clearfelling ceased. After many community consultations, agreements were made to help them find alternative work.

This adventure, my green experience, woke me up to look at what had been going on with governments agreeing to remove pristine areas from this planet without any conscious connection to nature, without seeing the value or connection for *all beings* when they chop and destroy these magnificent areas. We do not have many old growth or ancient forests left in Australia thanks to so much clearing since the white man arrived. It's sad that so many people have never been to a forest of this magnitude, and haven't experienced the healing of their hearts and souls just by sitting and being present to the energies the forests provide for humans, other beings, and the planet's health.

I am no scientist, but I do know what my mind, body, heart and soul feel when I visit these magnificent, ancient, living sacred places. When the politicians were taken to the forest, they agreed it was an enlightening experience. Feeling the energy of the ancient forest was a memorable time for them. The opposition party at the time came on board to save the forest, and they became the new government because they listened to what thousands of people wanted. We thought it was a miracle to save the forest, with so much money at stake and contracts with corporations in opposition to our cause.

Miracles can happen when people band together to a *power of one*. Trees remind me of the importance of community, because they thrive when together in community (like a forest). Their roots are strong through community connections, so they are able to weather life's storms, yet be flexible and not break when the winds of time and change arrive. They support the younger trees to grow tall, strong and healthy, and older tree spirits are protected with a place to share their wisdom, to remind the community the seasons change and nothing in life is permanent.

The cycle of birth and death is a constant reminder not to be stuck, because the cycle of life is ever-changing.

33

How I Commune With Trees

Have you ever communed with a tree to find yourself transported to another realm of existence?

How beautiful it feels to hug a tree when I commune through my heart intelligence. They listen to me, and I feel warmth in my heart as they embrace me. They do not have a voice in the way that we do, but you can hear them loudly as they talk with you through your heart. It goes beyond the words of our limited language and gives me a strong knowing of what is being shared between us.

I try not to let my head interfere with the communication, and hold the messages in my heart and trust my soul knows what's being shared. It is the same with other species. I connect with my heart, then the mind does not misconstrue or interfere with what I am receiving, which keeps it pure. The heart has a knowing that goes beyond the limited language of words—it is the portal to the soul, our feelings and intuition. I energetically interpret my communication, bypassing the mind of logic. This helps me tune in more easily, like in meditation, bypassing the mind and going to your higher state of consciousness, enabling pure understanding without the egoic mind of judgment and misunderstanding.

When your egoic logical mind is communicating with another species, you may be limited to the physical 3D realm. This can lead you astray and take you from the purity of what's being shared in the heart. The egoic mind can only work from logical sequences that are already known from the past and held in the subconscious mind, and will have judgments attached to them that create doubts and limitations.

Working from the heart space, truly listening with your whole body, is such a fulfilling and magical experience. We can never predict or know where it will lead us in our interactions with other species. That is the magic of using our heart portal to our soul, feeling the communication—as opposed to thinking of what it is all about. Pure communication across the infinite space of time and beyond matter, soul-to-soul, gives such power to the interaction in interspecies connections. The only catch is you have to be totally committed to being in the present moment or you'll miss the magic it holds for you because you won't be open and expansive to receive the greater learning. You may feel you had no communication, but in fact you did on a higher conscious state, so you missed that moment in time by allowing the mind to interpret, which will only take you back into judgment and doubt.

Trees inspire me by their very presence and strength. I always feel held by them when I sit with them. I love to tell them I love them when I wander through the bush and forests, and I feel that returned to me for acknowledging them. I thank them for being here for us. I'm so sure they're fully aware of what I'm feeling with them at an energetic level.

Pia the tree was saved, surprisingly, by a simple act of creativity and acknowledging her respectfully. I had been staying by the coastline in a caravan park in a small regional town in Western Australia and connected to a tree beside our van. I could not stop looking at her and wanting to commune with her. My heart won, and I received guidance to highlight her face. She looked at me with big joyful eyes every day as I sat outside eating my meals. I could feel her beauty, and that she wanted me to create with her, so I gathered my paints and highlighted her face on the trunk, as I could see it, and she gave me her name—Pia.

A surprising creation, everyone in the caravan park passed by our campsite to go to the beach and started to notice this tree and comment, using her name of Pia, which I had painted under her face as she requested. Pia's name gave her icon status in the park and she was seen as having beautiful eyes. She was not the oldest or biggest tree in the park, but she got all the attention, and I felt this pleased her. What happened next, I could not have imagined.

Twelve months later, the caravan park was going to be redeveloped for villas and all the trees were marked to be taken down. Many trees were quite old and majestic, with big shady canopies for people to sit under in the hot summers by the ocean. The small community were upset with the builder's decision to cut the trees down and tried to stop the development. It didn't work. They were all taken down except one—Pia still stands today, twenty years after the redevelopment was completed. She has a special place amongst the villas along the path to the beach.

I was so happy to hear this I had to go back and check it out when I last visited Western Australia—and there she was, looking happy with her painted face. It seems the builders had a change of thought around her, maybe it was her beautiful eyes they noticed? Did being acknowledged save her? We never know where our guidance from the heart can take our actions. I believe I saved beautiful Pia because I listened and trusted what she wanted me to do, even though it was against my own belief of not wanting to be disrespectful of the tree by painting all over her. It was a moment of trust. Pia wanted to be heard and seen for whatever her mission was to stay in that park, and I respected her wishes, with a surprising outcome.

Pia's message to me.

It gave me strength to be on the earth to be heard and seen. This supported my mission on earth, and I appreciated your joyful time with me as I held the energy of that park joyfully.

I'm reminded of a beautiful tree in the front of my rental home who I commune with each day when I eat my meals under her canopy. I call her Grandmother Tree, and believe she protects our house. She has many birds visit her and provides seeds and flowers for many species to be nourished. I found a wild orchid growing on a branch under her canopy one day, showing me the exquisite beauty to be found when we stop and look around us. I hadn't long moved in, and passing by on the path to my car had not noticed this superb wild orchid until the day the splash of colour took my attention, stopping me in my tracks. It grew from a low branch of the tree, close to the ground, with five branches of exquisite flowers in full bloom. The flowers were the most amazing shades of pink, such as the tropical type you see in Singapore. They were growing in my own backyard and I had almost missed this!

I wanted to pick the orchid, then stopped myself and thought *no, I can admire its beauty every day as I pass by, this will keep me present to the beauty I often miss by living life without being present to the moment.* Over the years, it has continued to produce the stunning flowers once a year. The wisdom message I received was to come out and sit with my guardian tree, to commune and observe all the birds who visit her. She is my relation, grandmother. Interesting how I have always called her my Grandmother Tree, and then I received her message, "You are my relation."

Sometimes as I sit with her a bird will sit beside me, on the branch hanging out over my table, not really doing anything but being with me. It is such a treat to see and to be with its beauty and song playing. At these times I will ask, "Do you have a message for me?" If I'm in my heart space and open to the present moment, I'll receive a profound answer for myself and my life at that moment in time.

Grandmother Tree is quite beautiful. I have seen her expand over the past few years since we moved here, and she supports many other smaller trees who have grown up under her large canopy. I have noticed grandfather's beard plant, a type of air plant that lives off Grandmother Tree's trunk and branches, grows under her canopy now and is spreading to other smaller trees below the branches. It hangs gracefully, looking almost mystical and getting thicker and longer, hanging towards the ground while living off the atmosphere Grandmother Tree offers.

I feel so blessed to have connected with beautiful Grandmother Tree, as she's given me so much joy and many personal messages in my life.

How many of us walk past the beauty we have at our home and on our way to work each day and miss the magical beauty that awaits us? Walk more consciously and look with awakened eyes, and you can experience these magic moments with nature.

Let me remind you, as Grandmother Tree reminds me, stay awake or you will miss magic.

I share here the sensitivity of feeling another species as your relation. Recently, our neighbours complained to our landlord about a large old pine tree branch that was over their driveway. They wanted it cut back. We were told the branch would be removed within the week, which was enough for me to feel uncomfortable, but I was happy they were not taking the whole tree down.

The day the contractors came to my home, I was inside writing when I heard a noise similar to a chainsaw, then something heavy fell to the ground—thud! My husband and I loved this big old tree, so did many other species in our yard. Birds and possums would sit in the branches for protection from wind or rain.

The noise made me feel uncomfortable in my heart, so I rushed outside to see what was happening. I was shocked to see the contractors had taken most of the tree down within two feet from the ground. I could not believe what I saw. I felt sick with shock. The contractors insisted the tree was not safe to be standing.

I sat in our backyard, so upset I could not watch any longer what was happening to the tree in the front yard.

"Help me! What's happening?" the tree was yelling. I felt so helpless. It was so painful to feel in my heart, what could I do? Immediately I thought *heart to heart, I will sit here and connect through my heart space to the tree and try to commune, explain what is happening.* I held her in my heart, which was so difficult when my heart was feeling so much tension. I cannot tell you how much this affected me and my husband, hearing that chainsaw and not being given the truth of what the property owner had organized with the tree contractors, omitting to let us know the tree was going to be taken down and removed, not trimmed.

Had I known the truth, I could have prepared this poor pine tree before the day, warning her of what was to come so she could release her spirit in readiness, instead of more pain and suffering being locked into the earth's energetic grid from the unconscious actions of humans. I could not even look at the site until many hours later. There stood a healthy stump. There was no sign of white ant infestation. That mistruth was just their justification to take this beautiful tree down.

What were they up to—collecting more tree mulch? They mulched the tree as it was taken down, then took mulch to another contractor who paid good money, so we were told. So much greed on this planet upsets me. Writing this now, three weeks after the brutal attack on the tree, is causing tension in my heart space.

On a happier note, later that day when I got myself together, I did a ritual to honour the tree. She came to me, thanking me for my kindness and love, and shared a message that she will rise again. They had not taken her totally down, and she will rise again from the stump. I was so happy and excited to hear that her spirit had gone down into the earth and she will grow again. I have been honouring her spirit and life over the past weeks with a candle and gratitude for her being here with us. She gave us great joy visually, aromatically and energetically by being in our yard nurturing us and so many other species. I look forward to her spirit rising from the wood chips and stump again for me to nurture her new beginnings.

That was a very emotional day, and week, feeling a relative being unconsciously taken down. The sad part was, of all the trees on the property, she was the healthiest. I had been communing with two others who were struggling to survive, to warn them of being taken down.

Sometimes we cannot control what is going to happen, but we always have our hearts to be a soothing balm for an injured species to feel loved.

Message from the Oversoul of Mother Earth.

Debra: Was the tree that was taken down in my front yard a soul family member of mine?

Oversoul of Mother Earth: Not really, remember

that trees have many souls, dearest, we explained that they are the gateways.

Debra: Do they have a single soul?

Oversoul of Mother Earth: No, they are a communal group of souls who need one another, that is why leaving one alone is not good for them. Because they are communal and need to be communing with one another. They are happiest together, as you have experienced in the forest or bush, how they commune, and how they make you feel. That is because they are so happy, and then humans gain the benefit of this.

Debra: Do the trees have an oversoul, like the crystals?

Oversoul of Mother Earth: Yes, dearest, you have worked that one out.

One of the most unconscious acts of humans is to cut trees down without respectfully honouring their life. If we commune with trees in spirit first, letting them know they are going to be taken down, they can prepare to take their spiritual energy from the structure into the roots, or choose to leave the earthly plane for another realm of existence. This practice also gives all the insects, birds and animals who live in the tree time to find new homes.
Understand the importance of ritual in consultation with trees, allowing the spirit to leave harmoniously, without placing them into shock when taken down, because that would cause more pain on the earthly plane.

We are here to heal our hearts and clear our karma, to find liberation, and some of us have chosen to come and heal the earth and our soul family karma, as pattern shifters. There is so much more that keeps being revealed as I evolve more consciously, that the ancestor souls share with me to remember as my heart expands and the planet expands in consciousness. I do know we live in a hologram of realities, so that in itself is very challenging to explain in a limited physical world of existence. There is so much more to our lives than most can see.

> *"Transformation of the world begins with transformation of oneself at the level of one's own heart."*
>
> *A Sacred Art Visionary, Alex Grey*

34

Conscious Trees and Plants

One of my favourite and most passionate subjects is trees.
Trees are magical beings of light—gateways to other realms of existence for spirits to travel between worlds.
Trees hold all the energy frequencies on this planet to keep the balance above and below Mother Earth.
I have always had a close bond with trees because they felt like my relations, and they are.
Trees hold great wisdom as guardians of the earth records of all time.

Feeling Trees in My Heart

Have you ever been to an old growth forest and smelt the fresh air, seen the moss growing around the base of the trees who make shelter for the creatures, and felt the invigorating energy that surrounds you if walking or sitting and being present to the moment? If you listen deeply, you can hear the whispers of the trees as they commune with the ancestors who travel on the breeze around them. If you speak to the trees, you may even feel them hugging you. These are some of the experiences I have been gifted to feel when I am with the trees. If I have felt sadness in my heart, they have consoled me with their wisdom and love.

Trees inspire me with their great strength, combined with the gentle nature that holds so many creatures under the canopy, including me at times when I have felt lost and alone. I call it the magic of the trees.

Sharing with Trees' Souls

I have sat with Mother Earth and the trees and shared my painful heart, asking questions in my sadness with challenges in my life, and I can say I have felt the trees hugging me as I do so. That is something I cannot deny—feeling supported and heard by nature as I have shared my sad heart. I always leave nature feeling stronger, supported, heard and loved by Mother Earth and the trees, something I have treasured all my life.

I love when I see trees in a natural circle formation. If you get the chance, sitting inside such a circle is a magical experience! I have a grove of trees near me, and I am always in awe of them when I sit and meditate in the centre. They are so loving towards me and commune with me, giving the most profound messages of wisdom.

I remember a favourite power place I would visit in a park, near where I lived many years ago, and regularly sat in a circle with huge old fig trees. I always felt them hugging me when I sat and communed with them. Sitting in silence or sadness, asking them questions, that circle took me to another place. I would feel my reality shift to another dimension, another space in time, and see their strong, unique facial features on the trunks and feel their wisdom surround me. Just being present with them uplifted me, the joy of feeling that they are my relations and I could commune with them so easily.

When I have seen a tree being cut down or a branch removed from the trunk. I feel for this tree with a part of them missing, how out of balance they must feel, as if it is part of my own body. I have shed tears for trees when I see how destructively and disrespectfully some humans take trees down.

Why do people keep cutting trees down so disrespectfully? Trees feel like my relations, brothers and sisters of the forest and bushlands. We gain so much from trees for the well-being of our mind, body and spirit. If you spend time with trees you will already know this.

I find it beautiful to be reminded of life cycles by the tree relations as the seasons change, such as the leaves changing colour and falling as we leave the active summer cycle of life and warmer months, getting ready for winter and a time of reflection. A new season in life approaches with the new beginnings of spring, when the new buds appear on the trees. Trees give us so much symbology to remind us to stop and feel our way consciously with all the senses and cycles with the planet, because nothing is immortal, everything and everyone comes and goes. As we become mature adults, we begin to realise how quickly!

Guardian Trees, Unmistakable When You Meet Them

I have been to places where you know on arriving it is a very sacred site, such as when you meet a guardian tree in all its majesty, standing tall and spreading its branches many feet up into the air above you. These are the times I will ask to hug the tree and gain permission to enter the site.

Visiting ancient temple sites in Central America, I found guardian trees scattered all across the sacred sites. What a beautiful experience to feel the high vibrational energy coming from the land. Some trees were up to 200 feet tall, and I believe they are the guardians looking after that magical site for all time, magnificent old trees who have grown over the buried temple sites, below the thick vegetation that covers them. These trees appear to be growing in the strangest of places—you would not think they could survive amongst the rock formations.

These powerful energy sites are gateways for souls, such as humans, to enter other realms of existence.

A Tree's Resilience

Trees are so resilient, surviving in many climates across the world. Some live to be thousands of years old! What wisdom they must have to share with us. In Australia, I live in one of the harshest climates in the world with its extremes. We have trees who have survived many droughts over hundreds of years. In arid regions, I have seen tree roots stretching twenty feet or more down into caves, where they find water and create unique environments for many other species to survive with them above and below the earth's surface.

Tree Spirits and Souls

My incredible experiences with trees have quite often shown me faces of ancestor souls stepping outside of the trees to make themselves known to me. The human forms who come out of trees not so often, but when it does happen, I see them as souls of ancestors from the past. When they appear to me, I am reminded we are all inter-connected across dimensions and they have wisdom to share with us.

One time, I remember travelling for ten days on safari along the largest river system in Australia, camping on the banks of the river each night. The first day, as we motored along in a small cruise boat, I saw spirits coming out of ancient gum trees. They looked like physical people with their heads in the branches of the trees—and they were greeting me!

I kept asking the other people travelling with me, but no one could see this dimension that I could see so clearly. The vision did not go away. I kept closing my eyes, thinking it would disappear, but it did not, instead lasting the whole first day of the cruise. I felt blessed they were acknowledging me, and that I was conscious enough to see them coming from other realms of existence. Later, I found out that trees are gateways to many realms of existence for souls to move through.

The most extraordinary experience is to go inside the trees beyond the physical world to find they are gateways into other realms of existence, forgotten worlds of inner earth, like parallel civilisations in other dimensions. In a deep meditative state whilst sitting with big old trees, I have been invited to leave my physical body and move with my spiritual body up to a tree and stand outside its trunk. A door opens and I am welcomed by a small being similar in features to Dwarfs, I am guided downstairs and along underground tunnels to another civilisation.

During these journeys the guide will communicate with me, sharing much information about my past lives, knowing my name and who I am. Intuitively, they feel like my family. I find it fascinating that I cannot recall their names, who they are or where we are going. The most exciting part is that I always feel I know them in my heart, even though I cannot remember them. They share much information about me from my past, always asking, "Do you not remember us?" I tell them they feel familiar in my heart, but I cannot remember their faces or names. Their beautiful villages are also familiar to me, like I have been there before, and the houses appear to be made from crystals. They are always friendly and have much wisdom to share with me on middle earth, where we humans live.

≈

Outdoors in nature I hear the birds singing. I hear the songs of the universe being played, making my heart sing with immense joy and emotion, overwhelming my mind. At this point it can crack my heart open to see or feel another realm of existence around me, such as stepping into another dimensional world of great beauty and feeling joyful. Maybe another species will come to be with me, and I will feel our hearts and souls communing together in a beautiful, unconditionally loving experience. Or they will share a message my soul can interpret to me in my own language of the soul. Sometimes other species bring their young ones to me and we all feel very safe together. They just sit with me and we all feel the love that is around us.

2019: An important message I received from Oversoul of Trees' Wisdom.

We hold the energetic field on the land, while dolphins and whales hold the energy field in water. We all assist with the balancing of the earth's energetic and magnetic fields.

Trees balance the energetic fields of the earth above the ground and below.

They are an organic web of communication and have played a part in humans working out how to make the artificial technological web.

They are doorways to other dimensions and advanced civilizations below the earth who can teach the human race much about surviving in harmony with all nature and species.

Where do you think your fantasy movies come from? That is how you think of us. These visions of what you call fantasy are real, you were sent them through the earth's communication system.

We exchange gasses in the air so you can breathe

oxygen. We provide you with nourishment with our delightful fruits, and support many species you need for your food chain with recycled matter, and seeds you ingest, and for crops.

We are the nervous system of Mother Earth, sending messages and making adjustments, like human nervous systems that send messages via hormones and electrical impulses received internally and externally.

Many souls live within the trees. They can move through the trees, like doorways in and out of many realities, as you, dearest, have experienced for yourself with the souls who have come to greet you through the trees, and on your journeys into the trees to other realms of existence, meeting other civilizations.

2020: An important message I received from the Oversoul of Trees, for all humans to know.

Oversoul: We are the ones who hold all the energy frequencies on this planet to keep the balance, as you may have already been told. We are the real internet of life as you call it, the organic version, as many of you are working out.

So much goes on underground and you will learn more as humans. What happens above goes on below. We influence the aboveground activities.

Your internet came from our messages and memories held for you humans to make sense of this system.

Debra: What do you mean here? How did you do that?

Oversoul: We ask you to come and commune with us, yes? Mother Earth asks you to commune with nature. Well, we have the wisdom and keys for humans to evolve, even though you humans believe you are the superior ones. You will be surprised to know this is not the case. And it will all be revealed to you soon.

Debra: Okay, do you mean that the realms below the earth are influencing above the earth?

Oversoul: Yes. You have been to those places, have you not? Did you not go into a tree to see those places?

Debra: Yes, true.

Oversoul: So, that is our place. We are the doorways to other realms below the earthly plane of existence, which you have seen in action and met all the other beings below. There are some very advanced civilizations below the earth. Yes, you humans have much to learn from their wisdom and knowledge. They were honoured in times past, but now they are seen as mystical/not real/a fantasy. Where do you think those ideas of fantasy come from—the realms below the trees. They send these messages up to the earth for you humans to tap into and learn about.

Debra: So, are you tree spirits or souls?

Oversoul: Souls, dearest. We are the souls of many. Some are your relations, as you have already shared. That is why you feel them so strongly.

Debra: Do you mean many souls live within you?

Oversoul: Yes, you have seen this, have you not?

Debra: Yes, I have.

Oversoul: Well, we can hold many souls. We are the gateways. Souls travel through dimensions through us, just as you did when you went below the earth to meet the beings and civilizations below the earth plane.

Debra: Yes.

Oversoul: You have seen many of us in one tree?

Debra: I have, and it was quite magical, but I did not really understand how it worked.

Oversoul: Well, we are like the antennae for accessing other realms, the communication wires we connect with all the trees. That is why we are needed on the earthly plane, not to be taken down, as humans keep doing, interfering with our antennae. Same as the dolphins and whales, we have much to do around keeping the balance of energy for Mother Earth.

Debra: Is it that you are part of the earth's nervous system?

Oversoul: Yes, you have it. We are this part, that is why we can transmit information to one another and into other realms. Our sound is something you have also found fascinating, is it not?

Debra: Oh, yes.

Oversoul: Well, that's also part of the system we work with to communicate, which humans are just beginning to understand and hear. This will be a big discovery for the human race when they get the technology to hear this adequately for everyone. It will change the thinking around us being ornaments in the garden.

Debra: I am so, so, sorry that happens to you.

Oversoul: We are also a source of nourishment to the human race with our fruits. Our important job is to balance the energies of the earth with outside worlds beyond this 3D dimension on the planet. Your bodies are the microcosm of the macro world. You know this.

Debra: Yes.

Oversoul: So, keep thinking of how the body works and take it to Mother Earth's body and you'll begin to understand how we're all connected, yes?

Debra: Did you want me to share this in my book?

Oversoul: Yes, dearest. Humans need to know this. Oh, some humans may find this very outlandish to read.

There is so much humans still don't understand, yet through our ignorance we make decisions based on the 3D reality—we lock up other species and chop trees down, all that sustains us on multi-dimensional levels. I believe some species have agreed to help humans, but we never ask them, so we don't know which ones they are. Are we causing misery and suffering with our human whims to other species who have chosen at a soul level to help Mother Earth's body?

I was introduced to the majestic Guardian Tree (la Ceiba) in Guatemala, Central America, on a sacred site pilgrimage of the pyramids in the ancient city of Tikal. Fifteen years later, I have not forgotten its power. Travelling with a group of like-minded friends and a Mayan shaman, we were taken into the site from a back entry by our local tribal shaman. He introduced us to the Guardian Tree, a massive 200 feet tall and wide enough for thirty people to surround and hug it by joining our outstretched hands in a ring. That tree was the unmistakable guardian of the temples it towered over. Standing straight and tall, a sentinel above the dirt walking track in the tropical forest and towering above the Mayan ruins, it demanded respect.

The energy I felt when I hugged with the group was extraordinarily powerful within my body. My heart kept expanding with love. This was the beginning of a big adventure into the temples and hidden mysteries of the earth and rocks. The ancient tree species were found all around the sites at different heights. They store so much history on the earth, many before man's arrival.

Why do we keep cutting them down? That is a question I find difficult to answer. They were here before us, yet we remove them disrespectfully and unconsciously, not knowing their mission here on earth of holding the energies to sustain Mother Earth's health and all other species who inhabit this planet. Before entering these temples, we did an honouring ceremony to ask permission respectfully. This set the tone for a very magical stay. We meditated in the moon temple under the stars of the full moon and received many messages for the human race, and our own healing was gifted.

I came home to feel my body and mind had shifted, as has happened repeatedly over many years visiting these sacred sites across the planet. They are doorways to other dimensions because the veils between other dimensions are very thin. If you are conscious and respectful when you visit these sites, you will find healing and real magic awaiting you.

35

The Power of Trees

Tree Wisdom Lost
I have intuitively always known trees are the silent, voiceless sentinels who hold much wisdom and have seen many changes happen around them over hundreds, if not thousands of years on this earth. That is way beyond human lifetimes, yet we treat them like a commodity that can be replaced easily. What we lose is places of peace and calm to find a balance in our lives for a healthy mind, body and spirit. Perhaps most crucial—we need them to exchange carbon dioxide into oxygen for us to breathe in life. They're the lungs of our planet, without them we can't have the wonderful air we breathe, yet we continue to cut them down like they are not needed and we can easily replace them by replanting, ignoring so many other qualities that are found in old growth forests.

There are so many other reasons on many levels of existence. On a 3D level, many science groups are now sharing how there is so much more to the trees that they did not know about. Did you know trees communicate with one another through the breezes and the biochemical changes that happen in the air? A tree can tell when a human is coming into their zone from quite a distance away just by what is carried across the air. They can change the chemical composition of their leaves to make the leaves unpleasant to taste when predators arrive to prevent overeating of their leaves. Humans do not know everything, and never will, because every species has a part in the puzzle of life on earth. I feel we need to honour them all.

Have you ever listened to a tree, put your ear against the main trunk and heard the flowing sound, like fluid running through its trunk? I find it absolutely fascinating to do this! It can only be heard with certain trees, and was shown to me by an Indigenous person, how to really feel and hear with your senses the aliveness of the tree's inner workings. I do not know at a science level what this sound is, but my heart feels it like the blood and life force of the tree.

In the past, as you know, I have meditated in nature and the trees have invited me to enter them. That is when my spirit body has gone inside the tree trunk and been greeted by a smaller species, like a dwarf, who has guided me to other civilisations of the inner worlds—other dimensions beyond time and space.

They have shared their wisdom and the importance for the humans above in middle earth to know about them and that we humans are damaging this planet in our unconscious acts of destruction. They want humans to know we need to heal our hearts, to feel connected to everything around us, then we will understand what we destroy on this planet is here to sustain us. Humans are also disturbing and destroying the habitat for many other species, making them become extinct in an astonishingly short time.

These beings remind us that Mother Earth is evolving, and many changes are always happening, but we are speeding up the process with devastating effects for all species. Mother Earth can survive without humans, and will, as she did before we came to earth. Evolution is a constant. Everything changes—the seasons change, the cycles of time and space change. Life is all about cycles and change in the physical world we live in. Mother Earth is such a large, conscious being compared to humans. You can feel that little breeze pass your skin as she breathes in at dawn as the sun rises, and you can feel it again when she breathes out at dusk as the sun drops down. One breath cycle per day—how magnificent Mother Earth's body is, compared to the many breathe cycles a human must take in one day.

Consciousness of Trees and Plants—Damanhur

Some years ago, I travelled to a unique community at the base of the Italian Alps, a magical place where the people have very close and respectful relationships and connections to Mother Earth and the natural world. They have been researching the consciousness of plants and trees for more than forty years—with surprising results.

I was blessed to have the opportunity to be taken to a secret and very sacred forest that is tended to by community members with reverence. In return, they were receiving extraordinary results working with the plants and trees. This community has many areas of interest. They are working for a new world that is now birthing with new understandings of how Mother Earth is interconnected to us and everything here on the earth. Some of the fields researched are advanced practices in education, science, spirituality and technology. Their research led them to find a way to capture the sounds and the communication frequencies between the plants and the trees, proving they have a consciousness as they interact with one another and their environments.

On visiting the community's sacred forest, I was overwhelmed with the beauty of the music I heard coming from the plants and trees as they communed together. I was not aware we would be recording the sounds, and thought we were going to have silent meditation connection in the forest. I never expected to hear the extraordinary array of sounds, loud enough to be heard by humans! It was like a high vibrational orchestra. Each of the plants had their own unique vibrational frequency, just as the whales and dolphins have when they commune with one another, as proven in research studies. When we magnify the sound through technology it sounds like the most beautifully composed and calming orchestrated music.

The community also has a shop with all the plants attached to little machines the size of a mobile phone that magnify the sound for our human ears to hear. It was a wonderland to visit, with all the plants interacting, their individual sound frequencies playing together. When they first went to the schools to test it out with children none of the plants would commune or sing. The teenagers showed no interest and wanted to go home. One curious child stayed in the room, along with the teacher and the Damanhur community member who had offered the experiment. After all the other students had left, the room shifted to a peaceful, calm environment. Then, the plants began communing with one another consciously and could be heard by the those who stayed, surprising them all.

Further research discovered that the plants and trees had consciousness—they had tapped into the energetic field of the room and read the teenagers' disinterest, so consciously chose not to perform their songs. This proved that not only do they have a consciousness, but they can read the energetic field of other species.

If ever you have an opportunity to listen to the sound of the plants, I believe you will be surprised how beautiful and calming it is to hear and feel in your body. That made so much sense to me after being in ancient forests. That is why it is calming to us—they are communing with us at a higher frequency our hearts know very well—the language of love.

How extraordinary that technology has evolved so far now that you can buy an instrument to hear the trees and plants communing consciously with the world around them through different frequencies of sound in real time. This is a subject close to my heart! I was so excited to be able to hear the music of nature. It is still quite new technology and needs to be made more affordable before I purchase one, but I look forward to the day I will have my own machine to take out into the bush. For now, I have the plant recordings on compact disc. Their frequencies always send me to a calm place of peace within.

> *"All that takes place in nature is permeated with a mysterious music which is the earthly projection of the music of the spheres. In every plant and in every animal there is really incorporated a tone of the music of the spheres."*
>
> *Rudolph Steiner*

On my travels in Australia, I have experienced trees calling me to stay in a region, to commune with them, which became apparent after I decided to stay. I listened to the call of the old river gums, hundreds of years old. "Stay and spend time with us," they shared, as I sat on the banks of the mighty Murray River. My heart said *do this*, so I listened, and found a home in the area and a job. Visiting the river almost every day to commune with the trees and the Indigenous ancestors within the trees, I was surprised to find so much bird life and other wildlife in the area. I was going through menopause at the time and many challenging health issues presented. Intuitively, I knew I needed to connect to the natural world to keep me inspired and healthy.

I felt I was receiving a wonderful healing, after previously living in the central desert of Australia where water was scarce.

Respect

36
We Are Not Gods

As I was reaching the completion of my first draft of this book, Australia was experiencing the worst bushfires in our history. Millions of hectares of national parks and private properties with farm animals were lost, as well as many human lives. It's estimated three billion wild animals perished in the devastating fires, so intense we could not stop the fire fronts that covered the east coast of Australia north and south for 2,500 kilometres.

This loss was felt heavily in the hearts of our nation. People rallied to get help for the wildlife and provide food and medical attention for survivors once the fires slowly burned down to ash.

My heart was so saddened to experience this loss. Sadly, within a month of the fires burning out, an international investor purchased a large parcel of farming land in southern Australia. It had a healthy wildlife population of wombats that the investor did not want on the land—unbelievably, the company gained permission from a government body to cull the wombats.

Local residents found out and tried to alert the people far and wide, but their cause was hindered and went under the radar as most people were engrossed in helping their communities get back to normal after the fires, which was not going to happen anytime soon as the damage was devastating, and some towns required a complete rebuild.

What gives a government authority the right to play god? We have no right to kill other species, dressing it up and excusing it as 'culling' for economic benefit. To hear this decision and learn it was not going to be overturned was devastating. After all the wildlife we had lost in the months of fires, it was insanity. These disrespectful acts of diverting and killing nature and wildlife using economic justification needs to stop. Until our nation stands up together, instead of just a few small groups speaking up, these acts of cruelty will continue, and sadly, be seen as acceptable!

> *Please—heal your heart and become conscious and aware of what goes on around you. Ask questions, and speak up for those who do not have a voice.*

Surely, we can commune with wildlife and ask them to move, or ask if we can take them to another location? I remember a story of a man in Africa who was trying to save elephants. A farmer in his region did not want them on his land and kept killing them (referred to as 'culling'). The farmer who wanted to save the elephants went to talk with them and tried to get them onto his land. The elephants seemed to know what he wanted, and moved to his land. He asked them to stay there, explaining the other farmer didn't want them and would kill them.

The farmer could not afford fencing for his whole property, so when the elephants wandered off, he met them and tried to commune with them at a deeper level, asking them not to go over the boundary he was showing them each day. They did stay, and they were happy. When the farmer passed away, the elephants knew and came to his home from many miles away to join the ones on his property. They stayed there for several days, which appeared to his family as if they were mourning for this dear man. They all left when they were ready.

The man who saved them was remembered because he communed with the language of love from his compassionate heart and the universe responded with love and respect. Those elephants knew this language and felt it in their hearts, a powerful story I felt to share. We do not need to be trained animal communicators, as this man was not, but he did have a compassionate open heart towards the other species.

This story has been my own personal experience too, not with the label 'animal communicator', but one with a sensitive compassionate soul whose heart is open to feel with other species, who know our open hearts and respond to us in magical ways. There are many other stories from other lands, such as with lions who remember their compassionate carer's love and will return to feel that loving heart again, never forgetting them. The heart does not lie or forget, such as my own experiences with wildlife species I tried to save, who returned to me in spirit with a message to remind me how they felt my compassionate loving heart, and to keep sharing my open heart with all species who cross my path.

All species really want to connect with humans, as crazy as it may seem when you know how unconsciously cruel humans can be to them, and sometimes consciously cruel! The voiceless and powerless species, unable to stop humans, often endure the brunt of human anger and are blamed for frustrations they are not responsible for causing. Humans will place their anger physically towards other species who cannot voice their sensitive feelings.

What amazes me is when animals turn up in a pound and are forgiving, ready to love unconditionally again with a new carer. Sadly, some are so traumatised from what has happened to them previously they become fearful and feel the need to protect themselves from humans. That is the saddest of all cases, because humans will say, "...they have a behavior problem," and euthanase them in the shelter. Such a loss of a loving life and a disrespectful act. Could this scenario have been avoided if more humans learnt to commune more effectively from the heart with other species? Life can be so cruel for so many species on this earth.

There is much to share around how we treat other species and how we can make some big changes to connect with them. It is not too hard—we simply need to heal our hearts. That has been my experience, and it has taken me on some amazing, magical journeys beyond this 3D world. As a child, communing with other species kept me feeling loved and heard, something I felt was not available to me in my home. Other species were my family relations, dogs, bees, trees etc., so many species to commune with. As an adult, I have healed many layers of my wounded childhood years, and have found more magic that keeps opening up for me.

The sound I found with Mother Earth has given me unexpected moments with other species. I know they are feeling the sound from my heart and the earth as one. Living in a region with much wildlife around me, I feel privileged to hear their beautiful bird songs every day. They keep me inspired and I feel my heart open with the sounds they sing. I have learnt the difference between when they are singing a happy song or when there is a predator in the area.

We have many snakes here, and although I cannot hear them, I do get a sense of them being around our backyard. They rarely show themselves, as they are mostly shy, but we do find their rather large skins splashed around the yard at times. Only yesterday, a beautiful green tree snake turned up at my study window. I was on the computer, and looked up to see the green snake was sitting up and looking at me through the window. "Hello, we are out here." When he was done eye-balling me, he gracefully slid off along my garden furniture across the lawn. Living in harmony is sharing habitat with other species and not wanting to hurt one another. I love those moments when they come to say hello!

As a volunteer with the wildlife rescue service, I often took phone calls from the region I now live in. That was interesting, because if a snake appeared in some people's backyards, they would want them disposed of by the snake man. I would talk with them and say, "… they'll leave your pool area when the sun goes down," and the snakes did, while the people would share later how they had not seen them since. I suspect they had scared one another. I learnt snakes are generally not aggressive unless you are near a nest with babies, or you are threatening them. Ninety-nine percent of snake attacks are because people are scared and try to kill them, so the snake tries to defend itself. Who would not defend themselves under attack? That is a primal instinct. I hear so often that people use a shovel to try to kill a snake, then get attacked. That is so unnecessary! We must have respect for other species. If a snake is a threat to the family and needs to be removed due to its location, use a professional snake handler to take them safely to a new home.

On a walking trail many years ago, I stepped over a snake, unaware of its hidden location alongside a wooden step. I was not attacked, but my husband was behind me and the snake reared up at him. We suspect that his heavy walking over the ground disturbed the snake's sleep and he went into fight and flight mode. The snake quickly saw a place to disappear to in the bush and went at full speed after he reared up at my husband. We did not try to kill him. We stood very still, and the snake found a way out. Try not to corner a snake or they will try to defend themselves and rear at you.

> *My wisdom message from the snake soul, "…walk lightly on the land."*

A few years ago, my cat disappeared in an area known for snakes while we were staying on a friend's property. I eventually found him, sitting, looking eye-to-eye with a red-bellied black snake only a foot away. The snake, one of the deadliest in Australia, was reared up in attack position. I managed to grab my cat and the snake quickly slid away into the bush, almost faster than my eye could capture. Thank goodness he did not attack my cat, or me for that matter! I grabbed my cat without thinking about it, but that snake could easily have bitten me as I had placed myself at awfully close range. Later, I thought about my actions and what a dangerous position we were all placed in for a fatal incident. I guess instinct kicked in and I did not really think about it, and the snake, not cornered, found a way out. Lucky for me it turned out well for all of us.

Mother Earth is a powerful entity and force. She has her own natural cycles of balancing and knows how and when she will do this in divine timing. We are merely parasites living off her extraordinary, large earthly body. We will be recycled and returned to nourish her body when we also die. Only visitors to earth, we come as custodians to care for earth and other species, to live in harmony and peace within the cycles of life, not gods and masters who come to conquer and destroy the earth and all who inhabit her.

I am probably talking to the converted here, but I plead with you to think about what you support in your purchasing choices, and what you can support to improve the situation on this planet and stop the destruction. When the earth's resources are gone, we'll no longer have a home, nor will our future generations.

I'm not advocating everyone become a vegetarian/vegan, even though I'd love to see that. I realise we all have our own unique paths to follow. What I am suggesting is that we highlight the disrespect and dishonoring of animal's lives. Think of the toxic energy and chemicals you ingest into your own body when not consciously aware of how your food is mass produced. Do you think it might be time for us to question the practices of where and how food is farmed?

I hear some members of the next generation refusing to eat anything on their plate that has 'eyes, a mouth, and a mother.' These children are showing signs of being very evolved, with sensitive hearts. Do we need to consume such large quantities of animal products to be nourished? Eastern yogic traditions advocate tiny quantities of animal products in the diet, while the Western diet goes way beyond levels suggested for good health, causing dis-eases in our bodies.

Do you think because our lifestyle has become more sedentary, we may need less food consumption to reduce obesity—a health issue for Western cultures? Cancer sufferers who try alternative treatments usually omit animal products and go to plant-based options. Those I have spoken to who have healed after dis-ease report they feel more energy and the changes supported their healing journey. Enjoying the feeling of their body functioning more efficiently, many do not want to return to eating animal products after feeling the benefits. This has also been my own experience. I healed quicker, felt lighter and my body was working more efficiently.

I grew up on meat products at home with my family, but I became a vegetarian when I left home. It was not long before I noticed how I was not so easily triggered into being angry or frustrated in life. Do you think humans eating meat with toxic chemicals and the energetic memory of animal suffering held in their flesh could correlate to strong emotional reactions from toxicity, if consumed?

I have not done the research, nor am I a scientist, but I do know what I felt and there was a shift in my emotional triggers. Spiritual yogi training has taught me to reduce or avoid eating animal flesh due to the toxicity of the energy stored in the body of the animal, which is passed on to us when we ingest it. What we eat as fuel for our body will make us emotionally, physically and spiritually healthy or unhealthy.

Try it for yourself and observe any differences in your emotional state when animal products are omitted from your diet. The old argument that we need animal products for good health is being weakened these days by many great athletes and sporting professionals, even weight lifters, winning competitions as vegetarian/vegans. Do your own research, but I'm confident you'll also find people are living longer, with good quality of life, when on healthy vegetarian/vegan diets.

Changing to a vegetarian/vegan diet is not just a matter of leaving animal products out long term, or you will become deficient in some nutrients. It is also necessary to change your mindset around the type of recipes you use for healthy vegetarian/vegan options. There is a great deal of information on the Internet, making it easy to find healthy options to follow and learn a new way of eating. Our bodies have lightened up energetically, and with our sedentary lifestyle changes, would that not lead to needing to consume less food? Why would we not make some changes to our diet for better health and harmony in the body, knowing that without toxins we can vibrate at a higher frequency?

Humans disrespect our own kind. This is a true story I experienced in a remote community in Australia that I found very disturbing, but a reality check. Many people lack compassion as their own pain and suffering clouds their unconscious actions. How can we have respect for other species when we treat our own species disrespectfully? What follows is a story of disrespect for a fellow human I witnessed while working as a Remote Area Nurse in a large community clinic of the central desert region.

A young Aboriginal woman presented at the clinic in pain. Six months pregnant, she had been healthy until that point, but now complained of back pain and requested pain relief. Assessing her, my gut feeling was she could be having a miscarriage. Communicating with the flying doctor service, I explained the case and asked if she could be flown to a hospital as she had a history of miscarriages. Something kept telling me there was more going on for this young girl and she needed more complex specialist care.

The flying doctor on call was new and did not agree. He suggested strong pain relief for her back pain and observing her response. I felt he did not take it seriously, even though I had shared her history of miscarriages and her vital signs, and my own personal experience of miscarriage.

Over several hours, we cared for her and gave the prescribed doses. Then she became more distressed, so I made an urgent request to get her on a flying doctor flight out of the community to Perth or Adelaide hospital. He said he was sorry, there was no available plane. The medical team were delivering complex births on a property many miles away and there were two more bookings ahead of us—not what I needed to hear.

Another nurse on duty worked with me to comfort this poor young woman and care for her with everything we had available to us at the clinic. When she began having contractions we had to prepare for the baby's delivery, as the flying doctor team would not be with us for several hours yet. We were experienced nurses, but not midwives, and dealing with a complicated delivery. The midwife was on holidays at the time, so we had to deliver the baby on our own—something we had not done before.

We contacted the flying doctor service again and all agreed the doctor would talk us through the delivery process, communicating via two-way radio. Sadly, it was a difficult birth for her. The young woman began haemorrhaging and her baby was stillborn, devastating for her and us.

When we spoke to the doctor, his reaction was to say that had the baby had survived it would have needed an intensive care unit in a hospital to thrive. *Yes, if we had sent her earlier that would have been available,* I thought! As we completed the delivery process, the flying doctor service rang to say it was too dark, and there were too many camels on the runway for the plane to land. I had to jump in our clinic ambulance, turn the lights on and go scare the camels off the runway.

The young mum's husband was not at the birth, a cultural decision, as birthing was seen as 'women's business'. We called him to see the baby before the mum, and the baby in a little padded container, were taken to the tarmac to board the plane. That was the last we saw of the baby. Working in the remote clinic we always honoured the cultural requests and customs of the community, and one important custom was to have the body returned to do ceremony and release the soul.

This part saddened me so much. I rang the flying doctor service the next day, and the hospital ward, and the pathology department trying to find the baby's remains, but no one wanted to help or seemed to know anything about it. Apparently, when the young mum arrived on the ward her baby was taken, and she never saw the baby again. We had to check the baby before leaving the clinic—it was twenty-six weeks old and appeared to be perfectly formed, looking like a healthy baby. I had never seen a baby at that development stage out of the womb. What surprised me was how perfect and fully formed the baby boy looked, with no apparent external dysfunctions. It was hard to believe he had been a stillborn delivery.

All our hearts were heavy after this event, as we all knew the girl and her family. I continued to ring the hospital for days and could not believe how rude and uncompassionate staff were when they found out it was an Indigenous baby from a community. I was embarrassed to say I was of the same species.

The girl received a couple of blood transfusions and returned to the community very depressed. I visited her most days to sit with her in silence and know I felt her pain. I felt she responded in positive ways to my visits and looked forward to them, but I had to leave the clinic myself with a health issue and was unable to return. This has been heavy in my heart as I know the importance of doing ceremony for a soul who has passed away in the Aboriginal culture, as I was privileged to be invited to their ceremonies and burials. The disrespect for the cultural needs of the girl were sadly overlooked. She struggled to get on with her life, and the family were also affected by the ignorant actions of the hospital. A piece of her heart may never heal due to this cultural disrespect.

If we treat our own species in this way, how can we respect other species? We need to be respectful of all beings who cross our path. The human species still has much to learn.

Have you witnessed disrespect and exploitation by humans towards other species on this planet?
Do you have any ideas on how you can be part of the solution to stop it?

37

Human Interference

I was excited to witness the annual pilgrimage of sea turtles on the north coast of Australia as they made their way from the ocean up to the beach to lay hundreds of eggs. There were many people across the beach, I thought too many, but we were directed to stand around a hole where a turtle was laying her eggs.

I noticed a number of junior and senior researchers rush to the turtles as they laid their eggs in the holes they had painstakingly spent quite some time digging. The science people were all over the turtles, taking measurements of their shells and checking them in any way they could while the turtles were laying their eggs. I felt this was disrespectful towards this dear, beautiful species who had been doing this for thousands of years, and now had to contend with humans interfering. I really felt for the turtles with all the distractions going on, and had to question this activity with the researchers.

"Is this not disruptive to the turtle when she's trying to lay all these eggs?" I asked.

The response, "Oh no, she's in a trance, she can't feel us around her taking all these measurements."

The researcher's answer did not convince me at all. I believe all species are aware of the energetic unified field that surrounds us all. If you have been a mother and given birth, you will know it would be very disruptive to the birthing process of this miracle of life. If you know anything about quantum physics, you'll know observing an experiment can change it because our energy field is interacting with the observed object (person or turtle). Because we are all interrelated energetically, if we interact physically or observe another species, we are changing the unified energy field with our frequency and our focused attention.

Speaking to some local fishermen the following day, I mentioned the turtle sanctuary and they shared that they also had been watching turtles for years and seen them in the ocean. They had a lot of knowledge about them and told us they had never been asked by the researchers about what they had observed and learnt over many years of living with them and watching them arrive annually. I assumed it might be the type of knowledge the Indigenous people would know while living with turtles for many generations, watching them and interacting with them, respectfully honouring them. I felt so upset about this I tried to write a letter to the research team, but it kept coming out passionately angry, which would not be helpful to someone unconsciously trying to help them, so I stopped and decided I would try later.

Whilst cruising on a wildlife tour around the south east coast tip of Australia into the Bass Strait, the skipper shared his past as a deep-sea fisherman in the region, which gave him exceptional knowledge of the water currents we were passing through, seen as unpredictable and dangerous at times. The skipper had experienced a change of heart and began taking tourists on wildlife cruises. Witnessing extraordinary beauty and much change over many years working on the ocean, he was passionate about helping others to see the great, unique beauty of wildlife in the region and became more sensitive to saving it, through educating and showing tourists all the wild inhabitants of the sea.

On approaching a small island, a huge monolith of granite rock dwarfed our large cruising boat. It stood upright out of the ocean, with steep sloping rock faces on all sides. Its inhabitants were an Australian fur seal lion colony. The seals were using it as their home, birthing place and nursery for their babies, and we could see them all sitting along the steep slope of the rock face. The skipper shared a story of the insensitivity of scientists who visited one time. Just telling the story really upset him; we also felt his compassion for the seals. He was out fishing on his trawler and noticed dead baby seals and young adults floating around the ocean near the seal island. Confused, he went to see what had happened.

Apparently, a well-known scientist from overseas had come in a helicopter to research the fur seals up close. He could have landed by boat, but chose to land on top of the huge island rock in a helicopter.

The seals had never seen or heard a helicopter before. The noise alone must have been terrifying for them. The seals went into a frenzy and the huge male bull seals, larger than the others in the colony, charged down over the steep rock face, stampeding the babies and mums as they all tried to get away from the noise and unknown object.

Babies landed in the water and drowned, as they were still in nursery stage and not ready to go to the ocean. Others were crushed. I was horrified to hear this. My heart sank. All this occurred because of the insensitivity and unconscious actions of the scientist. Their clumsy actions left them without seeing or tagging the seals. What a sad story. The skipper was careful not to go too close to the island as he shared this story. It was months after the event, and he was still traumatised by what he had experienced in the ocean waters with the wildlife.

I struggle with scientists who don't have sensitivity in their hearts and treat other species as objects to be exploited for their own benefit. Another time, I witnessed this firsthand while camping at a famous national park in south-eastern Australia. I had been walking and exploring the park trails and came across a grassland area with kangaroos grazing. It appeared they were free to come and go, but they each had six coloured tags punched into their ears and radar collars on their necks. Extremely sensitive to Wi-Fi waves, I feel cloudy-headed and get headaches if it is strong, so I immediately felt for the poor little kangaroos.

How can we justify a kangaroo wearing all these devices when we have studied them for many years in Australia? The sign I found stated the tags were for research for a science student's thesis. I felt so sad. How was that going to help these poor kangaroos? At the same time, only a short distance away, kangaroos are being culled across Australia because some believe them to be pests or a problem on their properties, eating the grass or drinking from the waterhole the sheep or cows drink from. Am I crazy, or is this disrespectful to another species to be killing them and limiting their activity and causing harm for research projects?

The question here is will animal wildlife research bring more respect to the wild species? Will it change our disrespectful and traumatic practices towards them, to honour them, or is it the illusion of the ego taking over, thinking we are so intelligent, know it all and are more important? What happens to all this research? Is it used against the species—because I am not seeing changes to benefit them? They come to earth as souls wanting to feel peace and share love with us. We need to stop seeing them as separate from us. We are them and they are us energetically. We all share the same universal field of energy that surrounds us, connecting us.

We are All One.

There are so many examples of disrespect for other species on this planet. Humans are not superior, yet our vanity sees us unthinkingly accept the belief we are more important than animals. I highlight that as the beauty and pharmaceutical industries test products on animals and rodents, leaving them blinded, tortured and maimed for life, or dying slow deaths. I believe these to be some of the most insensitive and blatantly cruel practices on earth, and it has been allowed to go on for many years, accepted by the human race in our research institutions.

If our hearts were sensitive and felt connected to everything in oneness, we wouldn't be able to do such cruel things to another sentient being, because we'd feel their suffering and disrespect in our own bodies. Sadly, many are desensitised, and I feel we still have so far to go in this area of feeling separate to other species on earth.

I have worked in the corporate marketing sector, so I know if no one buys the products the industry will change their practices to accommodate the market needs, but they hide the truth as it continues behind doors. We have the power as consumers to change the marketplace so easily—by silently protesting, only buying products that state on the packaging 'not tested on animals' and by asking questions of the industries. I beg of you, please be a conscious buyer. You can make a difference by changing the marketplace, saving the lives of many sentient beings.

There are too many exploitations on this planet that we need to question. It's time to change our thinking and behaviours towards other species by respecting them as souls equal to us. I am deeply passionate about other species because I have communicated with their dear souls. They deserve a life of peace and harmony on this earth. They all have much wisdom to share—you would be surprised at what they know about the planet and life. The saddest thing is that they want to help us. Why, I wonder, when we are so disrespectful towards other species?

**A message from Charles/Grandfather.
Subject: Wisdom on Respecting Other Species.**

Charles: Animals are still not respected, for these beautiful souls also have a mission they come to earth to do. It is not natural to have them in handbags, to be indoors with no outdoor activities when they are needing to be earthed. Just as the human race does, they need the energy source of Mother Earth to keep them healthy, as well as good quality organic foods, not the foods mass produced from other dead animals who may have died due to a disease like cancer. The animal food authorities do not have any regulations for manufacturers to ensure that quality food is prepared for animal species.

Please let your people know it is quality food they need, sunlight, and earthing with their paws on the ground. They have many superior senses to humans. Their sense of smell has a greater wisdom than most humans—they can detect disease. Their smell is so developed it's similar to the detail you see in many things around you, that is why they are used for the police and military groups, as they already know this sense to be highly developed.

Sadly, they are exploited in these environments and have short lives as they wear the physical body of these animal souls out at a younger age by over-working them.

Why do humans have to keep doing this to other species—because they do not feel connected to the world or other species around them. Their hearts are full of wounding that needs to be healed to find their sensitive side to be connected and not feel separate from the world. When they do this, when the heart heals, as you dear one, have realised, so much can be experienced on the planet and so much more love can come to you. When people's hearts are healed they feel more love, and then more love is sent out around them.

If you feel connected to everything around you, like all nature and Mother Earth, you cannot in your heart of hearts injure another being or species because you will also feel their pain within your own heart. This is why so many on your planet need to be healing their hearts at this time. If they stay disconnected they will become dis-eased from this separation, will not resonate with Mother Earth's new resonance, their energetic field will be out of balance and they will be taken off the planet by an unhealthy body (diseased).

Healing comes from the energetic body, then moves down to the mental and physical body. That is how healing is done.

Mother Earth can also help with this healing. If the people go to her, she will help them, as she has done for you dear one, many times. If you remember, you could share some of those times Mother Earth has helped you heal. This will help others understand how it works and how it feels to have that experience, and that it is real for them when they feel it.

Each soul is an energetic vibration of force that is contained in a human body when on earth. When not in a human suit or other species' bodysuit, it is part of the consciousness all around us that we can feel.

There is no separation, dear ones, it is an illusion to the human race.

We are all connected as energetic beings of the light and love in the ocean of consciousness. That is what you really are.

38
Cows, Calves and Karma

Hopefully, when humans gain the concept and believe that we are all connected energetically, we will have the courage to start questioning many unconscious, disrespectful actions taking place in our world that may not resonate with our sensitive hearts as we raise our vibration.

A practice I've long questioned is the exploitation of cows, disrespected as a commodity for dairy and meat products in mass production farming. I have friends who owned a dairy farm many years ago that had been passed down through generations. When I visited and camped on the land, I learnt a great deal about the dairy industry that maybe I'd have preferred to not know in some ways, but was glad to be enlightened to share this information.

Have you ever questioned the constant supply of milk from cows on a dairy farm? For us to have dairy products, cows are forced to fall pregnant constantly to provide milk. That means most young calves are taken from their mothers within a few days.

I do not know about you, but I have felt the emotions and love that cows give us and have watched them with their calves. The sadness cows feel when they lose their calves is heart-wrenching. Male calves are most often taken to the abattoir to be killed for veal meat that goes to your table if you eat veal. As animals are very sensitive to energies, they can pick up on the pain and suffering of other animals who have died in those abattoirs. Can you imagine what suffering a little calf feels when he is going to that place to die?

I did eat meat before I became vegetarian in my early twenties, but my body has had a sensitivity to cows' milk since I was a child. Maybe my soul knew at a deeper level and was trying to tell me not to have dairy? If a human mother and child are separated it is incredibly traumatic because they are connected energetically for up to three years of age before energetically separating. That is wisdom of the yogic traditions, and my personal feelings on the subject. Here in Australia, we hear the stories of stolen generations of our Aboriginal culture where children were taken against their will and how this has traumatized generations of this culture. My own mother was traumatized in her early childhood, when taken from her family.

I find it so painful to know that is what we are doing to these poor cows and calves on a consistent basis for the cows to provide milk for human consumption. Their whole life is traumatized by having offspring who we keep taking away from them. Have you heard cows cry for their young when they are taken away in trucks, and the calves crying for their mothers?

If we have compassionate hearts, how can we see this going on without questioning if it is right? We have become desensitized over generations, justifying it is acceptable for them to experience this trauma and suffering.

Looking again at energy when trauma is experienced—it is held in the body energetically. If we drink milk from a mother who has been traumatized and is depressed her whole life, do you think we may be taking that energy into our own bodies when we consume their body flesh or their milk?

While at my friend's dairy farm in the '90s, I found out that cows experience mastitis. It can be an ongoing problem, so the dairy industry's solution was to mandate farmers to mix antibiotics with the milk. Every time we drink cows' milk products, we are taking in these antibiotics, the milk is thus a toxic combination of emotional energy and physical chemicals. My friend had stage four advanced cancer and had to stop his dairy farm and heal himself. He chose to become vegan and detoxed his body with the support and guidance of a naturopath. He successfully cured himself, surprising all the doctors. When he healed his body, his heart also gained healing and he was unable to practice dairy farming in the mass production approach any longer, even though that was all he ever knew after thirty years.

He loved his cows and treated them kindly. I believe he never really wanted to give the antibiotics, and deep down he struggled with the separation of the cows and calves. When his body detoxed, he became more conscious, lightened up, and was no longer desensitized to what his work entailed, finally able to question the whole system he had grown up with on the family farm.

> *I believe that deep down in all our human hearts we do not want to harm others, but we live in a system that brainwashes us to believe we have to do this for our own good, at the expense of other species. And that is when we are setting up karma on the planet by leaving all this pain and suffering in the energetic field around the earth.*

I remember reading a doctor's research on breast cancer and dairy products for women, comparing Asian and Western cultures. She reported that Asian women rarely experience breast cancer problems on dairy-free Asian diets, compared to Western women who experienced high levels of breast cancer when they consumed dairy products on Western diets. If we truly believe we are all connected energetically, it makes sense that when we cause harm to another species it will return to us in some way. Do you think that may be karmic? What goes around comes around—could this be the result of our own insensitive actions towards another species, directly related to our unconscious actions?

I highlight here that there have been less abusive practices used by humans to collect milk in past generations, not the mass scale we see happening now, with cows turned into robotic machines, like many other species who provide us with food. This so saddens me. We need to be more conscious of how we do not honour other species and how poorly we treat them, mass producing them for food. I feel this needs to be addressed, and one way that I know works is to educate people on how their food reaches the table. This has been kept secret over the years by the industries involved.

Humans have become so desensitized by our culture, almost robotic with no questioning, to go to the supermarket and buy food, unaware of what the poor animals souls have suffered or the toxic energy stored in their bodies. When humans have cancer, the first change made if they take a natural approach will be ditching meat products, or at least reducing consumption, to assist with their healing. Do you see a link here of us all being connected? When I stopped eating animal products many years ago, I noticed a shift in my personality to feeling more passive and sensitive, to being less angry and reactive, and my body health improved.

Are you aware of the culling that takes place in Australia?

Australian government authorities agree on culling our precious wildlife, as they believe it is so abundant—or is it because they gain monetarily by taking habitat from wildlife who live on land, seeing wildlife as less valuable than profit?

Instead of honouring the wildlife and animals, they remove them to gain what they want from the land. Those species have a right to be here too. We need to share our land, not take it for our own selfish gains. Every species has a purpose as part of the ecology balance and each species' soul growth.

Australia is a land of many extremes, quite different to other continents, but this land knows how to find the balance. When we are in abundant cycles with rain, many of the animals and wildlife have big breeding numbers. Then the cycle changes and we go into drought, and much of the wildlife struggles to keep offspring. The weakest do not survive, that's nature balancing, but they also try to survive to the best of their ability, and that means finding waterholes and grasslands wherever they can, even if it is on farmers' lands. They do not see boundaries unless the farmer has erected an electric fence. They are simply surviving, as humans would in hard times, and will do whatever they need to keep surviving.

Sadly, it becomes a battle of the species in Australia, as many farmers believe they have the right to shoot any species they do not wish to share their land with for food and water. Take the kangaroo species—they mean no harm, they are just living and surviving, but they can be shot if found on a farmer's land.

It is always about the money, and we disrespect the beautiful wild species who have lived in harmony with other species, sharing the grasses and waterholes. Man comes along and changes all that as they are greedy for money and feel separate to the other species. Unconscious humans can be such a beastly species with their disrespect of other species, destroying the peace and joy on this planet, not understanding that other species could be living in harmony with us if we rethink our harsh practices.

Eating animals is unnecessary and selfish when we can learn new ways. There is no need to kill other species disrespectfully to eat them when we can practice honouring their lives respectfully. Many humans live healthy lives without eating meat. When our animals are seen as a commodity, we treat them poorly and condemn them to a life of misery.

My friend has a wildlife sanctuary next door to a property where sheep are bred for the abattoir, and she tells me how upsetting it is to hear the call of the lambs and mothers as they are separated when the trucks arrive. And yet, the farmers seem oblivious to this fact and continue to breed and separate them, placing them onto trucks for the abattoir for more money. We need to be more conscious to the emotional needs of other species, not to ignore their needs. They have hearts that are being broken, as ours would be in the same circumstances, or they would not be fretting for their young ones.

If no one wanted meat there would be no need for the farmers to keep breeding and causing all this pain and suffering to these beautiful animals, and taking more habitat from wildlife species. We treat chickens like they are a piece of dirt, throwing them onto conveyer belts. I have seen the chicken industry scoop up baby chicks and throw them down into death machines. Alive and fully conscious, they are crunched up for some food source like they are worthless. They are not, they have a consciousness and can feel like our own children. They share the earth with us and have a mission here too with family.

Just because we do not understand the consciousness or language of another species is no reason to think about or treat them so disrespectfully. Keeping them in cages where they cannot even move, as is the case for many farmed pigs and chickens, makes my heart feel painful with the thoughts of what they must be feeling. We are sending out more pain and suffering in our energetic field—this is not the way to bring peace and harmony to this once beautiful planet that has so much to offer all species. Every species has a part to play. Our lack of understanding of the puzzle of life is no reason to disrespect another species the way we do.

We waste so much food on this planet now and throw it away. This killing and waste has to stop, and can only do so when we heal our own hearts of pain and suffering and become kind to ourselves, for then we feel the sensitivity to respect and be kind to other species who do deserve to be respected and not brutally killed.

The oceans fare no better, for we reap them of sea creatures with such disrespect, dragging everything within a wide distance into fishing nets and throwing them out if they are not to be kept, such as dolphins, killing them. This is so shameful. Sea creatures have no time to replenish due to the high rate at which we take them from the oceans. We disrespect them further by throwing away any who do not fit our market criteria of buying and selling. Humans are so greedy, not taking only what we need. The Indigenous tribes took only what they needed, and have kept the food chain going for thousands of years. It is time to honour another's life and give gratitude for what is given to us as a gift from Mother Earth so all species can all live in harmony with humans. I find having gratitude for every meal a good practice to remind me of all the species who contributed to my food landing on my plate.

39

Killing with Kindness

Writing about the abusive and disrespectful behaviours of humans, I feel so much tightness and discomfort in my own body, as I know this is so true and needs to be shared. The problem is we are trained in our Western thinking to believe humans are superior, and we are not acknowledging other species have wisdom too. What if their souls have greater wisdom than humans to share? The soul chooses to come and experience and learn through another body form, such as an animal species. They also come to support us, as many already know our souls from other lives, something I know about from my own experiences with many of my beautiful furry soul companions. What if, in past lives, we have visited earth in many forms?

Many species come to show us what unconditional love feels like and how they have great strength, to inspire others no matter what happens to their physical bodies, such as amputees or those with severe injuries who continue to be joyful and keep trying to accommodate the limitation with great gusto. How could humans not be inspired by what some animals endure from humans' unconscious behaviours? I do hope from my sharing with many species that many will see there are other ways to treat our furry companions and wildlife, firstly with respect.

I should mention too that there are also people killing their furry friends with kindness. How is it that some are carried in handbags and treated like ornaments? We need to touch the earth often so our bodies can be healthy, getting the energy from the earth's organic battery that's powered by the sun and by the crystals beneath the earth's core. Animals need to feel the earth with their paws to get this healing energy from Mother Earth's organic battery. This keeps our energetic field tuned up to feel more alive, and importantly, reduces inflammation that can cause dis-ease to our bodies. When we do not spend time barefooted with the earth to balance our body's energy system, our bodies can become unhealthy. The life force of Mother Earth is crucial for the good health of all species.

The food we feed ourselves and our furry friends needs to be healthy, organic and compatible for our bodies. The animal foods are mostly processed foods made from other dead animals with diseases, which passes the diseases to our companions. Dogs who live off the land and fresh kill will often live longer, healthier lives than many dogs in domestic homes who die young from cancer and other dis-eases that their bodies cannot heal when they are not receiving Mother Earth's energy to help them stay healthy energetically. There is so much I have learnt from my furry soul companion friends, and I share this with you here, to question and research the sources of food processing. If you can offer the best for your furry friend and show the respect you would for your own children, they will love you for it.

> *What if your animal companion was the soul of your ancestor, a relative from your past who chose to come to help you in an animal body form?*

Would that change your actions towards your animal companions and other species?

We can learn much from the souls of our children, they can be our teachers. I never had children. I chose not to when I was quite young. My furry soul companions have told me they came to me in animal form to help me as they knew I would not have children, so this way they could reach and support me. I've many stories on this subject, how they have come to help me even when I did not know I was going to need them. They knew I would need help, and did not leave my side, giving me healing even when I was unconsciously aware.

One time, I was visiting a dog pound and my heart felt broken on hearing the dogs' plights. I offered the dogs healing if they wished to receive it. My hands were burning with the heat coming from many of them. I had to do distant healing from a park nearby. The dogs were trying to communicate with me, but I had trouble concentrating due to the barking distracting me from receiving their messages.

The message I heard the loudest and most often was that they were confused. "Why are we here?" The dogs were going to be euthanased after fourteen days if no carers were found. Hearing that reality absolutely broke my heart.

Please, I beg you—if you would like a furry companion,
please consider a visit to a dog pound.

You will find the most loyal, loving and beautiful souls—souls who shouldn't be discarded simply because people are tired of them. And still, people will go to a pet shop that supports puppy farm breeding for dogs, and others only want pedigree breeding, while we have so many souls without homes being put to death by the painful death needle.

I ask this of you: Please consider what you are supporting for a more peaceful world.

40

Horses and Me

I do not believe humans have the right to play God over other species.

And yet, exploitation is what I see every day, wherever I look. Since childhood, I have witnessed humans disrespecting other species, exploiting them, not hearing their calls, their wisdom, nor honouring their lives for who they really are and their missions on earth.

What other species really deserve, and need, is unconditional love.

Writing this chapter has challenged me, taking me to painful memories that I felt vividly in my youth, but pushed down as I grew into adulthood. Observing this in so many others, I believe humans tend to become desensitised when we see the suffering of others, as it can be too paralysing to do anything.

My passion is to be the voice of the voiceless here on earth. By sharing my experiences, I hope that you will relate to your own sad feelings, giving you an opportunity to heal your own heart. My dream is to motivate and inspire people to help the voiceless species, instead of the human pattern of avoidance and ignoring what we know in our hearts to be unacceptable disrespect, with so many species kept in captivity for entertainment, killing them, eating them, allowing them to starve, and using them for research. This is what we try to ignore, but this is the truth of what goes on.

Our food chain is so well hidden that many have no idea of the suffering other species experience before ending up served on the table as food. Worse, if they do know, many do not want to acknowledge what really goes on in the mass production food processing plants. When we block this out of our radar, the suffering of the species is sent out into the energetic field of the planet and keeps us in a cycle of pain and suffering. If other species suffer, so do we. While many do not feel the connection to all species, what we do to them we reap for our own karma, causing our own unhappiness.

> *If our hearts can never find the freedom and joy of unconditional love, they become dark with pain from denial. All suffering we send out will come back to us—it is called karma.*

Can we not see this cycle? Please know this is what we are setting up for ourselves—more unhappiness and less peace in the world. Send out love and peace and that is what will be returned to you. We cannot send out unconditional love when our hearts are heavy with hurts, grief, and pain from not forgiving others. This is a recipe for a heavy heart that will not find freedom or joy, and will not know unconditional love when it's sent to us.

The distortion that pain and suffering create in the energetic field of a species affects everyone and everything around us. This is how the human species is seen at this point, distorted energy moving around the earth, unable to hold pure unconditional love for ourselves, and so it's not possible to share with others. It is necessary to find love within before we can share it outside of ourselves, otherwise we are in delusion, or as the Yogic tradition calls it, the Maya mind (delusion of our reality). So much can be changed so easily, as I have shared with you. It can be done—healing the heart is possible and feels very freeing and joyful when you go beyond the fear of your mind and follow the heart's way.

As I sit and write my story, it triggers old memories of the pain stored in my body. I know it rises to be healed. I observe as the witness so this shadow can be released, for allowing more space for light and love to enter into my expanded heart allows unconditional love to be present. A lot of pain has shown up. I had no idea how much occupied my heart space, keeping me in unconscious discomfort. This pain body has probably triggered me often and I have not been aware of it.

Unconsciously, I stored so much pain and suffering from what I have absorbed, seen and heard in this world around disrespect for other species. I have tried to desensitise myself when this painful feeling arises, as so many do, finding distractions because we feel unable to do anything about it. We keep the pain in ourselves, where it shadows the light in our hearts, so we miss feeling unconditional love for ourselves and for other species. When we disrespect another species and feel it in our own bodies, we suffer too. Our body will need to balance this energy at a later time, that's karma.

It is time to acknowledge we are all ultimately connected to one another, and not energetically separate from anything on earth. Thousands of years of pain and suffering felt by all species needs to be released from the human race. We are here on earth to heal ourselves and support Mother Earth to evolve, free of pain and suffering. Everyone has their own journey of healing, and it helps if we do not take things personally from others. If we can remember this and keep our own heart open, we can release the hurts as they arise. It is not the time to be holding on to toxic emotions. We humans are destined for greater things, like finding freedom and joy, for that will assist our own and Mother Earth's evolution.

Next, I share here some examples of exploitation that came to mind whilst I wrote this chapter. They arose for me to share with you to offer healing.

Step into magic by physically spending time with a horse and feel their spirit take you to places you cannot imagine possible.

Although I never had the privilege of owning a horse, I have had many experiences with horses. I learnt you do not have to own a horse to have a joyful and powerful experience. As a child I was fascinated, wanting to ride and care for a horse, but my parents would not agree to buy one.

That confused me, as my grandfather had a large property where I could have left my horse. I believe they were fearful of the cost, which I guess was realistic given that we were not a wealthy family.

Horse riding schools were a favourite place for me. From a young age, I would pay for several hours and always loved feeling their strength, power and spirit when we went at speed. I was never scared of horses. I would talk to them and encourage them to take me faster and faster, wanting to feel the wind and freedom of spirit within me. At about twelve years of age, I was enjoying a fast gallop with a horse, but when we came to a fence, he stopped dead in front of it, which left me in the air, then crashing to the ground on my bottom. I was with my cousins at the time, and everyone came running to see if I was alright.

I stood up a bit sore and with a few bruises, but that did not stop me in any way. I got back on and walked back to the stables. Nothing was going to stop me riding horses. I found them so exciting to ride, travelling powerfully in oneness, feeling our free spirits together. The day I came off I blamed myself for pushing the horse to go faster, not realising there was a fence hidden in the bush. Lucky the horse knew, or we may have become a big, tangled mess and I could have been a lot worse off. Back at the stable I patted him and thanked him for letting me ride him. I always found out a horse's name and used it, talking with them while I rode, my respectful acknowledgement of them as kindred souls.

In my late teens I would go riding with a friend who also loved horses. I still did not have my own, so continued going to riding schools to hire them for a few hours. One place I visited had a beautiful horse, a white palomino, not a tall horse at fourteen hands, but the first time I rode her it was like we were best mates. She was such a gem to ride! I felt like we were one as she did turns and spins with me and I found it easy to hold on. I was not exactly the best rider in those early days, but I picked up enough techniques to get me through. Every weekend we went to the riding school I asked to ride her, because I felt her heart to be big and kind, even though she was a smaller horse.

Apparently, she had been a camp draft horse in the Northern Territory of Australia and the owner had given her up to the riding school. I never did find out why. Maybe she was past the fast action stage they need to be in for competitions? That did not worry me, she was plenty fast enough and a real treat to ride as she rode like she knew I was with her in spirit. I always felt safe, like she was protecting me at every turn. I sure did like those barrel turns she would do on the track.

I have always felt it a privilege to ride horses and feel their spirit, strength and speed. The connection of one species to another—you cannot explain it, you just know it in your heart, and they are with you all the way.

In my twenties, I met a new friend who had three horses in agistment twenty kilometres out of Sydney. I did not have to think about it when she asked if I would like to meet the horses and go riding! We ventured out many weekends to check their feed and water and groom them, ride them and spend time simply being with them. The first visit was interesting, for as much as I loved horses and never felt scared of them (unlike my cousins and sister), I would jump straight up and ride any horse, I was a little taken aback when I saw these horses. At seventeen hands they were so tall!

Ex-racehorses, they were lean thoroughbreds and looked majestic in the paddock. They always came running to the gate when my friend called them, amazing me with their sheer size and power. My friend showed me how to groom. I had never had that privilege before and was very tentative and intimidated by the size of them. A great help and teacher, my friend said, "They're just like big dogs, treat them like big dogs."

I did, and that was the point I realised I did not need to be intimidated by their size. They *were* like big dogs, and I already had a great rapport with many dogs. I had no fear after that day of grooming. Later, we went riding through the countryside, in rivers, and swimming in dams. I could not believe it! It was like heaven on earth for me with those majestic animals, such joy to feel the power and wisdom they showed with such intelligence and sensitivity.

I have ridden many horses in many locations over the years. I remember I thought the riding school horses knew who you were by psychic means, so knew how to treat each rider. I always ended up with the most spirited horses, even as one of the youngest riders at times.

One special experience was at the disability riding school. I volunteered with Riding For The Disabled, a group who take children with severe disabilities for rides out into the paddocks one day a week. The children experienced severe limitations. Some needed braces, while others could not even sit straight on the horse or hold the reins alone. Many had no language and were unable to move their limbs. When they met the horses something truly magical took place that I can hardly describe, but we could all feel it in our hearts. There was so much excitement, but also a peace and calm around the horses' behaviours. They knew the children were special and had limitations.

To see and feel the connection the horses had with the children was miraculous. They really knew the children's capabilities and took it slow, even though volunteers like me were holding the rains as they walked with the children. The bliss and joy I witnessed from those children, and the kindness I saw from those gentle ex-race horses, was extraordinary. I felt so blessed to be there to have that experience.

I believe they showed me great wisdom, and that all horses have immense wisdom and the intuitive ability to know things way beyond what we see or feel with our own senses.

I choose not to ride horses any longer. In my heart, since I became more conscious of the souls of other species and began communing with them at a deeper level in the language of love, I no longer feel it to be right for many reasons.

What I find unbearably painful and upsetting at this time is that this incredible species is being culled—wild Brumby horses in the Snowy River Mountain country, part of our history, helping stockman for as long as white man has settled in those areas. I am devastated to hear reports of hundreds of them being seen as pests because they are sharing the same feed land as the livestock farmers' cows and sheep. The argument is they are destroying the natural ecology of the land. I believe it is the farmers over-stocking their properties with farm animals who do the damage kept behind fences. The horses are on the move, having learnt to live there in the wild, and are not doing the damage livestock confined to a paddock can do.

Recently, the culling shooters were in helicopters shooting these beautiful wild horses from the air. When I tuned in to them, remotely viewing them in meditation, I could see and feel the pain and confusion they were going through—mothers shot down and young foals confused as to what they had witnessed. The adult horses were in shock and running in circles, lost and confused at seeing the cold-blooded murder of their herds.

This is so inhumane!

These are sentient, intelligent beings who feel with their hearts. How could we do this to them? It is criminal. I believe those who allow and enact such cruelty are unconscious humans and do not know what they are doing, or the impact this has on the herds, filling them with fear and shock. None of these horses have ever experienced this before. They are trembling with fear as I remote view them.

Billy Dean, a friend who has a sanctuary 'A Place of Peace', a home for injured and rescued animals, sent a truck to the killing area to collect as many Brumbies as she could before they were culled in this act of cold-blooded murder. That is all I can call this heart-breaking action—murder. Billy has so many animals on her property she had to limit the number, but even so, she still took quite a high number. Tragically, it was nowhere near enough to save them all. Billy is a shaman, consciously awake, and her compassionate heart feels for all species and communes with them all, a soul who walks her talk to support peace on earth. I respect the great work she is doing to offer lifetime peace to other species. I have been to her sanctuary and am humbled in gratitude. Those Brumby horses are so happy in the paddocks with others of their own kindred spirits. They know they have been saved to live a life of peace.

The Brumby horses left behind in the mountains were wounded, not dead. They were left lying in pain, until they were taken to the cannery for dog food. It makes me feel ill to think of it. How can we do this to another species in cold blood with no respect for their life on this planet? Every time we kill animals inhumanely, they are condemned into fear when they pass over, their souls not able to pass over completely into a higher realm of existence energetically. Their pain and suffering are left as an imprint in the consciousness of the earth's energetic field, for more pain and suffering to be played out. Bless those horse souls not released respectfully, as they died feeling shock, despair, and pain, and suffered dreadfully and unnecessarily.

My interaction with horses has taught me how psychic they are. They know me, and I feel their great power and strength holding me in their caring ways. They remind me of my free-spirited nature, and I have felt their unconditional love expand my heart immediately, feeling sensitive to their great love and in oneness with them and all nature around me in those moments of unconditional love and joy we shared.

Have you ever thought about a horse's power and mystery, seldom seen in other species? And their nature—quite independent, yet majestically strong and beautiful, they befriend us, they care. They can express unbridled rage, yet can be gentle and sensitive with strong psychic awareness. The worst pain they endure is isolation, as they are a herd species. Horses have lived on earth for millions of years, roaming freely before humans tamed them. The gift a horse gives to humans is freedom and power (still used as a measurement). Horses, more than any other species, have assisted in human evolution with our travel, at speed, and giving humans mobility.

Do You Feel Humankind has a Debt to pay to Horses?

As I write, I feel their pain in my chest. It causes me such discomfort to think they are lost and unable to leave this earthly plain in peace as they so deserve. They did not hurt anyone—they simply ran naturally around the mountains with the other wildlife. This is such a problem on earth—we keep killing animals cold-heartedly, leaving their shocked and fearful energy imprinted in the conscious energetic field that surrounds our planet. This is not helpful when Mother Earth is raising her vibration and wants to have a place of peace for all. She will do this with or without humans, but we are making it more difficult for ourselves to move beyond the cold 3D reality of pain and suffering and making more karma for ourselves, not finding the joy and peace we could all have if we simply respected other species.

41
Value all Life

Lack of respect is a problem for our furry companions. For example, we kill them with a special needle called euthanasia if they are too old, have no home, are disabled or are ugly to us. These souls come to help us and support us to evolve. Many are more evolved than their carers, yet we treat them like they are lesser. There is no hierarchy here on earth with the body type each soul chooses to return in. We are all one, there is no separation. If we humans could heal our hearts and raise to a higher vibration of love, allowing more sensitivity, we would feel this, and I would not need to share how damaging and awful this lack of compassion for all species is for the planet and our furry companion friends.

One of my soul companions, Charles, shared a sad message with me on euthanasia for our furry soul companions, how it feels painful and is not a comfortable experience. He said carers and veterinarians need to know this, "...it's like having acid go through your body... it's not calming and is very frightening to us animals when humans use these injections."

Humans need to respect each soul who comes to them and ask when it's time for them to leave the planet, not decide for them. Other species know when it is time for them to leave, as they are souls like us—but without a voice that can be heard. Here as their voice, I now share that it is inhumane to do this to our furry companions or wild animals who come to us. Our interaction with an animal is a precious connection that needs to be honoured, for they come to help us evolve and grow to understand them more, yet we discard them like they are separate and do not matter, as though they are soulless.

We are throwing away an opportunity to heal and evolve by being so disrespectful. I feel it deeply, as I have had very deep and extraordinary experiences with my furry soul companions. They all came to me with a different lesson or message for me to grow. I hope by sharing my experiences you will view animals with more compassion and not see them as separate to humans.

We have so many opportunities to have deep meaningful lives if we are inclusive of all beings and start to commune with them from our expanded and loving unconditional hearts. We need to stop controlling them and start asking what wisdom do they have to share with us, and the planet, to help us evolve and grow into more conscious humans.

Wisdom Received from My Soul Companion Charles on Euthanasia.

Charles: Humans do not understand that they are not here to play God and to be making decisions for furry companions living or dying because it makes them feel uncomfortable to see them suffer.

Do humans not understand it is the will of the furry companion's soul to decide? You must always ask them if it is time. You must always ask them before you make decisions, not base decisions on your own feelings.

Please understand, this is part of the respect you must show for other species. Humans are to allow free will and let the soul decide when it is time to leave their contract on earth. Many who have a problem with this may be needing to learn from their furry companion something they have not yet learnt about dying and suffering.

When humans decide on euthanasia, they are cutting the contract short with their furry companion's own soul's free will.

Remember these are souls just like you and me. I am like you, but I chose to come to be your furry companion to help you evolve, as your teacher. Many furry friends who have a strong connection with their carer have a contract to come down to be with that carer for whatever reason, or for however long. It is an agreement. The only difference is they have chosen another species' body form.

We are all the same, souls on a journey of service to others in one way or another. It is not your place to interfere with another soul's contract ending on the earth. It is up to their soul to decide this. Humans always want to be in control of everything, but there is a divine timing for all that happens in your world and beyond. Many still do not know this.

You also have free will in your human body form. We would not be respectful if we were to come and take you off the planet or assisted you to leave before your soul calls it is time. We can support you to do what you request, but we cannot do it for you or give you a magic needle to end times of suffering.

The human bodysuits have much to learn about respecting other species, even their own species, to be honest here. So, there is no reason to use euthanasia for other species.

Debra: What about when they are injured and really suffering from pain, like in bushfires, what happens then? How can we help them then, or when they are dying of cancer and suffering?

Charles: The same applies, dearest. We do not interfere with the contracts of other species, or our own, to aid them to leave the planet of the 3D world. It is one of the accepted spiritual laws of nature to not interfere with another's soul contract.

When the contract is shortened by another without permission the soul is left in the ethers, lost to suffer further as they were not ready to leave the earth plane. This is the same for those humans who commit suicide. They will suffer further by being caught in the web of the astral field around the planet. This is full of those who have suffered and are lost, unable to find their way back to the light as their contracts have not ended. They have agreed to live out the contracts of their souls as a particular species.

You do know many are stuck in the energetic field of the earth, called the astral field, because they are lost and confused. That is why many spiritual healers can see them and try to release them back to the light if they show themselves and request to be helped. This is really a whole other subject which we can touch on at another time or book.

Currently, we will stick with communing with the voiceless. They are so in need of help from you to speak for them, dearest. That is what you came to do—be their voice. You know how to do this. You have had many lifetimes communing with them, and that is why they feel your healing heart when you hold them.

When others learn to heal their hearts, they will also be able to make a difference to any other species' suffering. As your wildlife rescue friends have shared with you, they were very nurtured and happy to feel all the love you shared with them at the end times or if they were suffering. That is something humans can do, heal those hearts so they can share the love with other species in good times or painful times. That is all they ask from you.

It is not complicated, but it is a big ask for the many with wounds in the heart blocking them from feeling their own hearts. You need to convey this to them. When they heal their hearts, they will feel the magic of another species as you have done and be able to commune with them through the heart.

There is only one language—it is love, no other.

Drugs cannot give the same comfort as pure, deep, unconditional love from another species, it soothes the body and soul of whomever is receiving. Remember your own furry companions, including me when I was your dog companion, how I sat with you for all those days, weeks and hours holding you with my love. That is why you were able to find the strength to carry on when everything looked so dark and hopeless.

This is how we help another soul to be soothed and grow from the experience, it is our service to the greater force of all that is, that surrounds you every minute of every day.

Love is the only drug and the only healer for all species, and they all know it when you share it from unconditional love. You have done this numerous times in many lifetimes. Remember your beautiful heart and heal that sadness and hurt that haunts you, dearest one.

The tears wet my keyboard now, as I remember my past of being connected to so many species. Only this week, I saw pictures of so many species being injured and killed in the huge Australian bushfires. My heart felt like it was breaking, I could hardly hold the tears back for what I was feeling for them all. I feel helpless when I feel the pain and suffering that is being released into our planet's energetic field. My heart feels so sensitive to the pain of other species that sometimes I can hardly move, paralysed with guilt for what they suffer, particularly those who suffer at the hands of unconscious carers who do not have the love to share with them.

This is so hard for me to see and feel, as I often see images on the media which break my heart, as they did in my childhood. I try not to feel paralysed, rather to use this pain to motivate me to write my book on the voiceless. If anything, it has created an urgency to get my book completed and out for so many to learn from and to acknowledge their own pain that may arise. When it does, I encourage you to feel it. Try not to push it deeper down, for in doing so you become even more desensitized to the pain and suffering that is all around us in the earth's energetic field. This will not be helpful to you or the earth mother, adding to the pain and suffering that needs to be released.

My Australian Bushfire Diary 2019/2020

42

Apocalyptic Fires—November 2019

Mother Earth is transforming through fire all that does not serve her body any longer. She is preparing to raise her vibration for a new earth.
The question for humans is whether we are ready to raise our vibration to go on a new journey with our Earth Mother.

For six months—from September 2019 until February 2020—Australia endured the most horrific, apocalyptic bushfires in our country's history. Wildlife habitat areas larger than some countries, millions of hectares, were lost (some sources suggest as much as 46% more than the Amazon fires of late 2019). Tragically, billions of Australian native animals are believed to have lost their lives, along with domestic species and people. So many lives and properties were lost. The intensity of the fires has changed the landscape forever, turning it to ash, devoid of life. Many months later, much of the bush struggles to recover, but we do see some new green shoots. While humans have managed to destroy, control and pollute the earth, water and air, fire is the one element we have not been able to control or contaminate, and it continues to remind us of its power to transform and regenerate new life.

I share here some of my experiences over this horrific time.

Diary entry from two months after the fires began.

I am struggling to write, thanks to the strong emotions I feel and the gruelling physical effects on my health due to smoke exposure and inhalation for two months now, causing eye and respiratory tract irritations. Massive bushfires are burning along the east coast of Australia, many now out of control. Wildlife and farmed animals are burning as I write, unable to be saved. This is happening in my home state of New South Wales. So much death and destruction of the land, flora and fauna has hit our lands. Many homes have been lost, but most sadness for me is for the death and destruction of wildlife habitats and lives. How must it be for them, confused, lost and injured with no food or water.

Fifty kilometres from the closest fire front, we have dense smoke, while black, burnt leaves and debris falls from the sky. The whole state is on alert as the fires are raging out of control across many locations. They're flaring up instantly and spreading across the trees at such a fast pace, taking out huge regions of the land along Australia's coastal areas. Some towns have been wiped out, and many properties are turned to ash, with what were once personal belongings for so many now burnt debris.

The bush is burning at an unprecedented speed across vast areas of land, abundant with wildlife, that no one can reach. Water-bombing airplanes and helicopters are but a spit on the fire, making no real difference where they have taken hold. It is horrible to see on the TV. Winds are predicted to be fifty-plus kilometres per hour today, combined with a temperature of thirty-six degrees Celsius, making it catastrophic.

A state of emergency has been declared, so all schools and parks are closed and many public facilities in our region have shut down. We live on the central coast of NSW, covering 100 kilometers of beautiful pristine national parks to the north, south and west of us, with inland subtropical hinterlands and ocean to the east.

The risk for us is heightened due to the low rainfall over the past few winters. The fuel load is high on the ground, with dry mulch stacked deep on the bushland floor, observed on my bushwalks.

Fire and rescue crews say they have never seen fire behave in these ways before. They cannot predict anything, or stop it when it takes hold, they just have to evacuate people and keep everyone safe. But what about the wildlife?

Is Mother Earth trying to wake us up right now? Are we paying for our past actions of disrespect towards her body? Today has been an intensely emotional day for me. I am deeply feeling the pain and suffering of the wildlife and burning earth. Limited water from years of drought conditions and no food, and now everything burnt to the ground. We are in dire need of rain here right now. I feel this devastation is not being acknowledged by some, as they seem to be doing business as usual, like it is not happening. Are they finding ways to distract themselves from feeling in their hearts? That is something we do as humans when it feels painful.

I am saddened by the suffering and pain Mother Earth and all the species are experiencing along the fire paths of destruction. I fear for what it will take to make people wake up to what they need to do to respect our Mother Earth.

Our culture is so materialistic. We keep wanting more and more without thinking of the consequences of our actions, discarding everything without thought. So much wastage is just not being acknowledged by so many who fail to comprehend how it impacts all on the planet. Most people do not see where our rubbish ends up. Even horrific photos of the oceans full of rubbish do not seem to be enough to make people change their buying habits to respect this planet for us all to survive together. My heart feels so sad to witness this disrespect for the earth and nature.

What will it take for humans to not feel separate from earth and other species, to feel connected and understand their actions are causing massive repercussions for all species? We waste water and food, and continually buy material goods that become throw away—while that rubbish is turning up in oceans and landfill is overflowing, taking precious habitats from native species. When did we decide our rubbish was more important than nature? This land-grabbing is causing a negative impact on the habitats of many other species.

We need to make some giant steps to change. Our leaders in government do not want to know about climate change. They do not want to make any changes to their greedy actions of raping the earth and destroying our beautiful country. It all seems quite hopeless at times and my heart feels heavy with grief for our planet and feeling for the voiceless species for what is happening to earth, ignored as their habitats are stolen from them for large farming and mining projects.

Our government authorities have mismanaged our waterways and the flow has almost ceased on our biggest river systems. This has not honoured the water element of earth—the mother's blood flow to nourish and regenerate regions.

These current fires are devastating to our already dry landscape in my own country, one of the driest in the world, burning what small areas of green we had available into ash and bare blackened soil.

We have a history of poor land management practices, not caring for or supporting what the land needs. Nor have we listened to the traditional custodians, the First Nations People who understand and know this land and have carried great wisdom for over 45,000 years. Within just 200 years of arriving, white settlers have denuded and devastated this beautiful country. Rubbish pollutes the land and water, while the air is extremely polluted from all the air traffic, land transport fueled by petrol vehicles, energy resources depleted for industry and coal mining, while our oceans are mined for more oil to fuel our vehicles. Poisons run freely into our oceans—pesticides, agricultural chemicals, medical drugs—it all ends up in our oceans and affects our sea life and what we eat. These are just a few examples, as the list just keeps going on and on, year after year. There is so much to say about our planet and the poor state it is in from our disrespectful practices.

Are enough people making a difference by their actions? Many are protesting, but are we all thinking and acting at ground level by what we support ethically when deciding whether or not to purchase goods? We impact other species by not thinking about the end result of our actions—how it affects their habitats. We need to act now, consciously, before they become extinct, as some unfortunately already have. All species have a consciousness and were on earth before man arrived. Not separate, they have wisdom to share with us. Are we choosing to ignore and disrespect them for human greed of money and power?

We can have meaningful interactions with other species to learn more about this once beautiful planet. We can all live in harmony, joyfully and peacefully in abundance, if we can work together respectfully on equal terms, rather than humans believing they are superior and separate to other species. My heart is so heavy when I hear that the priority is to save property over other species during the fire destruction. Such unconscious thinking to believe a material possession that can be replaced is worth more than the life of another conscious being who shares their life with us and befriends\ and supports us.

There is proof that our flora and fauna have a consciousness just as we do, and that they communicate with one another at levels we are still beginning to record and understand. Evidence-based research has shown that plants and trees commune with one another, and us, in a conscious way. I wish for many more people to begin to experience and know this to be true. Many of us already know this intuitively and do not need to be shown by scientific research, however for those who need the science, it is here and available to find and experience right now, on the planet.

43

Loss of Habitat, December 2019

Diary entry three months on.

We now have hundreds of fires on Australia's east coast, raging at apocalyptic proportions. We do not have the manpower or resources for such large areas of fires burning wild bushlands and properties, unsafe now for anyone to get near enough to stop them. I am feeling for the wildlife we are losing and the impact this will have on our country.

Terrifyingly huge, the fires are making their own weather systems, producing lightning and striking more fires up to twelve kilometres ahead of the wide fire fronts. Fires are turning and twisting without any way to predict, and many lives and buildings have been lost. Cyclonic fire plumes and fire rise fifty to one hundred feet up in the air, bizarre to watch on the media.

Desperate now, fire crews have stopped saving buildings and are focused on just getting people to safety as towns are engulfed with flames and smoke. Some towns have burnt to the ground. While my heart really feels for the humans injured and dying from the fire fronts, it is hurting and heavy for the wildlife and farm animals we can't possibly save, as they're in the path of the fire, which keeps changing direction, suddenly encircling the animals. These sinister fires take everything in their path as they jump across containment lines and rivers.

Fire has now burnt twenty-five million hectares of our prime national parks, taking out agricultural communities and resources for power, water and communications. Planes and helicopters water bombing to save towns and people are taking water from dams, pools and rivers and dumping onto the fires. We now have water shortages, with no water for people in towns, then no water for wildlife, so they are left with no shelter or food.

So many native animals have perished now, but people are trying to search for and rescue the injured. In blackened landscapes of ash, no vegetation remains. We see pictures of kangaroos and koalas hugging humans who arrive with food and water. These fires are so hot that the Aboriginal people believe the bush may not regenerate. They have never seen such outrageous fires, yet they've been here for over 45,000 years and used fire to keep our land healthy and well. Two hundred years after English settlers arrived and the practices that the Aboriginals learnt as the caretakers of the land have largely stopped.

Our country will never be the same. I believe the rest of the world will be affected by these fires too. They have burned for three months now, and our neighbours in New Zealand are beginning to receive the heavy ash and smoke plumes, causing the fogs we have been suffering from for a couple of months now. Whilst New Zealand, three hours away across the ocean, has been flooding, we are on fire and have sunburnt soil that has not seen any decent rainfall for some years now.

Our ancient forests, damp and wet, are alight with fire and burning intensely, something the scientists did not believe possible. We cannot deny what's happening to our climate and we all need to stand up now. I hope it is not too late for us to really protest with our actions by not buying anything that ethically does not help the earth, or investing in anything that does not support a clean environment. Government leaders need to place our earth care and all species at the top of their agendas now, or we should not be supporting their actions by voting for them.

It is time to listen to the Indigenous people, the original custodians of this country, like never before—asking how to best manage and care for this unique landscape. Or is it too late? I hope this is just a wake-up call and the land will regenerate, but many people are skeptical, even the Indigenous people have doubts.

My heart bleeds for the wildlife who have no way to find safety and suffer from dehydration and starvation because we cannot get to them right now. We so need a balance on this planet. Scientists estimate we have already lost fifty million species of wildlife on earth, tragically epic proportions to witness and be part of.

The day of our earth's clearing has arrived. Are we going to wake up for the future?

Now is the time to listen to our inner guidance and observe the changing activities of the wildlife around us, for they have much to show us. The fire front has not been far from my home, and we have noticed greater numbers of bird varieties and bats arriving in our backyard. It is getting quite crowded as they all try to find a place in the trees, but they seem to be working it out. They have a lesson for humans, "We can all live together," and we have to—now!

Many of us were upset to hear the Amazon forest was on fire some years ago, at this point the Australian bushfires are five times larger in scale, and we have not entered the summer season yet. The responses from overseas nations have been heart sharing and supportive. Hopefully, this is a reminder to humans that our hearts are all connected and we cannot be separated by government borders, cultural beliefs or as another species.

While the loss of wildlife brings such sadness in all our hearts, we have no idea of the repercussions at this point. For example, the bats carry the seeds for our forests, so we can enjoy our fruits, whilst the bees need the flowers to produce honey. Koalas cannot survive without the seed dropping and pollen dispersal that only bats do in their natural movements. The food cycles have been interrupted now. We are going to see first-hand the inter-relationships of all species and how they affect our food chain. Time for more respect and to honour all species, as many humans still think they are more important and intelligent than other species. This is so far from the truth! All species are amazing beings, with wisdom for humans to learn from them to support our planet to stay in balance and harmony.

When we remove a species, we disrupt the balance of the landscape and earth. Humans so often interfere with the balance by culling native animals. For example, after the fires we will have a greatly reduced native wildlife population to keep our land in balance and to interact with us. Kangaroo Island is burning furiously as I write. It was set up as a sanctuary for every species in Australia in the 1920s because someone had the foresight to see we were unconsciously interfering with the ecology of Australian native species by introducing new species from other countries, without really understanding how this large island keeps the balance with all species on the landscape. Every species has a part to play, even if humans do not yet understand how it works.

Australia has an opportunity to find a new path, and maybe lead the way for the world to follow after our devastating fires. No more ignoring the obvious or the mindless destruction that is taking place right now. Let's act, united with all species, with respectful actions for our earth's balance.

44
Disrespect, January 2020

Dear diary, for four months now we have been experiencing these fires and it is having a devastating effect on our nation, physically and emotionally for many of us, especially the sensitives like myself. I feel the souls of those who have left the planet traumatized. I know this because I can feel it in my own body. When beings leave the planet traumatized, their distorted energy of pain and suffering is stored in the memory of the earth's energetic field. At the time of a traumatic death, the spirit can be shocked and lost, unable to find their way back home to realms beyond this earth plane. As we are connected energetically in our hearts to everything, we also feel their pain.

Not to forget this trauma also happens when we kill animals disrespectfully for our food supply. We kill them in ways that traumatize them, and that imprint is left in the energetic field of Mother Earth, so we will not find peace and joy on this planet until we stop sending other species to their death using disrespectful and traumatic practices.

On a metaphysical level, during the bushfires many groups have been using meditation and prayer to support these beautiful souls who have been traumatized, to assist them to leave the earthly realm surrounded in love.

All species have their own free will to know when it is time for them to leave the planet. If we interfere it is known as karma, the same as when we kill another human—the memory is held in our own bodies. Known as cause and effect, when we cause harm to others it has an effect on our own energetic body memory, held as a distorted energy that needs to be released in the future, even if we think our actions were acceptable at the time. The distorted energy agitates us forever more, or at least until it is released, as it is not held in harmony with the energy of love, which vibrates at a much higher subtle frequency, giving us peace within.

Our animal companions have free will, and it is universal spiritual law that we do not have a right to take free will away from another being. This applies to our companion animals when we feel they may be suffering and we do not want to feel their pain, so we euthanase them, saying we are taking them out of their pain and suffering. Do we ever ask them? That is the most important part of respect. We need to ask them if it is their time to be leaving the planet. Maybe they have come to teach by showing us what the pain feels like in our own hearts and bodies when we feel another species' suffering, and so they are not ready to leave until they have their own conscious calling to do so. We should always ask. It is just not acceptable to take their life just because it is uncomfortable for us to feel.

The images received during the bushfires have been heart-wrenching, to see the young sitting beside dead mothers, waiting for them to move, and others lost without their mothers. Sadly, I remember a koala with his head down, sitting beside his mate who lay dead on the ground, half burnt, as if the live koala had been grieving his mate. This is what rescuers were confronted with in the bush each day.

Another distressing image was of two young kangaroos sitting next to their dead mother amongst the ash and burnt soil. Some rescuers found dead platypuses in a river that had dried up. They placed the burnt little bodies on the riverbank to show the sheer numbers taken by the devastating fires. Such a big toll on our wildlife.

On a happier note, we had light rain some days ago and two kangaroos were captured on film jumping up in the air together, drinking the rain and appearing quite excited as they played in the water, as many waterholes and rivers have dried up due to drought.

Hopefully, the heartache so many are feeling at the loss of wildlife and their precious habitats will change thinking around government decisions and encourage them to stop culling our wildlife. They are not a commodity. We cannot keep killing them and expect no repercussions. These little souls feel pain, suffering and emotions just as we do for our partners and families. Sadly, they've no voice to tell us. We need to be more vigilant and spend time communing with them, using another more powerful language—called love.

Love, the powerful language of the universe, is used to commune with other species. So many do not feel other species in their hearts, as they carry trauma from the past. Time can heal our hearts to feel that deep peace and love with other species. We also carry our ancestors' trauma, held in our energetic memory. Fortunately, we now have an opportunity as humans to clear this energetic distortion we carry, for as the planet evolves, so can we.

That is why we are here, to heal our hearts of the past to find unconditional love for everything. Then Mother Earth will feel our healing hearts as love, peace and joy in her energetic field. She so wants to evolve in a place of joy, peace and love, with or without us. We have an opportunity to heal our hearts to evolve to a new level of conscious awareness, to find the joy, peace and love with all species, to feel great love in our hearts again as this planet once felt eons of time ago—before the killing of other species began.

For some months now I have felt compelled to keep writing about this fire tragedy that has consumed my sensitive heart and life. Writing has been an especially useful tool to release the pain I feel.

I guess that is my message here—use writing to release the pain and trauma you feel. Try it and see how it works for you. Better to let it go here and now than keeping it, causing you deep sadness to be released later.

In Australia we've been praying and meditating, in local groups across the country, sending out blessings and honouring the earth elements—water, earth, fire and air, for balance to be restored on the earth mother at this time, consciously aware it is all in divine timing.

We are all learning from one another how to be a powerful force to work together and not be in judgement, to just allow everyone to find what they can do to help in their own way. Many people are coming together to find ways to help irrespective of their personal beliefs or religious practices, finding ways to work together to help people with losses and to care for the wildlife injured. I view this as a positive outcome, as it is bringing people and all species together in love at a time when many are feeling the loss of wildlife and of human lives deep in their hearts.

It has been inspiring to witness at this time in the earth's evolution. Life is a kaleidoscope of magical happenings and events that we can never really understand, for in the bigger picture there is so much more than we are capable of understanding at this point in time.

So many hurdles for our nation now, but I feel this event may just accelerate our learnings and respect for all species and Mother Earth, as we learn to live in harmony and to consider our impact on the earth with each action we take, instead of aggressively taking down and destroying places for short term gains, for such nonsensical reasons.

In the end, anything material does not last.
Only love lasts forever.

The water element has been lacking in Australia for many years. Have we not been honouring this element of water? Many groups have felt called to perform blessings to honour the water element, encouraging it back to our land. Groups have been dancing, singing ancient chants and blessings of all kinds, and using meditations and prayers for water offerings. We are also very aware we don't want too much heavy rain all at once, so we keep asking Mother Earth for divine balance of the elements so our land can be hydrated once again after so many years of drought. Schools have even been taking part, doing rain dances with the children. And now I can say the rain has come very gracefully, and it is making a huge difference to our landscape, wildlife and people.

45
Climate Change, February 2020

Diary entry, six months since the fires started.

I feel there is so much to say about climate change on earth right now. It is not in the future any longer. The 11th hour has passed—we have arrived here now!

It is showing up in Australia and we cannot ignore it any longer. The pain from the devastation of our land and wildlife, which many of us feel in our hearts and bodies, makes it difficult to live our old 'normal' life. What is a normal life anymore? It is gone. We're just getting on day by day, while the heavy smoke keeps us locked in our homes and reports of the devastation continue as the fire fronts burn across the land, many out of control, despite the drizzle of rain that arrived and is now gone.

On our news and social media, we are now seeing people returning to their burnt-out homes and towns, and driving past many dead and burnt native animals and farm animals who died in paddocks because fencing prevented them from getting out. Their burnt little bodies form morbid mounds of charcoal that mark the spot where fire devoured them. So cruel.

I hope Australia's bushfire experience sparks people and governments to re-think the climate change situation and make some big changes promptly, changes we needed to make thirty years ago. It was all predicted so long ago. Growing up in the 1970s, I remember many environmental scientists were proclaiming all countries needed to make big changes because we were heading towards a catastrophe. Well, hello—forty years on and the environmental scientists were right.

Towards the end of our catastrophic fire season, we were ravaged by a massive storm that swept across the state with strange weather patterns. It hit our capital city with hail the size of cricket balls, damaging cars and buildings and covering the ground like thick snow. Only 100 kilometres to the west, country towns were consumed by a massive dust storm that rose hundreds of feet into the sky. Extending many kilometres across the landscape, it left a trail of dust and debris covering people's homes—inside and out! No one was prepared for that. They were taken into darkness in the middle of the day. Meanwhile, regions in the south only fifty and one hundred kilometers away experienced flash flooding.

All these weather cells were occurring at the same time, and unexpectedly, within 100 kilometers of one another. Mother Earth is really living up to the predictions of hazardous changes occurring on the planet now. After these storms, the next day was the most beautiful, perfect day, with blue skies, a slight breeze and warm weather. Mother Earth had shown her wrath to the people, a warning to be ready for what may come next. 'Be prepared for the unexpected' is the word on the street now.

Many are beginning to get the message now. It can't be denied any longer—the planet is evolving. We can all feel it with the catastrophic changes occurring. Drastic changes are now needed across all countries or each will be heading towards their own catastrophes.

There is so much to say, but words aren't going to help those who haven't experienced this to know how deeply it hurts to see so much death, and for empathic souls to *feel* the deaths of those who have passed over. I cannot even go to the bush to see what it looks like, as the pain in my chest is so intense and I would be terribly traumatized to see dead wildlife. I help in other ways. Fourteen years ago, I volunteered with a wildlife group in my region. I learnt so much about helping injured wildlife and I cared for quite a few, but many I could not save. That is the reality of being a wildlife carer. You are told at the start to be prepared as they may not make it, but to do your best and know they do appreciate it.

I remember a little possum I cared for. I thought he was going to make it, but unexpectedly, after a week he suddenly let go of life. This possum soul returned to me in spirit sometime later with a message in my meditation. He told me he was deeply appreciative of the love and care he received, most of all, that feeling the love from me when he passed was the most wonderful part. He thanked me, and told me not to worry if I cannot save a wild animal, for the most important part is that they feel love, and that is what he felt gratitude for receiving.

The possum told me he had his own timing, and humans are not able to interfere with the life that another species has agreed to. They have free will, just as we do, and if we use euthanasia, we need to be respectful and let the animal tell us when they are ready to go. We need to respect the decisions of other species and not jump in unconsciously, doing what we think is the 'right thing' to do. Always ask the animal and leave them to decide, which can be difficult if you cannot commune with other species through your higher heart. I believe it would be beneficial for all humans to learn heart-to-heart communication so we intuitively know how to be respectful.

My communication with Wildlife souls requested to be shared with humans!

The fires have caused us great loss, but it is more devastating for us to lose habitats due to human urbanization and being left or killed without our homes and food to sustain us. Think of us in your actions.

An important message for humans I received from an Owl.

Debra: Dear owl, how beautiful you are sitting in that tree. Do you have any messages for me today?

Owl: Yes. We are tired of you humans taking our habitats. Please tell your people to think of us when they are taking trees down. We need homes too. There is too much fear around nature—humans need to be more compassionate for us the other ones, your relatives.

Debra: Yes. I understand this, it saddens me, but many do not understand.

Owl: Yes dearest, we know this. It is why your book has to be a priority in your life to get others to see this with the messages. We, the winged, are also feeling the tension on this planet from all the fear and anger that is rising from Mother Earth and the human race. Please tell humans to heal their hearts so we can all live in harmony once again as we have done before. Tell them we can help them do this. We are a species who know how to do this with our relatives.

The humans are putting so much stress on their other relations such as us, the owls and birds. This is a very important message. Please share this with the many, as they do not seem to see this or understand what they are doing unconsciously—changing the balance on this planet for every species, not just themselves, for we are all interconnected.

They need to consider when they are making changes to the natural environment around their homes, for they have other species also in homes around them trying to survive with their families. We winged ones have been trying to connect with you over past days. Have you not noticed all the birds coming to your grandmother tree?

Debra: Yes, I actually have noticed many varieties turning up and loved seeing them.

Owl: We are showing you how many are here with you at this time, supporting you to share these messages of disrespect for all species' habitats. Humans are unconsciously destroying their neighbours' habitats. The repercussions will present as Mother Earth will call her allies, the elemental forces, to clear what has been done to her other children of earth. This will be most uncomfortable for humans when this occurs, if you are around at this time.

More and more compassion is needed. Tell your people not enough is happening to respect the other relatives—we deserve to be here just as much as humans. Humans were the guardians and custodians many times past for all species and nature. They seem to have forgotten their role here on earth to protect and care for earth and all the other relations. These past times need to be remembered now!

It is the time to make the changes before Mother Earth calls her elemental forces to make the changes, in ways humans may feel much discomfort with and not be prepared for.

This is a warning to humans—change your unconscious acts to find compassion and respect for all species. You humans cannot keep going with these disrespectful acts any longer. It will not sustain you humans in this new earth that is arising, which is now evolving towards peace and harmony with or without the human race. Please share this with the many humans, dearest one.

Debra: Yes, I will. Thank you for your message here today. Many blessings to you all who are feeling this disrespect of habitats by humans. I will share your message in my book.

Please do not forget the winged ones near your home when you make decisions to change the environment and habitats of the other relatives.

Only yesterday, a tree we had admired with possums in it was taken down by neighbours because they were fearful it might come down in a storm. There were no weakened areas in the tree. We could see it stood up right and strong, with no branches falling down, yet the fear consumed these people. Unaware of what was happening until we heard it fall and hit the ground, Nigel and I were deeply saddened once again by a beautiful habitat taken down due to fear, with no compassion, even though the property owners did enjoy seeing the possum. Where do they think he will go now? Possums are very territorial and do not relocate easily, causing great trauma and stress to them. The property owners shared later their concern was where there was a hole in the tree, "... it might be weakened and fall." That hole was the possum's home. We humans are causing much pain and suffering to so many other species, not just our own human race, with our fears and anger. Healing our hearts to find compassion for all is so needed right now.

Honouring in Life

46

Honouring and Ceremony

Are you ready to heal your heart at deeper levels to raise your vibrational frequency?

The earth is a living being, and everything on it is alive, has a consciousness and wants to commune with us. We can consciously connect with Mother Earth, the ancestors, all elements, and every species when we travel across landscapes on this planet. When we honour and respect Mother Earth and other species we feel connected, then we will never feel separate or alone as everything and every being is our relation, and we will remember the land owns us, we are only the caretakers of the earth.

"Everything is for us; nothing is ours to own."
I love this quote from Puma F.Q. Singona,
(Shaman Teacher, Peru)

Whilst consciously sitting or walking across landscapes, I am mindfully engaged with all my senses. I feel the wind caressing my skin, reminding me to listen deep inside to the ancestors' messages carried on the winds, whispering to me. I hear the birds singing as my heart feels joy from the songs of the universe. When I hear the water running and splashing, I feel cleansed of unwanted emotions, leaving a space to feel peace within me. I feel the fire of passion in my heart as I commune with everything around me, and I feel Mother Earth under my feet as she gives my body nourishment, warmth, comfort and strength. I know I am supported by a magnificent being of light, my mother the earth, as my body, mind and spirit are regenerated for another day on this planet.

Wilderness Calls Me, with a Metaphor for Life

In 1998 Nigel and I felt a strong calling to wilderness and trained for six months to trek for eight days with Mother Earth in Tasmania. We arrived at Cradle Mountain lodge in the National Park to spend our first night—the last time we would have a comfortable bed for a while. Travelling in early Autumn, we imagined milder weather conditions for the trek. Little did we know what was ahead of us! On the morning of day one, our first decision was which trail? There were two—the horse track or the lake view track. Of course, we took the lake view over Cradle Mountain. Bad decision! We had to go vertically up the mountain trail, while carrying heavy backpacks filled with eight days' supplies.

Mother Earth was getting us ready on day one. I lost my footing on the rocky mountain trail, and the weight of my backpack swiftly took me backwards down the mountain. Getting up, I thought *that was bloody scary and hard—what on earth have we done?* We continued on, sliding down the other side of the mountain, and found a lovely trail full of wild grass and native wild plants. We finally arrived at the first hut for an overnight stop at dusk. Sleeping on a wooden-boarded bed with no mattress after carrying heavy packs left our bodies sore and aching. We only had two sets of clothes in our packs, so we took them out and laid them beneath our bony areas for relief from the hard boards. Nigel had thought the trail would have mattresses in the huts, like New Zealand's Milford Sound track. Wrong!

Only seven more days to go ... a test in so many ways. This was my first challenge after healing my adrenal stress and chronic fatigue, and having experienced a miscarriage three months before, so I was not going to give up. The next day we pushed through gale force winds and drizzling rain and crossed a high mountain plateau, walking for hours. The force of the winds shredded our wet weather jackets as it hit us horizontally.

The beauty of the flora and fauna kept us going. Each day all the elements challenged us, but we embraced them with gratitude. We had to pass through dense, ancient old growth forests with tree roots across the path so huge you had to climb over them. I so loved the forest and trees, even though it was hard work. I was physically aware, feeling the trees and ancestors helping me to get over each large root, holding me as my legs became ever more tired by day three. I felt that beautiful ancient forest supporting me. Feeling so many energies and so many realms of existence in that forest kept me fascinated, like a child, and I just knew I was being watched by the ancestors.

The next day snow and sleet fell, so heavy we had to find shelter in an old historic hut. It was unsuitable to stay in overnight, but we were happy to have shelter as the temperature had dropped dramatically due to the snowfall. The unpredictable nature of the national park meant you had to have a tent with you for shelter—we were learning why that day! We were now deep into the mountains, moving through valleys with stunning scenery all around us, and feeling nature communing with us every day. Towards end of the week, with extra kilometres to walk from previous days, Nigel was checking the map for landmarks ahead to get us to the overnight hut, using the mountains we had passed. Making the next hut by nightfall was looking unachievable.

I remember we both took a great big breath and said, "We can do this, one step at a time." Rather than getting fixed on the distance we had to go, we needed to stay present in the moment of walking the trail. We did, and passed each mountain. The mental process worked. It was dark when we made the hut, but we had shelter. 'One step at a time' became our metaphor for life and has taken us through many challenges over the past twenty-three years.

Mother Earth tested us every day with the elements and the conditions, but walking with nature's beauty all around us was inspiring and unforgettable. Living simply with Mother Earth, our senses fully alive, we were being reminded of life generally and the challenges we all need to get through—staying present and smelling the flowers along the way works!

That wilderness journey was insanely beautiful with wildlife, fauna, flora and mountains. My eyes could barely believe the beauty, especially the different terrains we crossed, the little groves and rivers, rarely seeing any other trekkers, no aircraft, no electricity wires, motor vehicle or train noises, and you could hear yourself think! Some days you could see forever, perhaps to the ends of the earth. It was certainly an adventurous journey, I still smile remembering our bathing, which consisted of dipping our bottoms quickly into the icy water of a river.

We did a lot of meditation, communing with nature and receiving many beautiful messages along the way, and left that trek with elation in our hearts to have achieved it and communed with Mother Earth every day, inspiring us. Also, we were quite a bit skinnier, having lost some excess weight as we had miscalculated our food supplies for eight days. With some adjustments to reduce daily food intake, it was not really a problem, because we were very fit and so inspired to keep walking in wilderness every day.

This was a real adventure for us. Navigating our challenges and decisions to make each day, we learnt how the resources are within us when we are challenged. This journey became our metaphor for life, and we later measured our challenges in life against it. Nothing seems to be that big a challenge compared to what the wilderness offered us to grow as humans, with a new level of what is important in life. Nature is so inspiring when we make the time to be with her mindfully and commune.

Joyfully Honouring Everything

For many years, I have communed with the ancestors and elements in ritual and ceremony, even before I had initiations into shamanic practices, and always found it a powerful practice to connect to all our relations on earth. When I married in 2005, I felt a strong calling to design my own autumn equinox wedding celebration ceremony that honoured all the ancestors, the elements and Mother Earth. It had to be outdoors, and I found a beautiful location on a coastal region near a national park that held a strong Aboriginal history and presence.

The day we chose was autumn equinox, as we had experienced many wonderful new adventures in our relationship around this date each year. The autumn equinox is important on the Mayan calendar, which includes many levels of understanding for cycles of time with earth cycles, beyond 3D timelines, while our Gregorian calendar is limited to a 3D system of time. The whole ceremony was designed around a grand old Norfolk pine tree, under whose canopy we performed our earth and ancestor honouring celebration, our union ceremony.

All the elements were acknowledged within the four directions, held by burning fire poles. Participants of the wedding party were invited to take part with each element honouring with prayer blessings. The ocean to our east provided a natural boundary as the grand pine tree connecting us to the three worlds and the souls of our ancestors stood majestically strong. We had invited music and songs to be played by the wedding participants, so were gifted with the sounds of crystal bowls, a didgeridoo and clap sticks, all blended beautifully for the day's event. Many friends came from interstate, so we did not have time for preparation. It all just flowed beautifully and powerfully.

The elements had made themselves known as guests arrived the night before to the house accommodation where the Grand Pine Tree stood by the seaside for our weekend of celebrating. The skies broke open with lightning, thunderstorms, gale force winds and heavy rain as each guest arrived. *Now that was a cleansing!* The next morning was overcast, with small rays of sunshine trying to break through the clouds, but no rain in sight.

The moment we were making our vows the sun found a way through and we were covered in sunshine, with warmth and strong light added to our ceremony as the fire element finally arrived. Nigel and I performed a welcome dance to country, gifted to us from a well-known Aboriginal elder who has since passed over. I feel he would have been proud where his teachings had landed on that day, honouring the earth in joy and love. Gifts from our guests were from the heart, in the form of blessings through stones and the beautiful food they had all prepared.

It was a magical and powerful weekend to have all the elements and ancestors letting us know they were with us. We also received beautiful messages from the ancestors that day on the wind. It was a magical day that took us and the wedding participants to deep connections with Mother Earth and the elements. This is just one of many ways we can honour everything here on Mother Earth, to feel connected to all our other relations. So many stories I have to share on my travels, honouring my connections with all our other relations here on earth, and how it has transported me beyond the physical world to places of bliss and joy.

Power of Honouring Mother Earth

In Northern Australia, where the land is honoured regularly by the Aboriginal people through ceremony, the land is alive. Travelling that land, I hear the loud whispers of nature spirits in the bush and the ancestors in the landscape. It is important to always ask for permission to visit the land and acknowledge the ancestral custodians of the land—past, present and future generations. Call the ancestors any time and they will come; they are already walking with us. I invite them to join me and ask them to keep me safe crossing the land. I share that we take nothing and leave only love and joy with the land.

Sounding and dancing with the earth gives her energy to be alive and strong, and that is why the Aboriginal lands in the northern regions of Australia are so strong energetically. Mother Earth responds to the regular ceremonies with songs and dances honouring her by the Indigenous people, who have done this for thousands of years, with many wonderful healing energies and magical experiences. If we are awake and conscious, we are able to feel the shifts in reality.

The ancestors who walk with us always want to be called to help us to heal and do our practices on the land. They want to join us as our support team to be the caretakers of the earth. Their souls are part of the landscape on many levels of reality. We need to remember them so we can be a powerful team working together for the benefit of humanity and Mother Earth's body, and go beyond the physical world of limited thinking.

This can be achieved by expanding our minds and accessing our heart intelligence. In shamanic practices and journeys we acknowledge the three worlds—the upper world for the bigger picture of life (etheric element), the lower world to heal us, and the middle world (slightly off the 3D) where we can do anything, go anywhere and commune with any soul energetically. The middle world is where we get things done here. Our ancestors are part of our landscape, so when we honour them we keep them alive, which in turn keeps us alive and healthy. We are all connected to everything, so remember to honour all who live with us across many realms of existence.

I experience Mother Earth to be a magnificent, conscious being of light, supporting so much life. She can balance her body at will when out of alignment, sustaining micro and macro environment worlds.

She is a guardian, teacher, nurturer, healer and transformer. We have so much to learn from her on unconditional love for everything. I believe honouring her through ceremony is a way of showing our gratitude for her motherly love for us.

Honouring the Elements, Balancing the Karma on Earth

In 2012, I was invited to a Celtic gathering in Ireland to welcome and honour the new race of children coming to the earth. A large number of Ancient Earth Wisdom leaders were invited from many countries to share in a five-day ceremonious honouring with Mother Earth and the elements. Each day was full of ritual and joyful ceremony that included art, meditations, adventures to sacred sites, music, songs, ceremonies, prayers and sharing wisdoms. We honoured Mother Earth and the future children coming to the new earth who were expected in the next seven years.

Every day we focused our theme on one of the elements of fire, water, earth and air. At the end of each day we presented an organic gift to be added to a prayer bundle. The prayer bundle was handwoven, crafted with local materials and symbols by the local Celtic spiritual community. It had taken many women several months to make the beautiful wrap, measuring six by six feet.

On the last day, we celebrated with ancient rituals to wrap all the prayer items and add our blessings before it was taken to be ceremoniously buried in the belly of Mother Earth to receive her blessing. The males of the group dug the hole with love on a private property where ancient Celtic wisdom practices and learnings regularly took place. We sang, played flutes and drums and danced together in a parade of joy with the prayer bundle wrapped, ready to be buried. Large and weighty with blessings, it took four adults to carry it on the parade to the burial site. The bundle held the blessings for the new race of children who would be arriving on earth to guide our civilization to a new path with wisdom and respect for all beings on earth.

It's the most magical journey I have taken part in to date, and I have had the privilege to be part of many earth wisdom ceremonies across this planet. This honouring was highly emotional for all as we gifted our blessings to Mother Earth. Tears flowed with joy and heart expansion, with great love flowing from us all, feeling we had taken part in a very privileged event. A plaque sits above the buried prayer bundle site and states:

> "On April 29*th* 2012, an international group of shamans laid the healing medicine prayer bundle for Mother Earth, and all her children, at this place in Dunderry Park. For the time to come. Sli An Chroi."

The blessed bundle will be unveiled in future years, at the time of the new earth and next generation of children, to give them strength and hope and to inspire them. This was one of those events that can't be forgotten, and sits with light in my heart to feel hope for this planet.

Water Element Honouring—Cleansing of the Temples

In Mexico, I visited Palenque, a sacred temple site that represents the element of water. This visit took place on 12/12/2012, which was the shift in the Mayan Calendar, if you know about that ancient earth wisdom. Many Westerners believed it was the end of the world, so doom and gloom prevailed across the planet in many thoughts. We found it exciting and felt called to visit at that time on the earth with the Mayan culture, who celebrated this event, seen as the 5th world birthing.

We celebrated with a Western spiritual group and a Mayan shaman we knew from another region of Mexico. Our group came from many destinations on the planet—Europe, North America, Central America, and of course, Australia. Our ceremony began with dance and songs, holding hands in a circle at the significant moment in time and date—12 midday on the 12/12/2012. It was a sunny, tropical day, yet at exactly 12 midday, when we began the honouring ceremony by calling the ancestors and the elements, it poured with heavy rain. We all thought *wow, a cleansing of the earth temples*. The temples flooded quickly, with water flowing everywhere.

Many tourists and locals ran back to their vehicles and left the temple site, so it was all ours for several hours. We stayed and were blessed to come across a traditional tribal Mayan earth honouring ceremony taking place. Hidden in the jungle behind the temples, it was not for tourists or outsiders. We were exploring the forest jungle in the rain and walked into the ceremony unexpectedly. The elders wore highly decorated costumes, headpieces, and their bodies were painted ceremoniously. With the approving smiles of locals, we found a place to sit amongst the large roots of ancient fig trees and quietly observed from a distance. It was an extraordinary event to watch.

I had been to Mayan community ceremonies before in Guatemala, where I was invited to take part with an elder and his community on the equinox in 2006. That went for three hours and we sat in the sun in a large circle amongst the temples, a blessing to experience. Whilst we did not know the language, we felt the power of the ceremony honouring Mother Earth. The 12/12/2012 event was a different experience, way more elaborate with the ceremonial costumes and their uniquely painted bodies and faces. We felt honoured to be there, a powerful experience on a significant day on the Mayan Calendar.

After the ceremony, we left and witnessed water flowing down the stairs of the temples. It was up to our knees as we walked the paths, and overflowing down the stairs as it poured out of the temples, so we could not safely go inside. I believe it was a cleansing after years of many tourists visiting the temples. It was a sight I will not forget—waterfalls flowing from all the temples from every direction. Very apt for the temple that symbolized the element of water.

Two hours later and the sun showed its face, ready for the next event that took place with the world Rainbow Tribe of the earth, who set up a circle in the main square, where all the temples face one another. Eight hundred to a thousand people held hands in a circle, speaking many different languages, and families were invited with their children to join in, all chanting together at the temple site. What an awesome experience to feel all those hearts chanting OM! It felt like heaven! The new earth had begun for us. As we chanted, the sun kissed us all. Everyone was over-the-moon happy to be greeted by the sun's rays. In the centre of the massive circle (the size of a football field) a Rainbow Tribe member danced, dressed and painted like a serpent. What a spectacularly magical first day!

We still had two more weeks travelling through Mexico and Central America visiting temples. When I go to the ancient sacred sites, I call them power gateways into other realms, because they feel alive to me as Mother Earth is being honoured regularly by the local Mayan people with ceremonies for Solstice, Equinox and many others. I had also observed this in Australia when I first visited the Northern Territory, where Aboriginal people still practice their culture. I could feel the land alive and wondered why I had not felt that so strongly on the east coast. I believe that is because the Aboriginal people have been displaced and the traditional cultural ceremonies are no longer being done due to Western *invasion*. I believe Mother Earth responds to the respect we show, giving us land that is alive with energy and messages to help us evolve, and you can only feel it through your heart space. I am unable to really find the words to convey this feeling, you need to experience it for yourself.

Sacred sites that have had ceremony performed on them continuously for thousands of years are deeply alive and become gateways to other dimensions. I have learnt there is a very thin veil between other realms, dimensions and the 3D world, so I am able to gain healing and receive very clear, strong messages from our ancestors and other soul relations. Time has no place in the sacred sites situated on important energy vortexes and ley lines around the world.

Whenever I go to sacred sites with my soul family friends, as I call them, I always return home feeling a shift in my vibrational frequency, a change in my body and thinking. After weeks of integration, I reflect and realise I have had a healing, and new information comes to me about my life journey. It is all experienced in such a joyful, subtle and profound way on these travels. I almost feel like a sacred sight junkie! Travelling consciously with this group, we commune with the ancestors regularly and feel we are in a bubble of protection that surrounds us as our hearts expand in love and our vibrations feel remarkably high, like we cannot be distracted, very focused.

Something interesting happens when we all leave and go to the airport to return to our homes in different countries—the bubble disappears, and we all feel the heavy vibration of the earthly realms of being grounded. I always find this fascinating, and it emphasises how deeply we have been in the flow of the universal energy with our ancestors around us. I have noticed I come back remarkably high with love and light of heart, and know I have had a heart healing like no other. My vibration feels like it has shifted to a new resonance, giving me the inspiration to make changes in my life.

I have no doubt said this before, but I have so many stories I can share on this topic! This is just a shortened version on how I have experienced the honouring of Mother Earth and found the responsiveness of the land to be more alive and able to heal what has gone before us with the pain and suffering that's been imprinted into the energetic field of the earth. The healing I receive releases what does not serve me any longer, opening me to find more freedom and joy without being stuck in the suffering that keeps repeating itself on this planet.

Mother Earth is so happy to receive all our beautiful celebrative energy when we are in joy, dancing on her body. Keep dancing and singing, sound is a powerful healer. Of course, this only happens if you travel consciously, with all your senses awake. Most tourists visit these sites unconsciously and miss all the magic that is held there, just waiting for us to step into the other realms of existence.

I hope my stories help you to remember your wisdom of past times.

Message received when I asked the Ancestors for permission to visit sacred Mayan sites in Guatemala.

> We welcome you, our sisters and brothers. We will be united again back to these great energy centres of Maya lands.
>
> (We asked to be kept safe to travel across the country in Guatemala.)
>
> It is by design we have you all with us at this time. No need for fear, you are by design to be here, you bring laughter, love and joy. We welcome you.

When you go into nature and want to take a stone from the river, always ask the river keeper spirit if it allows you to take one of the sacred stones.

If you have to climb a mountain or make a pilgrimage through the jungle, ask the local spirits and guardians for permission. Important to communicate, even if you don't feel, hear or see.
We can enter each place with respect, because all of nature listens to you, sees you and feels you. Every move you make in the microcosm has a big impact on the macrocosm.
As you approach any vegetation, be grateful for the medicine it has for you.

Author Unknown

47
Communing with Mother Earth and Other Realms

In 2012 I returned to Guatemala Tikal Temple sites, six years after my first visit, and experienced another extraordinarily magical time with Mother Earth when we travelled with a local Mayan shaman. The shaman guided us into a temple that had tunnels closed to tourists, a tribal ceremonial area. We did honouring ceremony with ancestors and the elements outside, then individually moved through a tunnel, deep down into Mother Earth's belly, under a temple. When we returned to the outside air above, we all had to lie down on the grass to get grounded, to integrate the powerful experience of communing that took place with earth mother and the ancestors.

In the tunnel I felt the vibrational power Mother Earth holds in her belly and was taken with the Mayan ancestors to another realm of existence to have many amazing experiences. Some may call it drug-like, but I know we did not take any drugs. It was a totally natural state of euphoria and spiritual visions, meeting the ancestors as they guided us, as guardians to the underworlds and other dimensional realities. I believe, and felt, that we received healing.

My first visit to meet the ancestor spirits at that same location in Guatemala, in 2006, was an extraordinary experience. On my arrival to the ruins, our guide suggested any new members to the site be taken blindfolded and guided by another member of our group who had previously visited. Our guides directed us to enter from the back gate of the temple sites after ceremony honouring the guardian tree, Mother Earth and ancestors. I followed my guide and arrived in front of the Jaguar temple, the main ceremony temple on the site. When I looked up, I could see clearly all my Mayan ancestors who had connected with me at home in Australia before I had left for this journey when I asked if I was welcome and to be kept safe.

We spent a few days at that site on my first visit. It was extraordinary to do ceremony with the shaman leader every day and commune with the rocks and trees. I learnt how much knowledge they hold on the history of places. These are experiences that are held in your memory field for a lifetime because you have lived and felt them personally, and received your own messages to grow and heal. We also meditated in the Temple of the Moon at night.

We were taken by a local to the site after hours, and it was an extraordinary experience to go into the jungle where the jaguars move about at night. We heard many strange and unfamiliar noises around us in the dark of the night. Climbing stairs to the top, we sat on the platform in the temple under a full moon and were all downloaded with many messages and energetic codes for our bodies. None of us could talk on the way back through the jungle to our cabins. We were in a blissful state of peace and our senses were heightened as we heard all the jungle sounds, especially the howler monkeys, they were my favourite. Awe-inspiring experiences to behold in my body and memory.

Ninety percent of the temples in Guatemala at Tikkal are still buried and hidden by jungle as their government cannot afford to unveil the areas. So much history is held there, as we learnt through some of the meditation channelings received from the ancestors and Mother Earth on my visits to sacred sites. While these temples are hidden, they can be seen by satellite. I believe we, as a human race, may still not be ready to see what they have to show us.

The mysteries of the earth are my passion. I never read about these sites from Western history books, as they are limited and omit information through not understanding other realms of existence, so to me their accuracy is questionable. To visit and feel the energy and commune with the ancestors of these sacred places has given me so much more wisdom to know and remember from my past lives.

Equinox Fire Honouring Ceremony

Another time in Guatemala at Tikal Temples sites we were wandering around that sacred site and felt to wander to the back of the temples, where we walked into a ceremony being prepared by the local community elders and shamans of the temples. One of the local elders spontaneously invited us to join them, in sign language of course, there was no English spoken in the Indigenous community. Such an honour and a privilege to be invited was my immediate heart response, as this was no tourist ceremony.

We sat in a large circle in the sun with all the community members for three hours while the fire ceremony took place. As is so often the case for me, it was powerful to be part of and I could feel so many ancestors with us. The people were honouring everything using the fire element and organic items fed to the fire as offerings and blessings, from what we could make out, as they were an agricultural community. Preparing and building the fire base took the elders at least an hour of laying organic items, consciously placing them in a sequence of patterns, obviously with significant meanings for the people.

It was apparent this ceremony had gone on for generations before them with their ancestors, so everything had a precise purpose, consciously offered in divine timing to honour the earth and elements, fire—transformative and regenerative in nature—being the focus for transporting the blessings.

The ceremony became one of the highlights of my many visits to these temples of great power. I was shown magically by the universe why they are so powerful—because the earth elements and ancestors are honoured on a regular basis on Solstice times of winter and summer and Equinox times in spring and autumn. My own practice of honouring these same dates since 1995 made it more powerful to experience Mayan ceremony. I was overjoyed to have the opportunity to see it practiced in the traditional ways passed down through generations. Such a blessing, I felt gratitude for that unfolding in divine timing for us to take part spontaneously without expectation.

Messages from Our Galactic Families

Crop circles called to us when we travelled across the UK. There had not been any found when we arrived, but the night before we began our road trip to Glastonbury a fresh crop circle was found by air—an intricate butterfly in Wiltshire Avebury. Early morning, we took our time searching in nearby fields of tall grass and wheat, and bingo!

All credit to my husband's psychic ability, we walked into the newly created crop circle butterfly, the first to arrive. We were able to walk around it, feeling the energetic force field. It was the size of two football fields. We observed no damage to the wheat crop stalks at all, they were folded over and layered to make an extraordinary design of a butterfly. We felt called to sit and meditate in the centre, and I started to sound AAA with Mother Earth. Wow! It was like we were inside a dome as it magically echoed back to us. When rain began to pour down on us, we laughed and carried on. Our bodies were buzzing, full of joy. Our hearts expanded and we were full of excitement to feel the extraordinary energy coming up from the earth and surrounding us.

Eventually, we decided to leave, and in the distance saw many people coming up the path. They shared how we had helped them find it with our cars parked nearby. Funny how we ended up going in circles to find this butterfly circle, yet we had parked nearby without realising it. We felt blessed this crowd did not find us earlier, allowing us to experience the crop circle by ourselves. Our bodies vibrated with joy all day and the sun returned. At that time, the UK had been hit by a once in a hundred-year flood that had split the country into two parts, north and south. Everything came to a standstill, but we were supported and found our way to the south. It was so meant to be, with synchronicities along the way for us. These are the magic moments I have experienced over and over again with Mother Earth and the universe as I live a more awakened life and travel more consciously, following my heart and using all my senses.

When you have these experiences, calling the ancestors, communing with Mother Earth, elements and other species, your heart expands and you begin to feel sensitive to all that is connected to you here on the earth, and beyond into other realms.

48

Nature Mirrors Our Souls

Have you ever considered nature could mirror your soul to see life from a new perspective?

It was the early 90s, and I was looking to go for an adventure into the wilderness as I had been working in the city as a marketing executive. With two friends, we met a local guide at a small village that bordered the National Park of a Thailand jungle we were about to go trekking through.

The day before, arriving at the village after seven hours of rocking and rolling on dirt roads in the local bus, I had spotted a warning notice—a tiger had been visiting the village! Sadly, that week a community member was killed by a tiger. An agricultural village, there were no fences protecting the community.

Even knowing that, walking the jungle the next day excited me. So many amazing moments as I passed footprints of elephants and other animals. Suddenly, a great noise approached us from above. In the thick canopy of growth above our heads were families of gibbon monkeys (I called them rainbow bottoms) swinging from the trees. Keen to see more, we followed them for maybe fifteen minutes before we lost sight of them. They were moving too fast for us and the jungle had become very dense, closing in on us. Stopping to work out where we were, we quickly realised we had left the track—there *was no track* to see behind or ahead of us.

After two hours, we agreed we were lost and stopped joking. Dusk was approaching as our jungle guide admitted he had bought his compass from a roadside stall in Bangkok—and it was not working.

Then he confessed he was not local to the region. He had recently married a local village girl and was trying to make an income from the occasional backpackers who visited the region.

He had no more idea of where we were in the jungle than us—the tourists.

I kept trying to see the sun's direction through the canopy, but it was too dense and getting darker towards dusk. I believe we had been going in circles following animal tracks. It was getting scary, no longer an adventure, more like how to survive with tigers, and whatever else lived in that place, looking for prey at night. All we had were our three chocolate bars.

I suggested we could sleep in a tree, but the guide quickly told me tigers also climb and sleep in trees.

"Forget that idea!" I replied.

Everyone was quiet as we kept walking through the dense jungle. Some hours later, I caught a glimpse of a small opening in the jungle. Moving in that direction, I found a gentle descent. Yes! I remembered we chased the gibbons up a little rise. As we descended, I could see a large open area, and then a trail appeared. It appeared to be our way out, but which way—left or right? Intuitively, I guessed to the right, and it took us out of the park within a short time. I'm not sure it was the same trail we'd taken into the jungle, but we walked out unharmed.

I got my adventure—maybe not quite what I had envisioned. I suggest you be careful what you ask for, and who you take with you, as one of my friends was in panic mode most of the way so we needed to keep consoling her. She was my boss back home. You guessed it—the gibbons had led us into the darker side of ourselves. Being lost within, I observed how we all dealt with the scary moments of being lost in different ways. I learnt that I was lost in my life, I wasn't totally happy ethically with the work I was doing and it didn't fit my soul's calling, but I was fearful to move on to a new job and where that might lead me.

In Bangkok a few days earlier, I'd had a spiritual insight, where I suffered food poisoning that kept me in bed for a few days. I found a book in my hotel room, *The Life of Buddha*. Reading it felt like a message from my soul, telling me to follow my heart and change my work life. I did not make the changes on returning home, and within a short time my body made changes for me, as I became seriously ill and had to let go of my job and my old life. I was forced to go deep inside myself to dark places and reflect on my life. Only then did I find a way to rise up. A beautiful life awaited me, and without knowing where it would lead, I trusted my new life path. What awaited me was many new adventures of freedom, joy and love.

49
A Magnificent Conscious Being

Mother Earth is screaming at us to stop and change our ways. We humans are not making enough changes to help Mother Earth birth her new vibration, and we keep poisoning her with so many chemicals. It is time to make the changes or we will not be on this planet any longer and our children won't have a home to evolve on. Our wildlife, who come to spend time with us and Mother Earth, will be extinct. In a barren landscape, there will be nothing for anyone to stay for. In the short time we have inhabited this planet, compared to the lifespan of Mother Earth, we will have destroyed everything.

Do you know how Mother Earth breathes?
Have you sat and felt the stillness in the air as the sun rises?
A breeze will pass you — that's Mother Earth inhaling (breathing in) the fresh breeze of a new day beginning.
When you sit at sunset as the sun goes below the horizon, a breeze will pass you — that's Mother Earth exhaling (breathing out).
Ah! That sigh of a big day passed.

She breathes in at dawn and out at dusk, which is how long her life span is—one breath per day. As for humans, we take approximately 21,600 breaths per day. In yogic traditions your life span is determined by the number of breaths you have in your life. Does it make sense then that Mother Earth is a large, living organism, and we are so small in comparison?

Try this for yourself at the next sunset or sunrise. It does not matter what the weather is, it will happen as a subtle breeze or wind. I always wait for this moment to present, then I take a sigh. It feels so powerful to breathe with Mother Earth, there is something magical about this synchronised breath, feeling at one with no separation. I learnt this many years ago when I was practicing Agnihotra (a way to purify the atmosphere through a specially prepared fire performed daily at sunrise and sunset).

Mother Earth is such an awesome being! She's been through so many changes before humans arrived, and will again after we have become extinct once more. She holds the records of all time and is evolving at a fast pace. We need to keep up with the plan of evolution by healing ourselves, purging our unconscious actions towards ourselves and others (such as the wildlife and animals who support us), as Mother Earth supports us on this beautiful blue planet that's been seen from space as the jewel. It will no longer be the jewel if our destructive actions continue.

We need to support this paradise, heaven on earth, as it was before humans came to live here. Too few see what she does for us, and I fear the ones waking up are not enough to keep the light coming to Mother Earth. We are transmitters of light and need to keep ourselves clear to bring the strong light of peace and joy to the earth.

Mother Earth holds the records of all time inside her being, through the rocks, the landscape and so many other areas. We cannot ignore this knowledge, as it's shown to us so often through land shifting and so on. Mother Earth's body needs to be respected, something we have not done as humans, which is causing Mother Earth discomfort, just as it would if your body was being exploited for resources. What if ants were drilling into your body, or irritating chemicals were thrown across your body—imagine how that would feel! This is how we need to think when we disrespect Mother Earth, for she feels this as we do. Just because she is much larger than us does not mean she does not feel it.

If you had toxic energy in your body would you not want to throw it off? That is how she feels. All the toxic energy in her body from the pain and suffering that occurs on this planet is in her memory, and she is now evolving, expanding with the rest of the galaxy. To do that, she needs to cleanse. That is what we are feeling now, and if we do not listen to what our bodies and nature are telling us, we will be thrown from the earth, possibly in traumatic ways.

Why not heal our hearts and be part of the evolution on this planet, expanding our hearts to feel more, and increasing our awareness and conscious state? This will be the way we can commune with Mother Earth. We are not able to do this if we have heavy hearts full of pain, grief or anger, for that stops your light shining. When your light shines, you can accept the light from other species, and Mother Earth or other humans, then you will not feel the continual sense of separation that so many humans suffer from.

It is so simple—heal the heart, and practice forgiveness for yourself and others. Meditation can help you do this at deep levels of the subconscious more easily and faster than any other technique. We cannot rely on others to heal us. They can support, but are not able to do the deep healing for you. You may feel you have received healing, but maybe you have received some love as a balm to sooth your pain and suffering. The real heart healing happens when we do it for ourselves, and we then stop causing more pain to ourselves and others.

> *It is time to exercise our free will to do our own healing at deeper levels. It is a life of healing to evolve, as the layers will continue to show themselves, like an onion. One layer goes and we feel more light and love, then another layer is removed at a deeper level, and so the cycle continues.*

We have so many lifetimes to release! Lucky for us, this is a special time to be on the planet to evolve and release to heal our hearts quickly, as Mother Earth and the galaxy are shifting quickly. If we don't, we will find it seriously uncomfortable with dis-ease presenting in the body quickly for us to either look at and heal, or to make our way back to our star homes we came from. This is my understanding of our evolution. My suggestion here: If you can meditate it will be a faster and easier way to evolve and find your light, joy and love within, and then you'll feel to share this with the many.

Inspiring others to start healing when they see your joy and feel your love, as your energetic field will glow with light, is all that is needed. We cannot do the healing for others, only support them with a safe space to do their own healing work. We all need to do our own healing. If others do it for you it gives short term benefits, but you will need to do the work for yourself eventually. Whatever troubles you at a deeper level, not healed, will continue to rise up until you heal it. Let it go and heal the dis-ease in your mind, body or spirit. It is not natural or harmonious for the body to be out of balance with dis-ease. When you have toxic energy from pain, grief and anger the body will keep triggering you to release it. If you ignore your healing the body will become diseased and force you physically to attend to it. That has been my truth on this earth.

50
Mother Earth and The Elemental Forces

I find myself continually surprised at what other species come to share with me. These messages I receive are always what I need to know right at that point in my life, such as a message from my past life experiences to help me see my gift I need to use in this life, or they have shared a past life with me and have been called to come to help me heal my heart, as my furry companion animal. How beautiful is that—a soul incarnating into another species' form to help another soul in human form to evolve. Is that unconditional love?

We owe so much to other species for their unconditional love, and those special companions who come to support us to become more conscious beings and to remember our gifts from our past lives. This has been a big experience for me on that level and I feel such gratitude to all who have come to me in that capacity. So many people walk around with eyes closed, totally distracted by what is happening beyond the physical world around them. I know this because I have been in that place of 'too busy' to see with all my senses. I know it is necessary to keep monitoring myself to make sure I do not miss the magic that is waiting to greet me. This has given me great joy in my heart and keeps me passionate about life, reminding me of the extraordinary planet we inhabit to evolve on.

I cannot help thinking the massive fires in Australia are here to help us wake up to see the importance of all life that supports us. I hope the awful losses of life and habitat will change the thinking of many who take so much for granted and are complacent about our government's decisions that allow our land to be raped for greed, supporting the many who are not consciously awake.

I do not support aggressive actions, however we can use our money and buying power. Big corporations cannot survive and keep doing what they do if they are not supported by a market who buys their products, and they know this. We have the power as a collective group to vote with our money and buy products that support our Mother Earth respectfully. Look a little deeper into what you support with your money. For example, many are getting the idea now that we have unveiled the sweat shops that many Asian countries use to produce our merchandise, and this has been changing the marketplace. Now it is time to consider the impact on other species and Mother Earth when we buy anything—are people being exploited and are the products sustainable and ethical? Are we, other species and Mother Earth being exploited in the production of our purchases?

Do we need everything we buy, or is it false desires leading us to look for joy and happiness that will never be fulfilled by material things? Happiness and love can only be found from within our own healed hearts, no material objects or person can do this for us.

There is a change flowing through the earth. The apocalyptic Australian fires were a wakeup call to all nations to understand that the earth and elements are way bigger than us. It is time for us to learn humility, for we have become too arrogant, thinking we are superior to Mother Earth and all species, controlling in our ways without respect for other species or the earth, driven by greed, power and money. As a nation, I don't believe Australians are an aggressive culture, but rather laid back, in particular when it comes to political action, as we do not act enough to stop our government doing as they please to our environment. I often hear it said, "It will be ok, mate!"

I feel there is a change happening now. The fires brought together all nations, and many religions that do not get on in other countries, united to help one another. This country tends to do that, as we have lived through many disasters, with Mother Earth always controlling us. She has been in control in Australia way before white man arrived, the Aboriginal people will tell you this. They understand Mother Earth's ways and have full respect, having seen over 45,000 years of her being in control.

The natural elements in Australia have always dominated our lives with dynamic seasonal shifts and extremes in temperatures. If you have lived out in the desert with the Aboriginal people, you really know what it means to live with the whims of Mother Earth. She controls your movements at every turn. You need to be vigilant of her cycles or you will be caught out and can lose your life.

We cannot control Mother Earth in Australia. In outback regions some corporations try to work with natural seasonal cycles, but still come under threat and sometimes need to move on to save themselves. For example, with something as basic as the placement of a road—if it is built where it is not meant to be, it will be ripped apart if Mother Earth disagrees on the placement. Aboriginal people have tried to warn the construction companies over the years, but it is generally ignored, and the road has been seriously taken down by the elements of Mother Earth within months of ending construction. I saw the results of this when I lived in a beautiful region of deep gorges in the Northern Territory, many years ago.

Several years before my time in the Northern Territory, I lived in Western Australia and a building contractor had built a resort on an ancient burial site, which was unveiled during construction. The Aboriginal people warned it would not be a good idea to build there, that there could be trouble, but the construction company ignored the warnings and continued. A cyclone arrived and the new resort was taken down—twice. I was told they eventually built back away from the burial site, after the second attempt to rebuild.

I have seen this story play out in many other regions of Australia where I have lived in remote areas where the land is respectfully honoured. The Aboriginal people try to give a message of warning to a corporation building disrespectfully. Speaking for the earth, "She doesn't want you to build here, there will be trouble," they say, and sure enough there are problems. The Indigenous people have learnt much about our Mother Earth, as the custodians. In co-habitation for thousands of years communing with earth, they know the land and the spiritual laws of the land and they respectfully ask for permission. Sadly, our Western culture has absolutely no idea about respect and spiritual law of the land, because we believe ourselves to be superior to Mother Earth, the elements and all other species.

From my travels across Australia, I have learnt the land has a way of reminding us she is in control here. Ignore that and you will see the consequences of your actions in a future time, unexpectedly, most often.

Should we take notice of the other species and what they know? Yes, say the Indigenous people of many countries. The other species have a wisdom beyond our connection to the earth, so they can help us in times of great change. At this time, it is most important for us all to observe how nature moves around us and if there are any changes to note. Maybe try to commune with them, to find out what they know that can also help you as a human moving across this earth. Simple observations I have noted since I was quite young are the movement of ants and snails. In Australia, the ants go crazy looking for food a few days before the big rains arrive. Snails start climbing up to high grounds or walls if rain is coming. Frogs usually sing a few hours before the rains come too, a sign I noticed while living in the tropical northern states of Australia. There is a frog that goes underground for five years or more in the desert of Australia, reappearing when the rain comes.

The dark spaces between the stars in the sky alert Indigenous communities to what wild foods will be available for them to source, and so much more. We know so little of their wisdom. They see the world from many realities and feel all the energy frequencies we can only dream of knowing about. Interesting to note that Westerners make points of reference based on the patterns the stars make in the sky, whereas the Indigenous culture reads the dark spaces between the stars—the opposite almost. My point here is that they see a deeper story from the unseen areas of nature.

I often purchased paintings from local artists whilst living in community with them, and I found it astounding that they would paint with the dots and symbols, using them as maps of the landscape. The twist is that the elders who painted these artworks had never been in a plane to see the aerial view, yet their paintings were based on the aerial view of the landscape they lived in. These people are so connected to the landscape, it is not separate from them—they *are* the landscape, something that becomes apparent only when you spend time with them and see the artworks from their regions.

The message I received in the desert communities was that Indigenous people come from the earth and we, the Westerners, come from the stars. This was proved to me repeatedly in what I witnessed and experienced with them, and is why we will never fully understand them, for we are from different ends of the spectrum. They know and understand magic and have an exceptionally well developed sixth sense, from my observations. We do have a great deal to learn from them about communing with other species and Mother Earth, for they have firsthand knowledge.

I believe we need to be in acceptance of all of our differences and share knowledge from both cultures. I feel we need to listen to our first nation people, not try to make them like us. These people have a great deal to share with us on forgiveness, as they have a lived experience from what Western culture have done to them in ignorance of not understanding their earth wisdom. Now they share their wisdom with us—this could not happen without forgiveness. It is time—we need to respect one another and accept our differences to live in harmony. We all have pieces to the puzzle of life, that is, all cultures and all species. Combining all knowledge will support us all to be in peaceful relationship with all beings on Mother Earth, this beautiful planet we call home.

If we can accept and respect the differences of Indigenous cultures, they can certainly help Western culture to remember, and learn how to commune with our Mother Earth and the ancestor souls so we can all live peacefully and respectfully. These nations have been living respectfully with Mother Earth and other species for thousands of years and still hold the knowledge that we may have once had in our ancestry. Our lives could be so magical and felt at such a deeper level. When you start communing with Mother Earth, the ancestors and other species everything feels alive—including yourself. The inner child returns and so much magic starts to present to us, and greater love than we can ever imagine is possible.

At this point in earth's history, great changes are taking place and it is crucial for us to be tuned in to them. The most important message I have received is that we need to tune in to our intuition and trust our own guidance, for we will not be in safe places if we become fearful. Fear creates decisions that will lead us into troubled areas where dramatic changes will be occurring as Mother Earth expands her energetic field and detoxes all the pain and suffering held there from thousands of years of trauma on this planet. If we're not walking consciously on Mother

Earth's body, we will be recycled and our spirit will need to leave the body it lives in. This is a huge subject which I've mentioned quite a bit in my first book, so I'll leave it here and mention that there are so many more reasons why we need to be communing with other species. Not only for our safety and joy, but because a bigger picture is being played out in our galaxy with Mother Earth shifting to a new, higher vibration.

It is time to respect and embrace the Indigenous races who hold vast knowledge and wisdom of earth in their culture. The time is now to listen to them and work together to build a new earth of love, joy and peace for all, living respectfully in harmony with all species and Mother Earth. From my messages when I commune with Mother Earth and other species, I believe the Australian fires were only the beginning, we've so many more changes to come. All the elements will have their time to balance out Mother Earth's energetic field and sort out the toxicity that has accumulated on her body, with some areas perhaps more toxic than others.

A warning—be prepared for some rocking and rolling with the extremes of all the elements across the planet. Some say this cleansing will happen from east to west, as we see in Australia. We cannot know how long this will continue, but it is an alert to other nations to be prepared, because Mother Earth is a powerful being indeed. Do not underestimate her ability to create the changes she needs. Whether humans are here or not, she will keep moving and expanding her body.

There are messages that many will be sacrificed, and I feel that has already become evident from what we are experiencing right now in Australia. We are yet to see the real effects as we are still in the grips of the fire season, with many fires still burning even with the rains. Some of our fire fronts had flames 100 metres high and devoured everything in their path, turning everything into charcoal or ash. That goes for the wildlife, not just the buildings. Many animals were burnt trying to get through fences when the fire front passed them, turning them to charcoal.

I hope no other country has to endure what we have in Australia, as the toll is being counted day by day. The sheer number of species we have lost is unbelievable, while the survivors need medical attention and caring for by thousands of volunteers on the ground. It's the beginning of the end of the world as we know it, and the beginning of a new world. That's how I see it. What will rise from the ashes? That's still to be seen.

51
Our Evolving Planet

*A pivotal time in our planet's history,
as humans come to support Mother Earth's
evolutionary shift of the ages to a new vibrational
frequency of Peace, Joy and Love.*

Survival of the fittest will be needed now, as the planet evolves and changes with seasons, weather patterns and oceans tides—so many changes. This planet will survive without us, in fact, I am sure she would be better off without our destructive nature. If we learn to survive with other species, we can surely also learn to live here in peace and harmony with all species and stop destroying everything.

I find it difficult to understand why our governments are so fixed on looking for other planets to land on when I've travelled across the earth for the past fifty years or more, and can tell you it is stunningly beautiful. Every country offers regions that can inspire us. They are like paradise, and then I learn some greedy corporation has found a reason to rape the land of a resource and the paradise is lost to machinery or poisoned by chemicals.

There is no other paradise. We are privileged to live on this beautiful planet. Just look at all the planets in our immediate galaxy that scientists explore. The environments are harsh, arid, too cold or too hot to live on, with no compatible air for us to survive in our human bodies. Time for us to vote with our wallets! If we don't support the corporations who rape Mother Earth, they'll have no money or market for their goods.

How can we change this? Be discerning of what you purchase and where it is sourced from. I believe many of us do this already, but we need to keep it going in every area of our life when we make decisions to support a company with our money or time. We do not need to protest loudly, protesting silently with our wallets is powerful. There is a catch—we may need to live more simply than the ways we have taken for granted in the past, consuming more than we need.

I believe we are ready in the Western world. Questions are being asked and many are offloading possessions as they start to experience the joy of living more lightly. However, we still have many humans addicted to purchasing and supporting the manufacture of more than they really need. For example, my husband and I live in a comfortable economic region of Australia compared to developing world countries, but many here would say it is a lower demographic region. I disagree with this thinking, as I have lived in many different demographic areas and travelled across many regions of the world, and the waste I see here saddens me.

When I first came back to the east coast of Australia after living in remote areas of Australia, I was blown away by the amount of good quality furniture left on the side of the road as rubbish so more new items could be purchased. Such a consumable society we live in! In remote areas of Australia, I never saw anything wasted. Everything was recycled or upcycled into beautiful items. I have moved a great deal, and every time our goods were sold or given away and we would decorate our next home with pre-loved furniture. We have been surprised to find such incredible, good quality items for our home that others were throwing away, and we have been offered many items by friends and family.

Recycling for the planet, we only take what we need for the home. We have also found by posting on social media, such as a community Facebook page, that many are willing to give us their excess furniture. We have been able to decorate all our homes very comfortably, and sometimes have actually had to decline offers because we had enough. We always found it exciting to never know how our home would be comfortably decorated in each location.

Funny—one region we moved to, we made a conscious decision to use a minimalist approach. We agreed to have a surprise birthday party there for a friend's partner, and everyone who came asked if we were still waiting on our furniture to be delivered from our old address, three thousand kilometers away in another state! Our response was no, this was all we needed, what else did we need? We were happy to find what we needed at a second-hand store and it all matched our preferred comfort style for the house. The next week, we had neighbours dropping furniture on our veranda with lovely little notes stating, "We thought you might like this piece of furniture." We kindly declined.

Over many years, we have proven that you can live simply with used furniture items that are in good condition and be comfortable, and not be out of pocket trying to work hard to pay them off. I believe we have plenty of furniture available without using up precious resources making more. People get tired of their furniture even though it is still functional, or they feel it was dated? Dated from what, and when? If it works, why get rid of it? Our ancestors did not have the money or luxury to keep throwing away what was not broken, not like we do these days with no thought to where it goes.

We really need to take stock of what is inappropriate to be thrown away, to rethink our actions. If we cannot stop this crazy habit, perhaps we can trial leaving the dumped items in our own backyards so we can see how much space is needed to store them. Recycle and relieve the heavy burden we are placing on Mother Earth's body, causing it to be toxic. It is too easy to throw away, and people need to see where it ends up. When you go to over-populated countries with developing economies, you begin to get a sense of the magnitude of this problem for our earth, and the space we have available for so many people to survive on one planet now (seven and a half billion).

> *"Earth provides enough to satisfy everyone's need, but not everyone's Greed."*
>
> *Gandhi*

The situation is only worsening as developing nations have more income to spare. This is such a big subject, I am not sure I can do it justice here, but I would like to alert you to the facts so you might rethink before you throw functional working items out to buy new ones. I know it is hard with appliances because they are made to not last, but how many appliances do we really need? Do we need every appliance offered to us by the marketing corporations? They want you thinking you need their gadgets to make life easier, but at what cost?

When we keep purchasing, we keep needing to work harder to pay for these items, and use much energy looking after our possessions. By living simply, I can work less and have more time and energy to do what I am passionate about. Something to consider? I worked this out many years ago, realising the material things around me did not make me happy. The more things I owned, the harder I had to work to keep it all going. I became more stressed, and was forced to stop and reflect on my life. I did some soul searching and released old habits of collecting things.

I found my personal freedom and joy did not come from things from the outside world, it come from inside of me. That is how I live. If I find myself unhappy, I now look inside of me. I do not go looking for something to buy, because that never works, it's only short term, another distraction for the mind to not focus on what really makes you happy.

Travelling more consciously and awake to all the realities and dimensions that surround us on this earth with other species, I only take photos home with me, nothing else. I find it so enlightening to live this way, making my life journey one that has worked for me. There are many other ways to have experiences. Maybe spend time with people you feel happy to be around, or join a group of like-minded people with the same interests as you. Volunteer to help a group that assists others, like wildlife rescue organisations, a dog pound, or people less fortunate than yourself. There are so many ways to find happiness away from shopping. Try—it worked for me—it may help you too.

There is a message here to keep healing our hearts and open to the bigger, mysterious interdimensional world around us so we can all learn to live respectfully with Mother Earth and other species. Practice opening to the world beyond this 3D reality and we can all be rewarded with a happier, joyful life with a deeper connection to everything around us, which feels like the world is fully alive and wanting to talk with us all. You cannot help feeling a full heart when these experiences are felt at such a deep level and rise up within you. These connections go beyond anything possibly felt in the physical world that I know of. They are profound experiences to find your own wisdom and remember who you really are and what you came to earth to do, finding your purpose and mission to be here—maybe even find your gifts as I've done. How much better than that does it get?

It sure is a grand plan, way beyond the limited unconscious human mind of logic, is all I can say, but the heart knows greater things as it plugs you directly into the universal energy field that surrounds us and goes beyond the planet to other realms beyond time and space. The energetic field our heart plugs into is the unified field of unconditional love, source consciousness, which goes beyond our own physical bodies, a force unseen and unquantifiable. Maybe quantum science will one day find this measurement, but I feel it is a changing phenomenon as all of nature keeps changing through cycles. Even scientists agree we are in a galaxy that is expanding. How can that be quantifiable? The magic is that we do not know all the mysteries of life, but we can enjoy playing in them and moving about with them joyfully and peacefully, filled with love and light.

Our world is a marvellous place to reside in a human body form, don't you think? We have so much to learn and experience from our heart space, it would be a shame if you came to earth and missed out on the experience of feeling plugged into the many realms of this earth around you by not communing with the many other beings you share this planet with. I cannot stress enough the joy, heart warmth and connection that comes from being a more conscious being and connecting to all other species. You will never feel alone.

Here's a scenario to think about—the 3D earth or the multi-dimensional earth?

You take a holiday to a beautiful location overseas. You were on your way to Paradise Park, but on the path you were distracted by another location with minor attractions, a Wonderful Fun Park (3D earth). Sure, the fun park had many noisy rides to go try, giving you short-lived but exciting, fun moments, but you had to keep doing it over and over again to get the same kicks because it never lasted. Sadly, your holiday time has run out, you need to return home now, but you missed going to the location you came to experience, Paradise Park (multi-dimensional earth), a mysterious and magical location with access to many realities. Your heart could have received waves of unconditional love filling you with joy and freedom you could have taken back home with you for eons of time. At this point, you do not know if you will have another opportunity to return to Paradise Park. Will you miss out on Paradise Park—the multi-dimensional earth experience?

52

Power of Feminine Cycles and Earth Mother

Women honouring their wisdom and magic can work with the natural world to find empowerment.

Whilst living in outback Australia, I felt called to have an outdoor bath in my backyard. It had no roof, stones on the bare earth, and the water was hot and cold, sourced from our local river. The walls were bamboo, completely concealed by a scented star jasmine vine growing thickly over the walls. I was moving through a cycle in my life, the discomforts of menopause (some also call it men o pause), and felt a strong heart calling to be supported by Mother Earth and nature.

This life cycle, where the fertile woman leaves the body for the wise woman to be accessible to her, can be quite daunting, as many changes are taking place emotionally, mentally, physically and spiritually as a woman. She is detoxing her old life, shredding the old ways and making space to begin a new, powerful cycle in her life—the wise woman. This cycle can be uncomfortable if a woman is not connected to the natural cycles of life. I found it the most empowering time in my life. Some of the physical and emotional symptoms can be grief, depression, irregular menstrual cycles, cloudy thinking, tiredness, physical body changes with weight gain and erratic emotions as the hormones find a new balance in the body. On the positive note, my spiritual growth accelerated, finding my wisdom deeply empowering.

Menopause became a strong spiritual experience for me when I connected to nature, Mother Earth with the elements and the ancestors, and I felt their support. It was a great time for me to detox my body with foods, and my thoughts with meditation. Another powerful practice I found very necessary was to nourish and nurture myself with selfcare practices. A vital link in managing menopausal symptoms, this healed me emotionally, physically, mentally and spiritually to feel loved, nurtured and balanced in my life, and I understood I needed to practice this regularly.

How did I do this? With my beautiful outdoor bath and mother nature. My bath was filled with the element of water (warmed) from the river, and fresh herbs I collected from my garden, always asking which would like to be in my bath. The aroma from the star jasmine vine and the herbs in the warm water were incredibly soothing. I would choose the phase of the moon cycle that called me, so I was bathed by Grandmother moon whilst the star ancestors and the Milky Way sat above my head. As we lived in a remote regional area, we had no pollution from city lights. The candles around the bath reminded me of the fire and light in my heart, and the passion and transformation of my emotions.

In this enchanting world I created I was able to meditate and go deep into my body, emotions and spirit to witness the changes and what was arising within me. I so enjoyed the upper earth of cosmos above reminding me of the bigger picture of life we are part of, while the earth was all around me and offered many gifts for my bath. I visited the lower earth in my meditation, receiving deep healing for my emotions, mind, body and spirit. In the daytime I would regularly visit the local river and commune with wildlife and Mother Earth, making my heart sing with joy.

It was a magic time in my life. Sure, it was not all comfortable, but the rituals made everything easier to manage because I felt loved, nourished and whole, not afraid of the new cycle approaching that connected me even deeper than I'd experienced previously. I did have to go to hospital to control bleeding that had caused me problems for some time. That was a powerful experience with the hospital staff. All my practices of connecting in nature inspired and empowered me as a woman, which became apparent at my hospital visit.

The doctors mentioned I may need more done in the operation, perhaps the removal of my womb. I had consented to a minor operation, and advised the doctors I did not give consent to take any parts of my body, no matter what they deemed necessary, unless I was consulted first and agreed. This meant taking me out of the anesthetic to ask for my consent. They were surprised by my request, apparently it was not normal for a patient to ask this, thus the power is usually left to the doctors. I had prepared a letter of agreement to honour my request, and they agreed and signed it, shaking their heads.

I found it so empowering to voice my sovereignty. It was my initiation, and I acted as an empowered wisewoman. I was strong on the point of not removing body parts without my consent, for I knew for me to be connected to Mother Earth I needed my womb, a woman's power centre. I did keep my womb, and I left that hospital with the message that I had released some past life energetic attachments in my womb space that caused me dis-ease. I did feel the moment it energetically left my body permanently.

Before going into hospital, I had been doing rituals with the natural world and the elements, using visualisations to release what was causing my problems. It was all quite a journey, but I do remember how all the species I connected with gave me a sense of support in so many ways through my senses of sight, smell, and feeling them in my heart. I was also reminded of the cycles of life, that everything comes and goes, from young to older versions, then changing form through the gate of death to another realm of existence.

It was an inspiring and thought-provoking time, communing so naturally with all the natural world around me. I feel in a large city centre I would have missed so much on that healing journey of menopause. It was the trees who called me to that region to live when my menopause began. I spent time with the old river gums every day to be reminded of the cycles of life and the wisdom held in nature, as I communed with nature, other species and the ancestors of the land.

Before menopause, when I was still fertile, I used cloth pads. Sharing here for women a very empowering practice. Before washing the cloth pads in detergent, I had a ritual of rinsing them in fresh water and pouring the blood-stained water onto Mother Earth's body around my lemon tree. Within months, it began to bear fruit several times a year instead of annually. I found this a powerful practice that connected me at a deeper level to feel empowered and connected to Mother Earth.

For a fertile woman, I suggest you try it and see what it does for you. Be sure to do it with sacredness and consciously offer it to Mother Earth's body as a gift and she will love you for it.

Not Honouring Mother Earth's Blood

Some years after we left the region, the river that supported me to heal experienced a change in water flow. It had stopped and dried up in parts of that region due to disrespect and unconscious actions by governing authorities. I was sad to find out, as I received healing and nourishment from that river and all the species who relied on her flowing, the earth's blood I call it. The Indigenous people and the smaller farmers who relied on the river were never consulted to help with management. Large, greedy corporations had diverted the water supply.

I once heard an Indigenous elder share that when the landscape dies, so do the people and all species who rely on it, and that is exactly what had happened in that region of Australia. The rivers are the blood arteries of Mother Earth's body, she needs the flow, and we need her blood. The river needs to flow with nourishment to many places for all species to survive. Greed by a few wealthy investors changed all that.

I watched that river go through many seasonal cycles. I witnessed the ways it accommodated drier times with billabongs in concentrated areas for all species to have water. When the floods came it would be cleansed and transformed back to life with abundant wildlife. This is not the case for the river right now, sadly, it has struggled to flow.

Our ancient Indigenous culture in this region had never seen or heard of the river drying up, not once during thousands of years of their care. Now we are left with dead fish and other wildlife species who also relied on the water flow. Droughts are a natural cycle in Australia, but the Indigenous people know how to live with these cycles and Mother Earth has always been able to balance.

We face a huge problem—how to support Mother Earth to find the balance again. I'm not sure the governing authorities would agree, but it's obvious to me that we need to honour and acknowledge through ceremony, calling the ancestors and all the elements with Mother Earth to support her to be energized to find her own body balance. Thanks to so many unconscious decisions made by humans, Mother Earth may need a long time to find the balance. I am sure she will if we do not interfere. That is the challenge for humans, to let nature find a way, to honour the natural process.

Humans interfere unconsciously in nature, causing great pain and suffering to the earth and other species, including ourselves, as we are sustained by Mother Earth. This happens when we are not connected to the natural world around us and see ourselves as separate from everything. On top of this big challenge, we had the worst fires in history due to poor management of the land. Once again, our governing authorities weren't listening to the signs that presented in nature and ignored the Indigenous people's vast knowledge of the extraordinary landscape we live in, unique to anywhere else on the planet regarding the cycles of nature. The governing authorities are not communing with the natural world around them to learn how they damage the ecosystem for every species.

It's time for us to honour our landscape with gratitude, as the Indigenous cultures have done, to acknowledge everything we live with on the earth as our family, to call in the spirits of the ancestors, with all the elements (water, fire, air and earth) and do ceremony with Mother Earth. It can be a simple prayer blessing—it doesn't need to be complicated. We need to respect all we live with. It is out of balance, and it is time now to support Mother Earth to be energized and alive to do what she does best—to find a healthy balance for her body. When she is healthy, we are also kept in good health, being gifted with all we need to survive, in abundance.

Working with Mother Earth's Intelligence and Wisdom in Our Gardens

Consciously working with Mother Earth and the elements, honouring and being aware in our own garden landscape where we live, can be a powerful experience as Mother Earth offers healing to all who connect consciously.

When planting seeds in your garden try this tip: Place the seeds in your mouth and cover them with your saliva before you bury them. They will be sensitive and pick up from your body fluid nutrients that your body may be lacking, then the plant will give you what you need in its growth, ready for you to use, with gratitude.

Walk barefoot in your garden so the earth can determine what you need to balance your body and give you nutrient-rich plants. For example, I've noticed dandelions in yards lately, including mine, suggesting our bodies need to detox now, which isn't surprising with all the toxins in our environment, earth, land, sea and the bushfires of past months (dandelion is not a weed, it is a herb used to detox the liver).

You are probably throwing away or mowing over what nurtures and heals your body. So many wild weeds are still being found to have qualities we did not know about. Dandelion flowers are edible and have the highest Omega 3 of any plant. What would happen if we let nature's intelligence and wisdom act without us poisoning and changing the balance of nature?

Having lived in many climates, I have learnt how the earth goes through extreme cycles and the terrain is changed dramatically. When I have simply observed, without interfering and trying to change (by giving water if too dry, etc.), I've witnessed Mother Earth balance the cycle beautifully and been gifted the most extraordinary varieties of wildflowers grown from soil that was parched and dry most of the year, and grass suddenly appearing from the sand when the rain arrives after years. Mother Earth knows how to store nature's seeds to be activated at exactly the right moment.

When moving or planting a tree or shrub, a beautiful way to honour and respect the plant is to ask it intuitively where it would be happiest in your garden, or use your pendulum to ask the plant what it would like, such as which aspect (north, south, east or west) and whether near another tree or shrub. You will be surprised what you receive, and doing this gives the tree a good chance to survive, because it knows what it needs. I have made the mistake of not asking and the tree did not thrive. It is all about respecting other species, for they have a consciousness too.

All good reasons to have your own garden, don't you think? There are so many benefits, when you consider earthing our feet can keep our bodies healthy by reducing potentially disease-causing inflammation, and earthing energises us from that big organic battery (of crystals) in the centre of the earth, charged by the sun. The plant kingdom has a consciousness to share with us too if we let nature's intelligence and wisdom be heard and hold off on the poison. The poisons so freely used in gardens will kill us eventually, a karmic act. Why destroy other species when they can help us to heal our bodies? It is insanity to kill what can support us.

Many months ago, when the climate was extremely dry for our region, we had an explosion of a spiky bindi plant (little thorns in the lawn that many call weeds) taking over our backyard, as did all the neighbours. We live in a rental home, so the local real estate agent came on inspection, spotted our spiky bindi outbreak and suggested we use a poison to kill the 'bindi weeds' as she called them. We didn't follow her suggestion, but some months later the climate changed and they all disappeared, without our interference, and I walked barefoot again. Whilst some neighbours have continued to weed and poison their lawns, trying to beat nature, our lawn looks healthy, rich and thick with growth compared to theirs, with little interaction, just a cut occasionally, close to the house, so we can see any snakes who may pass by.

The earth element can remind us of letting go of things that die, in our gardens and in nature, so new things can be reborn. It is part of the natural cycle of life. Throughout life, sharing my upsets and loneliness with Mother Earth and other species has been a healing balm for my heart, reminding me I am not alone.

A beautiful practice I do every day is go outside for a few minutes, usually at breakfast, to connect with Mother Earth and other species. I stand barefoot on Mother Earth's belly and visualize my roots going down. I take three deep breaths, breathing in love and breathing out love through my heart space. Acknowledging the sun and divine light above, I bring it down into my heart and down to Mother Earth, then breathe in her love and harmony up into my body, allowing it to fill me up with love from my feet up into every cell. This lasts intuitively a few minutes before I disconnect and ask if there are any messages for me today. I receive her messages through her other children (the other species, our relations), observing who comes to visit me. I give thanks for all she gifts me to sustain my life. This is done by bending and placing my right hand on my heart space, and my left hand on Mother Earth's belly, sharing my love and my gratitude with her.

Recently, whilst I sat with Mother Earth, sharing my thoughts of the sadness and pain in my heart from the destruction of the devastating fires in my country and the loss of so many lives and species, Mother Earth shared her wisdom with me.

2019: Message received from Oversoul of Mother Earth.

I cannot support anyone who is not of the heart any longer. It is holding my evolution back and I have a much bigger plan here that needs to be unfolded, so many will start to realise this soon.

But in the meantime, keep sharing your heart, dearest. Many will listen. They want to know what is going on here on my body, and you've so much information to share with them in your own heart. You will feel the heart healing that's part of your journey, but you've so many here supporting you to do what you came to do. With great love and respect, they come to help you do your service to humanity. Remember you are not alone.

You have so much to share from eons of time. You have held back much in your life due to your trauma, and it needs to now be released. We were so happy for your insight on finding your mastery of not allowing your emotions to rule any longer so you can succeed in your journey.

You have a team of so many here supporting you to succeed in this lifetime. You have helped so many in so many lifetimes, it is time for you to now feel that returned to you in abundance and honouring, as you so deserve in this life.

Do not hold back any longer, you are offering a path to be enlightened, it's your time and it is now. All is as it is meant to be. Allow the cycle you are on to unfold in your timing. You do not need to push any longer. Practice using grace so the universal laws can come into play. You have already experienced this, and now it is time to remember that and how that is done.

Trust the process and your soul's direction. No need to do anything except write your story for many to read and find their own way. So many are lost, and more will be after all the changes that are going to be coming to this earth for humans to move faster on their evolution. It's a big time for all of you to really seize this moment in time.

In Peru, I loved the tradition of honouring Mother Earth and her life-giving gift to us by sharing a drop of our water with the land before we drank any ourselves.

How often do you honour Mother Earth and her offerings as you drink her water, enjoy a bath, breathe the air into your lungs, acknowledge the fire that keeps you warm and cooks your food, and acknowledge the ancestors and your other relations in everything around you—the rocks, trees, elements, other species and the natural world?

Travelling in Africa, I was consistently reminded of the cycles of life. Our group were getting ready to go and eat a meal at our safari campsite. There were no fences, and a pride of lions camped near us by a creek bed. We could see them and zebras in the vicinity of our tents.

As we sat down to eat this night, a huge, thundering noise passed the tent.

"What was that?" we all called out.

Masai Warriors, who patrolled our campsite, came to check on everyone. My husband Nigel was missing from the dining tent, so the warriors dashed off to find him. Turned out he'd seen the lion charging past him and felt its power at full speed as he sat outside on a deck chair, and had gone back to our tent for safety and to take a rest, shaken by what he had witnessed so close to him. Later, he shared it was like a freight train passing by, so much power and force he'd felt from the lion. Lucky the lion was focused on the zebra for dinner, and not him.

Whilst we sat, waiting for our main meal to be served, we heard screeching and commotion near our dining tent. It was a zebra trying to get away as a lion took him down. The Masai warriors reported back to let us know Nigel was safe in our tent and instructed us not to leave unless we were escorted by the warriors back to our tents, now it was dark. They also shared it was not good for the zebra—the lion had killed him. After the commotion had settled and finding Nigel was safe in our tent, there was no way I could stay and eat my meal, so I asked to be escorted back to our tent to rest for the night. The cycle of death up close and personal was so confronting.

Out in the 4WD the next day, we were privileged again to see lions. This time we witnessed two courting. A female was in the bushes within a few feet of our 4WD, then she came out into the open and played with the male, teasing him. After an hour of the courting game, she lay down beside the front tyre of our 4WD and the male was given the signal to mate with her. It was fascinating to witness the conception of a new being. We had witnessed death and a new cycle of life beginning, all within twenty-four hours. The natural cycles of life on earth continue without interference by humans.

With Gratitude

53

Souls from the Past

*I have so much gratitude for all the souls
who have come to support my earthly journey to evolve.*

Reincarnation is a reality for me. I've no doubt we return to earth for more lives to learn and gain wisdom. Over years of healing myself, I have experienced many flashbacks and memories from past lives that spontaneously appeared to me in meditation, or as messages at unexpected times. For example, while having a massage one day, my memory of a past life in Atlantis returned to me quite vividly. Remembering something that had upset me, this vision helped me understand my strong reaction to something I witnessed in this life. Another time, a different massage therapist stopped massaging me because she was receiving a message from my father. He had left the planet twenty-seven years prior, and shared a strong message of guidance for my soul's journey in this life.

Sitting in silent meditation and feeling into a dilemma that requires resolution, a clear vision of a past life will present to me, giving me greater clarity on what action I need to take in this life. So many past lives have presented to me since the early 1990s, when I started to heal my heart of deep wounds. These memories have helped me remember who I am, why I came to earth, my purpose, and what my gifts are to share while I live on earth.

Incarnating for a life journey on earth in a human bodysuit, we come with maybe 3% of consciousness, with limited memories from our past lives. As children, we have sensitive hearts that may remember some aspects of our soul's past lives, however as we grow to experience more of our earthly life our sensitive hearts can be traumatized, causing cloudy, heavy hearts and distortions in our energetic field. This blocks the flow of light and access to our akashic records (higher consciousness) beyond time and space, that energetically holds the past, present and future of our soul's core beliefs and the wisdom that can help to heal us and guide us on our soul's journey here on earth.

My soul companions have never left my sight, giving me healing even when I was not consciously aware of how they were helping me. It became clearer later in life when I started to consciously commune with them and they were able to share their stories with me spiritually, and why they came to help me and support me on my soul's journey as I walk on earth, evolving every day. It has been a big lesson, as I slowly remember my past lives with other species and my connections, which were natural back then.

Animals listen and support us unconditionally, without judgment. They read the energetic field from your soul to theirs, a most extraordinary ability animals have of reading our heart energy. Given a chance, they will help you in the most profound ways you could ever imagine. I have had magical experiences with many species, not only cats and dogs. It really is an amazing world when you open your heart to other species and make space for them to be with you in the present moment of life. They just know what to do and how to make you feel so lovingly supported and nurtured.

I encourage you to look past the moment, to allow yourself to be with other species and let them share great wisdom and messages with you. You do not have to have an animal companion friend, go outside and be with any species who comes to you. Be open in your heart and let them in for a moment and see what takes place. You may be surprised at what you experience and the depth of what is shared by them. Believe me, you will not be disappointed! I suggest you try it for yourself—go outside in nature and sit quietly with an open heart and see what presents to you.

Mandy is but one example. Her soul came to me in a puppy bodysuit and opened my heart. Her passing away showed me death doesn't mean permanently gone, rather it's transformation into another form to live in another realm of existence—that's how our companions are always with us.

You may remember from the channeling from Charles, also a soul in a dog's bodysuit, that he came to help me remember my soul's mission on earth—to use sound with crystals to work with the energetic grids of the earth, and to remember my special gift of connecting with other species, to be their voice on the planet.

Harley's soul has come to me twice in this life, first as a kitten and again in an adult cat's bodysuit. Harley came to help me remember my days in Egypt and that I needed to return to connect with the energy grids of that land, and to keep healing my heart and open my third eye so I might see more into other realms of existence when communing with other species.

All species can help heal us. Do not be fixated on believing healing can only come from animal companions. They all have the capacity to help us heal our hearts of fear and to feel love for all species. A beautiful example was Smartie, my niece's furry companion—a soul in a rat bodysuit. When I met Smartie many years ago, she wore a large white coat over a large-sized body and possessed a highly intelligent, curious and friendly nature. My niece connected with Smartie as a young child and had chosen her from a pet shop.

This dear soul had full run of the house and rarely spent time in her cage. Visitors who saw her for the first time as she passed them in the living room, particularly some of my niece's mother's friends, often screamed.

"A rat!" they would scream. My niece's response was always the same, "She will not hurt you."

After a cup of tea and the guest tentatively watching the little rat move about, they would start to come around to her. She always found a way to be near them and open their hearts. Before no time at all, that little rat would be on their laps or shoulders and they would overcome their fear as their hearts felt the love. They would leave saying how sweet and intelligent she was, no longer showing any signs of fear towards her, realising that maybe all species want to commune with humans joyfully and open our hearts to love, not fear.

I always found those brief encounters, witnessing people's reactions of fear turning to love, to be extraordinary skills of Smartie the rat. A very apt name! That dear little rat lived a long life, way beyond what the vet deemed a normal lifespan for this species. Why? My belief is because she was loved dearly, roamed freely and shared her love with everyone, and by healing their hearts she received love back from them. She so inspired love on this planet!

If you believe every species needs to be respected and has a mission on this earth, Smartie supports that. She was given an opportunity by her caring family to do her mission on this planet of healing fear in hearts. What an extraordinary soul she was to come to heal humans in a rat's bodysuit. How lucky she found my niece as her human companion.

When I practiced animal communication for other carers many years ago, I received a great number of requests. Some wanted to know what they could do for their furry companion's illness, and many asked about their companions after they had passed away—were they comfortable, did they have a message for their carer? I noticed many animal companions had been so sensitive they had been taking on the stresses in the home of the family, and their carer's illnesses (such as cancer), but the carers had no idea. How extraordinary that our soul companions come to support us, then take our pain and suffering. I so resonated with those messages. Being a sensitive empathic soul, I have taken on many pains of other humans and other species.

Are you a sensitive who takes on the pain and suffering of others? If you do, you may need to release it, or you may experience illnesses that are not yours. This has been one of my biggest lessons in this life. When we hold pain in our body energetically, ours or from others around us, if not released, it manifests physically to cause us dis-ease.

Sharing here an animal communication request I receive from a client named Vera, a woman who had a soul companion, a Persian cat named Minka. Before Minka died, she experienced many health issues, causing her to urinate around the house. Vera became stressed, causing her to experience an allergy to Minka's fur coat. This frustrated Vera so much that she no longer allowed Minka near her, or in her bedroom. Vera shared with me Minka was fed and watered, but they may not have been on such friendly terms because of the stress caused to them both before

Minka died. I wondered if Vera felt guilty for her frustrations, if that was why she wanted to have a communication session with her companion?

Message received from Minka, to support Vera through grief.

Minka: Tell Vera to keep trying to contact me to open her heart more.

Debra: Vera wants to know if you are comfortable?

Minka: I am very comfortable and peaceful on the other side, with no pain. Tell Vera I am not coming back to the planet, I am already with her, and that I want her to practice opening her heart to me in meditation to connect our hearts. My purpose to be with Vera was to help her open her heart.

Tell her yes, we did have many past lives together, but that is not relevant now. I came to help her open her heart energy. Tell her it would be helpful if she centred herself more often.

Debra: She wants to know if your passing was comfortable?

Minka: Let her know I felt her love when I passed over.

Debra: Does she need a toy to help her connect with you?

Minka: This can help initially to open her heart fully, then a physical item of me will not be needed, just to feel my spirit, then I will know my work has been done.

Debra: Any other messages for Vera?

Minka: Yes, tell her I have not gone anywhere, I am still here with her. Tell her to find a peaceful space and practice opening her heart. This will prepare her for new contacts and people in her life.

Debra: Many blessings Minka, thank you. I will pass this on to Vera.

The response from Vera, "I'm too busy this week, I'm getting healing sessions. I'll try to meditate with Minka on Saturday." I thought this an interesting response from the carer.

Our furry companions have many wise words to share with us if we find the time and space in our lives to stop, open our hearts and listen to their wisdom. They want to commune with humans and support us. They always listen to us without judgment and want to give us unconditional love to open and heal our hearts, to take our pain as their own pain. They sense danger and protect us, teach us and give guidance on our soul's journey on earth, while showing us courage and the determination to never give up, to keep us in the present moment of being and to feel joyfulness.

Can you find the time to commune with your furry companion each day?

Have you felt your heart expand with love when holding your furry companions?

54
The Joy of Communing with the Others

*Our planet and galaxy are going through an evolutionary shift of the ages right now. It is time for humans to embrace other species and offer the respect they deserve by treating them with love and adoring them.
It is time to feel the love they come to share with all humans here on earth.
We need to listen to their stories, for they are our relations who have come to support us.*

What have I gained from communing with other species? Every day I have gratitude for all the souls who have come into my life since my childhood to support my evolution as a human being. Life is a magical joy ride of experiences in my heart on this earth and beyond the physical world, to feel oneness with everything around me, never feeling alone or separate, living in dual realities of existence.

They support me to feel strong connections to everything here on earth, knowing all species are my relations on many realms of existence. They remind me what unconditional love feels like, sharing with me, as I do with them. I have great respect for all species and the wisdom and love they share. They have listened and heard me without judgment, and I have received many gifts and surprises from them. I have been shown the mysteries of life, which continue to unfold.

I feel supported on my soul's journey through life, as they remind me of my gifts, and remembering my past lives with each of them has helped me understand my life here on earth, to know myself more—my 'Who, What and Why' (who I am, why I am here, and what my purpose is on earth). They have shared so much healing with me for my soul's evolution, as other species on earth or as my soul galactic family from other dimensional realms. There have been no barriers, only my mind. My heart has expanded and healed every time I have communed with them all. They have enriched my life, giving me a greater understanding of the deeper meaning of life beyond the physical world. So much magic, greater joy, more freedom and deeper love has made my life experience richer.

I have received many blessings from across other realms beyond the 3D world of existence with my ancestors' souls presenting in many forms. The great mysteries of life have unfolded to show me what an awesome web of love and light we are part of. We land on earth as a spark from this greater, infinite force that holds everything together with love. I have felt so many wonderful blessings bestowed upon me at times, briefly it has raised my self-doubt—do I deserve so much love from so many?

So much gratitude I feel for my life journey with so many souls coming to support me, teach and play with me here on earth, as I chose a human bodysuit for my soul to evolve. I can only wonder what bodysuit I will choose next time to come and play?

The love I feel in my heart for other species goes beyond words, and this 3D reality, because we are all vibrating frequencies of divine love. As humans, we come to earth as a heart of the burning fire of love, then over the years we experience traumas that dampen our heart's ability to feel our divine spark and where we come from. When I spend time with my furry companions and other species, this love is rekindled for me to remember what it feels like to feel unconditional love. I then feel my heart begin to heal by expanding in response to what I receive from them.

Gifted to be this sensitive with other species is a double-edged sword, as feeling their love, I can also feel their pain. That has been too much for me to bear at times, and I would shut down and not feel love around me any longer, then begin to feel separate and alone from everything. That is when many souls from my family of light have presented to help me. They come in many body forms, such as my animal companions in cat and dog bodysuits. Other times they are in the elements, in the landscape or the trees, their souls presenting to remind me I am connected, for they are all my relations on earth in nature—I'm not alone or separate from anything here on earth. So many souls have come to me in so many bodysuits, such as the dolphins, crystals, rocks and the trees. I will never feel alone or separate again, as my ancestor souls are all around me.

I have no doubt when a soul comes from my ancestor soul family, for I know the vibration of a soul from my past in my heart. If my logical mind tries to interfere and confuse me with doubt of what I'm feeling and why, I simply ignore that little ego of chatter and feel deeper, listening to my higher heart's message from my soul, for it knows my truth. Sometimes, I may not find out until later why a family soul member arrives as another species, then it becomes clear they came to support my journey and remind me of my soul's purpose and why I came to earth.

Our heart is the portal to our soul, and does not forget our past life connections with other souls. Rather, it holds the records for all time of loved ones we have travelled with inter-dimensionally in the past, so when these souls come to us again, we know through our hearts without a doubt, even though our logical mind may be confused and cannot logically work it out. When our higher heart is ignited with a being we already know, it is a meeting of frequencies, communing soul-to-soul. Our heart-soul intelligence has all the answers, because our soul's memory holds the truth and cannot be deceived. We do not need others to tell us what our truth is, for it is all inside of us, our own wisdom.

Do you see—the portal gateway to our truth and divine love is through the heart and soul at a higher intelligence of wisdom and knowing. This connection keeps me present in the moment with my mind and body in reverence for all that is around me. I then feel connected to everything, no longer separate, and feel everything is alive and wanting to commune with me here on earth. When I commune with other species the connection of mind, body and spirit keeps me relaxed, ready to listen and be heard in the most profound ways that continually surprise me. My earthliness becomes so much more of a multidimensional experience beyond the 3D world, taking me to other realms of existence at that moment in time, reminding me I'm not my bodysuit, I'm a spiritual being having a human experience in this human form.

What Have I Learnt From My Interactions With Other Species?

I feel it has given me much respect for other species and has helped me remember my life is not more important than another species', and this gives me deeper meaning in my life. I look forward to communing with them all, as I experience living beyond the physical world that is so limiting, full of illusion and gives us a false sense of importance. The physical 3D reality simply does not encompass all levels of realities and dimensions, thus we miss many opportunities to find unconditional love and greater joy.

The spontaneity and magic that comes from interactions with other species cannot be compared or measured for me, it is so strong in unconditional love it makes my heart melt. Such as when hugging my cat Harley, I feel our energies blend together and the love I give comes back so much stronger than I feel I am delivering to him. It is unconditional love in nature, something not found easily in the 3D realm. There are no judgements or hoops to jump, other species just want to be respected and heard by us. They do not ask for much.

Humans are always wanting and asking for so much, to the point it is greedy, unnecessary and causes tremendous destruction and raping of the earth's resources, impacting negatively on the voiceless species. I do not understand this thinking that allows great damage to the very place that supports us by providing our food, air, water, warmth and protection from the elements. It is insane to be destroying our home, Mother Earth. I see her as my mother who nourishes me and supports me to feel so much around me, spiritually helps me evolve without judgement, and supports so many other species on this planet to be my companions in love and joy. Why would anyone want to destroy that relationship—unless they cannot feel it in their own hearts. Could their hearts be blocked by past wounds?

If you are not healing your heart of pain, suffering and distorted emotions, unable to forgive others, you are missing a life of joy, happiness and peace all around you. I love this thought from Indigenous groups:

> *"Western man does not feel his world around him with love in the heart, they are walking as dead people."*

From my experience of healing my heart bit by bit, my heart started to become the spontaneous child I remember, full of joy, curiosity and magic as I took everything into my life as something to enjoy, particularly the love I received when I sent that to other species who do not have a voice.

I feel many humans with a voice often talk with a forked tongue, not saying truthfully what they really feel for fear of one thing or another, and that is a heart not healed. When you open to healing the heart, you will notice you cannot accept dishonesty, it does not fit in the same frequency as a pure heart of unconditional loving energy. The voiceless do not talk with forked tongues. They speak with the most exquisite language, the highest vibration of unconditional love. I say this because it has been what I felt in my heart from them all, and as my honest experience I share this as my own truth.

> *The unnatural death of so many species for food and ownership of lands without honouring other species leaves a dark energetic imprint on the earth's energy field that will need to be cleared before we can evolve into a planet that supports love, peace and joy.*

How can we clear this dark, toxic energy imprinted into Mother Earth's energy field? Releasing our karmic actions will allow more light to enter the energetic field. We need to heal ourselves, so it can then be felt by Mother Earth as our actions become more conscious in not wanting to harm other species, then we can release this dark scar on the energetic field. This dark, heavy energy imprint causes our planet to carry the symptoms of abuse, anxiety, fear, loss, depression and struggles of survival. We then feel separate to everything around us. How can we have a loving, peaceful and joyful home on planet earth with all this moving around our magnetic field whilst we continue to make more karma, pain and suffering for next generations? After all, we are all interrelated.

> *This has been shared with me by other species and my ancestor souls, that humans need to start to respect all species and honour all their lives.*

55

A Blessed Life

The key is gratitude for everything.

My life has been such a blessing, thanks to my ability to commune with so many species and to my ancestor soul star galactic family who come as my soul companions to share great wisdom and support my earthly human journey. I have the utmost gratitude and respect for those souls and look forward to connecting with them again in the future when I travel across the veil to another realm of existence, returning to my soul star galactic family.

In my sixties now, the day I leave the planet may not be too far away. This keeps me on track to write my books to inspire others to experience the joy and magic other species can give us, as conscious carers and caretakers of Mother Earth. Living with them in respect and great love has been a privilege to behold. The love I feel with another species when my heart is open is the gift of unconditional love. If I allow myself to receive, I feel it reaching my heart like an explosion of bliss. This is what you can feel when you start healing your heart, a bliss bomb of love coming your way. You may become hooked like me, not wanting to miss any opportunity to share the love with another species. This sheer bliss of receiving becomes magic that unfolds in the body and heart.

I do hope I can always be conscious enough to feel with other species. Without this communication I would feel much magic missing from my life. I would feel separate and alone from everything we have available to support our human journey. Humans are so blessed to have these opportunities to commune with other species. If we could just see them as part of us, not separate, we could learn so much from their wisdom and stop treating them as inferior beings on this planet to be exploited, domineered, euthanased, given away or discarded, as we tend to do with everything on this planet at this time. If any object, or even an animal, is too much trouble to deal with or takes too much of our time, it is often discarded for something new.

A disturbing observation I have made over the years is the human fascination for the younger species who are considered cute, loveable and play a great deal. What happens when they become larger and older companions—the novelty wears off. Please also consider where you are buying your next furry animal companion, be that a dog, cat, or other. Ask where are they coming from—is it a puppy farm/mill, where they have not been bred or cared for in respectful and loving ways? If you would like a furry soul companion, consider the time you need to spend with them for their well-being. Can you give the time they require to have fun and love them, and allow time to simply sit with them in the day? They do get lonely waiting for you.

Please give your furry companions good quality fresh food, just as you would your human family members. They need to have outdoor exercise time, to go outside to smell the flowers and scents of the earth will make them happy too. Social time with other similar species to play is important too, and time with you—that is the most rewarding of all moments that you will ever be gifted.

Most importantly, animals are not toys for us to buy, then discard when they become mature dogs and cats and we have lost interest in them. This saddens me greatly, as the pounds are full of these souls, often having been gifted as presents to family members, then ending up in a pound for re-adoption. They are so sensitive. You become their whole life, then you are gone and they feel abandoned, confused and anxious on arriving at the pound, not understanding, after all, they gave you their hearts with unconditional love. What have you given them?

What if we all Healed our Hearts and Found our True Purpose Here on Earth?

The ego would no longer be running the minds of humans, instead, our souls would be guiding the minds through our hearts. We would be in loving respect for all on this planet and would be unable to hurt any other species, or Mother Earth, as we would be sensitive in our hearts and connected, thus we would *feel* what we were doing, making it painful in our own hearts. Humans would be respectful of one another, without judgment. Unconditional love would be the language. The world would be full of light, glistening. Imagine grass greener than ever, and everyone smiling with joy, dancing and celebrating life with all species.

The senses would be heightened for us all to feel magic and other realms of existence. Can you see how different this world would be if all communed with other species respectfully and all species were involved in our decisions and actions? The environment would be light in vibration, so every wave of movement would be felt by every human and all species across the landscape in loving ways, unlike now with distorted, painful feelings coming from so many places and humans. Peace and calm would be the normal emotion, and many would be in this state of high consciousness, wanting to serve the greater good of all beings using their own wisdom with other species to care for the planet as the true custodians we are meant to be here on earth.

In healing our hearts, we become more sensitive and no longer feel separate from other species or Mother Earth. Thus, we feel the devastation around us, encouraging us to change our distracting and desensitizing habits that have supported us to unconsciously store more pain in our bodies and into the energetic frequency of this planet earth. Sharing our stories to inspire others heals us, and inspires other humans to find their purpose too, so we will be helping to save many species and the landscape of our earth before it's denuded by the human race and we have to leave.

There is only one planet for our human evolution—Mother Earth, a paradise. If we can remember our own stories and share them, this will help others remember their actions to be more loving and respectful towards other sentient beings. Mother Earth has had enough. She cannot take any more disrespect from the human race and is showing us now with her body, rocking and rolling with her elemental allies in an effort to clear the toxic waste, and hopefully to wake up humans to be more conscious of our actions.

There are so many reasons for us to listen to the voiceless. Next time you are outside, be still and feel into your higher heart intelligence and see what happens for you. If you have a conversation going on, you are probably connected to your ego (smaller mind). See if you can bypass that chatter and be fully present in the moment. Mother Earth sustains us, all species, the elements and our ancestors within the landscape. If you can remember to honour them all and have gratitude for the offerings, you will begin to experience a different world from a new reality, one where magic is always present. As you open to it all around you, surprises will begin to present to you.

Communing from the heart bypasses the ego and words that are of a lower vibration and distract us or leave us wanting. Staying totally present to the heart space and connecting with another species is one of the most fulfilling experiences you can have as a human being. I have the same feeling when I commune with Mother Earth. It's a powerful connection of love, difficult to explain if you have never truly felt it, but when you do, you will not forget the joy, leaving your heart feeling fulfilled from the inside out. It would be a hellish and lonely life with my furry companions *not* to have the interspecies connections I have experienced after waking up to be a more conscious human being. It is so magical! I cannot stress enough how much unconditional love you will receive in return for healing your heart and opening to other species. They have many messages and much wisdom to share with the human race on how to look after this beautiful planet as caretakers.

Instead, as a race we have become destroyers and rapists of the planet, ruining our earthly home for all species, destroying every species' habitat. We can stop it right now if we choose to—by becoming more conscious of our actions, by respecting other species for who they are and listening to their wisdom from our hearts, not our minds. There is only one glue in this galaxy—the language of unconditional love that holds us and all other species connected, no other.

I share this from my own life experiences. Deluded by the egoic mind, we create a heavier vibration and our actions do not support the greater good of all species and Mother Earth. When working from a higher vibration, through the higher heart intelligence, we will be of service for the good of all on this planet, including other species.

Our actions affect our ancestors and beings in other realms on this planet. We are so much more than we are led to believe. It is time to

Wake Up to the illusion and stop being taken on a ride by the physical 3D distractions that keep us from our own authentic selves. What is true to your heart is what you need to follow. If all humans did that, we would be helping and supporting our Mother Earth and all species. Our egoic mind only knows judgment, competition and comparisons of past events, and analyses these subconscious memories to keep us from the present moment—but it is not the truth of who we are. Our egoic mind is an organic computer system that processes information logically, and it dies when we die.

> *Our soul is the real wisdom and mind of a higher intelligence. That is why we need to heal our hearts to connect to the soul, trusting in its guidance.*

Your soul is always trying to get you to heal your heart wounds by showing you triggers. When triggered, you can acknowledge the feeling and let it go, or you can hold it and deepen the wound within your heart so no light can reach you through the heart space. It is always your own free will how you manage triggers and make choices at every moment that your emotional imbalances are highlighted. What will you choose next time you have a conscious awareness of an imbalance within your emotions, or an uncomfortable feeling in your body/heart that is not joyful or loving towards a species or another human? Something to ponder when you are triggered by a strong emotion.

I have had to learn how to heal my triggers. When I did, a lightness filled me, I became elated and full of love that went beyond my own heart. I found that I just wanted to share the love that expands in my heart after healing some hurt or emotional reaction. Our strong emotional reactions do not go unnoticed, as the body is a computer and logs every thought and reaction we have at an energetic level. Wherever it is stored, the energy causes a distortion in the body with a frequency that is of a much denser vibration than the humming vibration we experience when feeling in bliss and peaceful, in a balanced state of wellbeing.

I hope you have had the opportunity to feel this blissful vibration at some time in your life. If not, I highly recommend you find a class, for example meditation, to learn how to bypass the mind of analysis and distraction that takes you away from your soul's calling so you may find that place of peace within yourself and experience freedom, joy and fulfillment. You will find it when you let go of the small mind's chatter. Our small minds want to be in control of us all the time! We need to train the small mind to be a servant to our thoughts, so we can decide what we will respond to or act on—then it is not our minds making the decisions. The small mind will always try to distract and control, because it runs on our fears or past experiences and attempts to protect us, so we become fearful, thinking this will happen and that will happen. In reality, does a fear ever materialize in the way you imagined it?

The small mind interferes with the soul's journey and purpose, stopping the flow and stopping us from feeling the great joy of life and feeling connected to other species. It is all about learning to control the small mind and allow space for the flow of your soul to enter into the body's field, a way to find the peace and joy we all look for.

> *Allow your soul to rise up and you will be in the beautiful flow of life, able to find the magic that surrounds us all, the peace and love that we all so deserve.*
> *Do not push it aside, allow it to come to you.*

We do not need to chase anything, as from my experience, the universe provides all that we need in divine timing. I have lived this now for many years. How? I meditate every day to clear my subconscious mind so I may be in a place of peace and allow the mind chatter to fall away whilst I connect to the unified field of source consciousness that surrounds us all. This allows me to tune in to my soul's purpose and direction, for my life journey to flow more easily, and to find a calm place within me, even when the world is frenetic. It reminds me of who I really am—a spiritual being having a human experience in physical form, with emotional intelligence.

> *I am not my thoughts. I am a soul being shown them to act on if I wish, to serve the thought or to ignore it, as I am the master of my mind.*

Meditation is a tool that needs to be practiced every day. We are not the master of our minds because we learn to meditate, we become the master by committing to daily practice. Just like brushing my teeth regularly keeps my teeth healthy, practicing meditation regularly keeps me spiritually connected to who I really am so I can live in the flow of life. That is a magic place to be in, because the universe will provide for you in divine timing without pushing or competing. It is a life skill I continue to practice with no goal post/no destination to get to, it is just a way of feeling freedom and joy, moving towards liberation.

I feel we are just starting a big shift on this planet, one that has been prophesied for many millenniums. The knowledge has been held in the ancient earth wisdom schools, and the First Nation peoples have all talked about these times to come. So brace yourself, and start to connect with nature and your own inner guidance if you wish to get through the times ahead. Start looking at where in your life you may not be respecting other species or nature. It is all about respect for ourselves, and healing the traumatised hearts we all have from many events of not being conscious of our actions. When healing takes place, our actions will begin to change towards other species and Mother Earth.

It is a force you cannot ignore—the real, deep heart connection of unconditional love. You will find yourself unable to justify any action of disrespect when your heart is sensitive and feels it strongly, for it will be too painful to ignore. I feel so many are not at this point of feeling into their own hearts yet, which is why so much is justified away in their actions.

I know this, I've been at fault of this by being distracted, and by being too busy to feel the discomfort when my soul doesn't agree with an action if I'm practicing against the connection with other species or caring for Mother Earth. I am sure we all have examples of disrespectful actions to other species from being unconscious, not honouring their life and having gratitude for their sacrifice to nourish us as humans.

Many children coming to earth at this time are not going to accept these actions any longer and will be telling their families of this. I have seen a few children already highlighting this fact by saying *if they have eyes and a mouth, we cannot be eating them!* My niece is a good example—in the early 1990s she refused to eat any animals or have her food contaminated by any animal product on her table or eating utensils. My sister, being who she was at the time and a naturopath, tried to accommodate my niece and supported her food choices with education on how to maintain that lifestyle with a balanced approach for her health and replacing meat protein with healthy options. She respected my niece's choice, and that has affected the whole family, as my niece has now educated us all on how to do this and gain the benefits. My niece, now in her thirties, leads many other young adults by example and shares her knowledge on the benefits of a plant-based diet and glows with good health and natural beauty.

Message from Oversoul of Mother Earth.

Mother Earth: It is your mother, the earth. I am here to share with you, dearest, from the high realms of existence, which you will learn more about soon. Here now, I share with you what has gone on today in the fires.

Debra: Please share, I am so touched you are here to share with me now.

Mother Earth: It is a big story, but you need to be sharing this with the many now. They are ready to hear the story of love and pain that this dear body of mine continues to feel with so much disrespect from humans for other species, not just my body.

This is a time of big change, which you have already mentioned in your previous book, but here we are going to talk about that a little further. It is important for the many to be listening to this as it will affect each and every one of them at this time.

I am very much into my evolution cycle and many humans have not been keeping up. They will need to leave the planet if they are not going to keep up, it is so important to make some big changes for my body to evolve into higher realms of existence. I have been here for many eons before the human race. You already know about the breath of life I take in the morning and at evening on dusk. Maybe you could share that for your readers, dearest one.

I feel it is such a big journey for humanity right now to be fully conscious, or practicing being fully conscious, because my body cannot sustain any more disrespect from the human race. This has become clear over the past weeks as your country has felt big changes afoot in fires. As you say, it will never be the same again. That is for sure, it is not.

And many of your people still have no idea of the many other changes that are about to take place. As you say, if more light is to enter the wounds of my body, human's healing must take place. As you have experienced, as you heal your heart you allow more space for the light to enter, and you become and feel lighter, is that not right?

Debra: Yes, Mother Earth, I really do get that from my own experiences.

Mother Earth: Well dearest, I am also like the human body. The difference is I am such a big structure. You are my body on a smaller, micro scale, so think in terms of what happens to the human body when traumatised—it is the same for me.

The only difference is that when I'm healing and detoxing trauma I have a massive effect on thousands, as many on your planet are about to find out, particularly if they are not listening to their own conscious guidance and intuition.

It is so simple, keep healing those hearts so you will be fully aware of what is coming your way and you will be kept safe, if that is your contract with your soul. Many have already made contracts that they will be leaving the earth, such as your wildlife, who have sacrificed their lives for the good of humanity.

This is what your human race does not understand—the souls who come to be these bodies are sacrificing themselves to help humanity, as have you, and have been in many other forms and species in your many lifetimes. You will start to learn this soon and it may be a surprise to you, but it will give you a better idea of why you feel so much for other species, dearest, for you are them. They are your kindred spirits. You know this, it's held in the memories of your DNA and it triggers you when you see suffering because you know it is you they are hurting, and not a separate species.

You understand the idea of oneness. You have lived it all your life and many lifetimes prior. Unfortunately, in this life you have had some big hurdles and challenges to get through in your heart and have had to keep clearing these to remember all that I am sharing here. Please talk with us all every day. We have so much to share with you.

Debra: Yes, I will.

Mother Earth: You are an author, and this is why you came to the earth—to share all you have experienced and what you know from your past lives. The masses are now ready to hear your story of the heart journey you have been on, dearest. It will help so many others as they feel your pain and you describe what that feels like. It is so important to do this work, it is your service to humanity. You signed up for this. This is not a hobby, please see it as a very important service you have signed up for, and it is so needed right now for many to understand what they are feeling for their hearts to heal and evolve on this earth.

Do You Feel an Overwhelming Tiredness When Using Technology?

At times, I feel overwhelmed when using technology for many hours. I may be on my computer trying to make a deadline and I start to feel tired or can't think clearly—sometimes even going into a meltdown phase when I cannot even think about it anymore, or become confused trying to correct or edit a document. I have learnt this is the time to stop and go outside to sit on the grass and listen to the birds and animals talk with ancestors, to feel the elements and commune with Mother Earth under my bare feet. This takes me back to my heart space, then I feel at peace and joy returns to my heart. I find the songs of the birds are the universal music of my heart and connect to the greater force that surrounds us all to feel connected—I smile.

Since early childhood, I remember going outside and communing with nature as a balm to heal my heart when I have felt stress and anxiety. That feeling of being disconnected from my heart and soul creeps in because I am working from my headspace, absorbed in a project. The balancing act is to get a nature healing fix to connect with my family outdoors. They keep me sane, peaceful and joyful. As I feel into being in the present moment in time the tension in my body melts away. I try to do this often in my day. The other reminder I need for breaks comes from my wise old cat, who tries to distract me by wanting attention or by talking with me. His timing is always perfect for me to take a break so I am not tired from overdoing the thinking—the logical mind activity that stops me feeling into my body and connecting to the earth.

I do not know how I would survive without the hours I spend outdoors with nature and Mother Earth. Travelling in Europe recently, I was in a city and missing the bird songs from home. Where I live in Australia, it's like living in a jungle with an orchestra and all players competing to be heard, birds and other wildlife who share the same air space with their families in the bushland letting me know they are there, some joyful and happy, others raising their voices to say a predator is nearby, and adults communing with their young as they deliver food to them. It is a magical place to be with all the song sounds around my home. I am reminded when I travel that not everyone has this privilege to live so close to nature, to have a blessed life and be inspired by other species and able to commune with them so closely every day.

I guess that is what travel does—reminds us of what we have and to be thankful for it. It is a blessing to have the opportunity to commune with nature at my front and back door. When I am momentarily present in my heart space, I can hear their loud voices competing to be heard and they fill me with great joy and love. That is not easy to find on this planet that humans have been re-designing with technology, with no respect for nature or other species. Humans always seem to be moving soil around, mining, fishing excessively across large areas of the ocean and filling the skies and land with transport needs. Do we really need all this stuff we move around and take from the planet?

I often wonder if this excessive moving and taking will ever stop—perhaps when there are no natural areas or other species left because we have killed them or have taken all their habitats? This is what I see, feel, hear and sense is happening to our beautiful blue planet. I believe we must not lose sight of who sustains all species on this planet. Mother Earth provides us with shelter, air, water, fire and food sources to keep us alive. If we ignore this fact, we send humanity and all other species to their extinction. I fear that is where we are heading sometimes with so much fear, greed and believing we never have enough—it is not sustainable.

We waste resources, unconsciously throwing away excess, thinking if it has gone from our sight it is gone forever. Wrong! It is simply sent to another area or zone on the planet. Mother Earth has only one body for us to inhabit, with limited space to store all our throw away excesses. If our excesses were left in our houses would you keep collecting more? No, we would run out of space! Rubbish turns up on our beaches and in natural bushland and parks because a great number of humans are still not taking responsibility for their buying and accumulating of things.

What will it take to have everyone making conscious decisions before purchasing? Our disconnection to where rubbish is dumped poses a huge problem not just for us, but for all the wildlife species who are forced to live with our waste in their habitats and environment. There are many examples of that in our oceans with sea creatures injured, becoming entangled and killed from our waste floating around the oceans of the world.

Consciously connecting will all beings, all species, will change how you feel about all beings and the beautiful planet we are privileged to live on. This is my truth, which I share with you for the good of all.

I have experienced an extraordinarily blessed life and feel tremendous gratitude every day for what I have received and how supported I am from other realms of existence across the veil of illusion from the physical world, by my family of light beings who co-exist in parallel realities, and Mother Earth. So many gifts and blessings I have received.

I sincerely wish you a magical and love-filled journey beyond this physical 3D realm of existence, that you too may feel supported with the Power of Love and never feel alone ever again, so our Mother Earth and other species can once again feel the love, joy and peace from humanity.

It starts with us, humans, one at a time.

It will change the world.

Many blessings to you for a joyful life into the magical realms with other species in love.

Everything is alive on the earth, and all species want to commune with humans, to show us the magic that is waiting for us when we wake up to become more conscious!

Debra A Lansdowne

Acknowledgements

I feel so much gratitude to all the beautiful species, our relations on earth who have come to share their wisdom and showered me with their unconditional love, reminding me we are never alone.

Thank you and gratitude to our divine Mother Earth for supporting my soul's evolution with her unconditional love, healing and nurturing.

So many blessings to my ancestors, my soul star galactic family of light beings who have kept me on track with my purpose here on earth, sharing their wisdom, unconditional love and healing light. Committed to supporting my soul's journey, they communicate with me inter-dimensionally, reminding me we are not separate from any other species and we need to be united in service to all species.

I would like to acknowledge and give thanks to the Ancient Earth Wisdom Keepers, Shamans and Ancient Mystery School Teachers who have crossed my path and assisted me to remember my past life gifts and my service to Mother Earth and humanity. I give gratitude to the Indigenous communities of this earth who have held the dream of the new earth and ancient wisdom for thousands of years.

Nigel, my beloved and devoted husband, I thank you for being my partner on all the adventures we've travelled across the earth, trusting, and opening our hearts to the magic that awaited us. I am forever grateful to Nigel for his patience and unconditional love in supporting my passion to share these stories and inspire other humans to follow their own heart's guidance.

And thank you to my beautiful editor, Karen Collyer, for her

Acknowledgements

patience, loving encouragement and gifted talent to transform my manuscript into a book that can be read with ease.

Gratitude to artist, Terri Graham, for lovingly creating and painting the heart of many species for my book cover.

Bless you all for the contributions you have made to my life and my author journey, it has been a gift of unconditional love. So much gratitude to you all.

About the Author

Debra has always enjoyed a close bond with animals. A sensitive child, she felt the pain and suffering of all species, while the unconditional love from her companion animals provided a powerful healing balm for her own heart, filling her with joy, love and hope.

A seeker of life experiences, Debra has followed her heart's guidance, living a life of adventures in the great outdoors, exploring nature and communing with other species.

Debra's metaphysical explorations began after challenging health problems in early adulthood called for healing outside of the conventional medical model. This healing became a life transformation with a Mystical Spiritual Awakening calling Debra to travel more consciously on the earth with all species and learn more about metaphysical worlds. Debra studied the Eastern traditions of meditation and yoga, trained in the Ancient Mystery School Wisdom of Masters from the Middle East, and Ancient Earth Wisdom practices of Indigenous cultures.

Training as a Shamanic Interspecies Communicator and Ancient Earth Wisdom keeper, Debra's initiation expanded her heart to commune with the souls of her animal companions who had passed over and were waiting to commune with her and share their wisdom. Other species also began presenting to Debra as she began

About the Author

communicating across realms of existence with her ancestors' soul star galactic family of light beings.

Debra has been a keeper of earth wisdom through shamanic earth honoring and celebration practices for over thirty years, in flow with Mother Earth's seasonal cycles and the natural world with all species, taking part in honoring ceremonies with Indigenous communities and like-minded groups who practice walking lightly on Mother Earth in sacred union with all species. Debra's earth-honoring practices have taken her on many adventures across Australia and the world to experience sacred, powerful energy sites.

This her second book, *Power of Love with Animals*, was born to be the voice of the voiceless, to inspire respect for all species and share their wisdom and the power of their unconditional love for humanity to evolve with Mother Earth.

Debra's first book *Seeker of Freedom and Joy* (Best Seller on Amazon, released in January 2020) is an inspiring life journey on relationships with the self, others and nature, with thought-provoking questions engaging the reader to find their own inner wisdom.

Author, Inspirational Speaker and Therapist, Debra offers workshops supporting others to write their own stories from the heart to heal and find purpose and joy in life.

Look for Debra's third book, due for release late 2021. Release dates check website

www.heartjourneyswithDebra.com

Facebook: Author Debra Lansdowne

www.ingramcontent.com/pod-product-compliance
Lightning Source LLC
Chambersburg PA
CBHW051417290426
44109CB00016B/1328